500 OF THE BEST

COCKNEY
WAR
STORIES

500 OF THE BEST

COCKNEY WAR STORIES

~❦~

WITH AN OPENING YARN BY
GENERAL
SIR IAN HAMILTON
G.C.B., G.C.M.G., D.S.O., etc.
Vice-President of the British Legion
President of the Metropolitan Area of the
British Legion

AMBERLEY

First published 1921
This edition published 2009

Amberley Publishing
Cirencester Road, Chalford,
Stroud, Gloucestershire, GL6 8PE

www.amberley-books.com

British Library Cataloguing in Publication Data.
A catalogue record for this book is available from the British Library.

ISBN 978 1 84868 424 9

Printed in Great Britain.

EDITOR'S FOREWORD

IN the remembering, and in the retelling, of those war days when laughter sometimes saved men's reason, Cockneys the world over have left to posterity a record of noble and imperishable achievement.

From the countless tales collected by the London *Evening News* these five hundred, many of them illustrated by the great war-time artist, Bert Thomas, have been chosen as a fitting climax and perpetuation.

Sir Ian Hamilton's story of another war shows that, however much methods of fighting may vary from generation to generation, there is no break in continuity of a great tradition, that the spirits of laughter and high adventure are immortal in the make-up of the British soldier.

Sir Ian's story is doubly fitting. As President of the Metropolitan Area of the British Legion he is intimately concerned with the after-war welfare of just that Tommy Atkins who is immortalised in these pages. In the second place, all profits from the sale of this book will be devoted to the cause which the Higher Command in every branch of the Services is fostering—the British Legion.

CONTENTS

~

SIR IAN HAMILTON'S STORY

THE Great War was a matrix wherein many anecdotes have sprouted. They are short-lived plants—fragile as mushrooms—none too easy to extricate either, embedded as they are in the mass.

To dig out the character of a General even from the plans of his General Staff is difficult ; how much more difficult to dig out the adventures of Number 1000 Private Thomas Atkins from those of the other 999 who went " like one man " with him over the top ? In the side-shows there was more scope for the individual and in the Victorian wars much more scope. To show the sort of thing I mean I am going to put down here for the first time an old story, almost forgotten now, in the hopes that it may interest by its contrast to barrages and barbed wire. Although only an old-fashioned affair of half a dozen bullets and three or four dead men it was a great event to me as it led to my first meeting with the great little Bobs of Kandahar.

On the morning of September 11, 1879, I lay shivering with fever and ague at Alikhel in Afghanistan. So sick did I seem that it was decided I should be carried a day's march back to G.H.Q. on the Peiwar Kotal to see if the air of that high mountain pass would help me to pull myself round. Polly Forbes, a boy subaltern not very long from Eton, was sent off to play the part of nurse.

We reached the Peiwar Kotal without any adventure, and were allotted a tent in the G.H.Q. camp pitched where the road between the Kurram Valley and Kabul ran over the high Kotal or pass. Next morning, although still rather weak in the knees, I felt game for a ride to the battlefield. So we rode along the high ridge through the forest of giant deodars looking for mementoes of the battle. The fact was that we were, although we knew it not, in a very dangerous No Man's Land.

We had reached a point about two miles from camp when we were startled by half a dozen shots fired in quick succession and still more startled to see some British soldiers rushing down towards us from the top of a steep-sided knoll which crowned the ridge to our immediate front.

Close past us rushed those fugitives and on, down the hillside, where at last, some hundred yards below us, they pulled up in answer to our

I*

shouts. But no amount of shouts or orders would bring them up to us, so we had to get off our ponies and go down to them. There were seven of them—a Corporal and three men belonging to one of the new short service battalions and three signallers—very shaky the whole lot. Only one was armed with his rifle ; he had been on sentry-go at the moment the signalling picquet had been rushed—so they said—by a large body of Afghans.

What was to be done ? I realised that I was the senior. Turning to the Corporal I asked him if he could ride. " Yes, sir," he replied rather eagerly. " Well, then," I commanded, " you get on to that little white mare up there and ride like hell to G.H.Q. for help. You others go up with him and await orders." Off they went, scrambling up the hill, Forbes and I following rather slowly because of my weakness. When we got up to the path, ponies, syces, all had disappeared except that one soldier who had stuck to his rifle.

All was as still as death in the forest where we three now stood alone. " Where are the others ? " I asked the man. " I think they must be killed." " Do you think they are up there ? " " Yessir ! " So I turned to Forbes and said, " If there are wounded or dead up there we must go and see what we can do."

Where we stood we were a bit far away from the top of the wooded hill for a jezail shot to carry and once we began to climb the slope we found ourselves in dead ground. Nearing the top, my heart jumped into my mouth as I all but put my foot on a man's face. Though I dared not take my eyes off the brushwood on the top of the hill, out of the corner of my eye I was aware he was a lascar and that he must be dead, for his head had nearly been severed from his body.

At that same moment we heard a feeble cry in Hindustani, " *Shabash, Sahib log, chello !* " " Bravo, Gentlemen, come along ! " This came from another lascar shot through the body—a plucky fellow. " *Dushman kahan hain ?* "—" Where are the enemy ? " I whispered. " When the sahibs shouted from below they ran away," he said, and at that, side by side with the revolvers raised to fire, Forbes and I stepped out on to the cleared and levelled summit of the hill, a space about fifteen feet by twenty.

All was quiet and seemed entirely normal. There stood the helio and there lay the flags. Most astonishing of all, there, against a pile of logs, rested the priceless rifles of the picquet guard with their accoutrements and ammunition pouches lying on the ground beside them. Making a sign to Forbes we laid down our revolvers ready to hand, took, each of us, a rifle, loaded it, fixed the bayonet and stood at the ready facing the edge of the forest about thirty yards away.

Even in these days when my memory is busy chucking its seventy years or so of accumulations overboard, the memory of that tense watch into the forest remains as fresh as ever. For the best part of half an hour it must have lasted. At last we heard them—not the Afghans but our own chaps, coming along the ridge and now they were making their way in open order up the hill—a company of British Infantry together with a few Pathan auxiliaries, the whole under command of Captain Stratton of the 22nd Foot, head Signaller to the Force.

In few words my story was told and at once bold Stratton determined to pursue down the far side of the hill. Stratton had told me to go back to camp, but I did not consider that an order and, keeping on the extreme left of the line so that he should not see me, I pushed along.

I noticed that the young soldier of the picquet who had stuck to his rifle was still keeping by me as the long line advanced down the slope, which gradually bifurcated into two distinct spurs. The further we went the wider apart drew the spurs and the deeper became the intervening nullah. Captain Stratton, Forbes, and the Regimental Company commander were all on the other or eastern spur and the men kept closing in towards them, until at last everyone, bar myself and my one follower, had cleared off the western spur. I did not want to cross the nullah, feeling too weak and tired to force my way through the thick undergrowth. Soon we could no longer hear or see the others.

Suddenly I heard Click! " Take cover! " I shouted and flung myself behind a big stone. Sure enough, the moment often imagined had come ! Not more than twenty paces down the slope an old, white-bearded, wicked-looking Enemy was aiming at me with his long jezail from behind a fallen log. Click! again. Another misfire.

Now I was musketry instructor of my regiment, which had been the best shooting regiment in India the previous year. My revolver was a rotten little weapon, but I knew its tricks. As the Afghan fumbled with his lock I took aim and began to squeeze the trigger. Another instant and he would have been dead when bang! went a rifle behind me : my helmet tilted over my eyes, my shot went where we found it next day, about six feet up into a tree. The young soldier had opened rapid fire just over my head.

At the same time, I saw another Afghan come crouching through the brushwood below me towards a point where he would be able to enfilade my stone. I shouted to my comrade, " I'm coming back to you," and turned to make for his tree. Luck was with me. At that very moment bang went the jezail and when we dug out the bullet next morning and marked the line of fire, it became evident that had I not so turned I would never have sat spinning this yarn.

That shot was a parting salute. There were shouts from the right of the line, and as I was making for my tree the Afghans made off in the other direction. I shouted to Stratton and his men to press down to the foot of the hill, working round to the north so as to cut off the raiders. Then, utterly exhausted, I began my crawl back to the camp.

Soon after I had got in I was summoned into the presence of the redoubtable Bobs. Although I had marched past him at Kohat this was my first face-to-face meeting with one who was to play the part of Providence to my career. He made me sit in a chair and at once performed the almost incredible feat of putting me entirely at my ease. This he did by pouring a golden liquid called sherry into a very large wine-glass. Hardly had I swallowed this elixir when I told him all about everything, which was exactly what he wanted.

A week later the Commander of the Cavalry Brigade, Redan Massy, applied to Headquarters for an Aide-de-Camp. Sir Fred Roberts advised him to take me. That billet led to unimaginable bliss. Surrounding villages by moonlight, charging across the Logar Valley, despising all foot sloggers—every sort of joy I had longed for. The men of the picquet who had run away were tried by Court Martial and got long sentences, alas—poor chaps! The old Mullah was sent to his long account by Stratton.

But that is the point of most war stories; when anyone gets a lift up it is by the misfortune or death of someone else.

IAN HAMILTON.

COCKNEY WAR STORIES

1. ACTION

The Outside Fare

DURING the third battle of Ypres a German field gun was trying to hit one of our tanks, the fire being directed no doubt by an observation balloon.

On the top of the tank was a Cockney infantryman getting a free ride and seemingly quite unconcerned at Jerry's attempts to score a direct hit on the tank.

" Hi, conductor ! Any room inside ?—it's rainin' ! "

As the tank was passing our guns a shrapnel shell burst just behind it and above it.

We expected to see the Cockney passenger roll off dead. All he did, however, was to put his hand to his mouth and shout to those inside the tank: " Hi, conductor ! Any room inside ?—it's rainin' ! "—*A. H. Boughton (ex " B " Battery, H.A.C.), 53 Dafforne Road, S.W.17.*

" Barbed Wire's Dangerous ! "

A WIRING party in the Loos salient—twelve men just out from home. Jerry's Verey lights were numerous, machine-guns were unpleasantly busy, and there were all the dangers and alarms incidental to a sticky part of the line. The wiring party, carrying stakes and wire, made its way warily, and every man breathed apprehensively. Suddenly one London lad tripped over a piece of old barbed wire and almost fell his length.

" Lumme," he exclaimed, " that ain't 'arf dangerous ! "—*T. C. Farmer, M.C., of Euston Square, London (late of " The Buffs ").*

Tale of an Egg

I WAS attached as a signaller to a platoon on duty in an advanced post on the Ypres–Menin Road. We had two pigeons as an emergency means of communication should our wire connection fail.

One afternoon Fritz put on a strafe which blew in the end of the culvert in which we were stationed. We rescued the pigeon basket from the debris and discovered that an egg had appeared.

That evening, when the time came to send in the usual evening " situation report," I was given the following message to transmit :

" Pigeon laid one egg ; otherwise situation normal."—*D. Webster, 85 Highfield Avenue, N.W.11.*

" No Earfkwikes "

O N a bitterly cold, wet afternoon in February 1918 four privates and a corporal were trying to take what shelter they could. One little Cockney who had served in the Far East with the 10th Middlesex was complaining about everything in general, but especially about the idiocy of waging war in winter.

" Wot yer grumblin' at ? " broke in the corporal, " you with yer fawncy tyles of Inja ? At any rate, there ain't no blinking moskeeters 'ere nor 'orrible malyria."

There was a break in the pleasantries as a big one came over. In the subsequent explosion the little Cockney was fatally wounded.

" Corpril," the lad gasped, as he lay under that wintry sky, " you fergot to menshun there ain't no bloomin' sun-stroke, *nor no earfkwikes, neither.*"

And he smiled—a delightful, whimsical smile—though the corporal's " Sorry, son " was too late.—*V. Meik, 107 King Henry's Road, N.W.3.*

A " Bow Bells " Heroine

FOR seven hours, with little intermission, the German airmen bombed a camp not a hundred miles from Etaples. Of the handful of Q.M.A.A.C.s stationed there, one was an eighteen-year-old middle-class girl, high-strung, sensitive, not long finished with her convent school. Another was Kitty, a Cockney girl of twenty, by occupation a machine-hand, by vocation (missed) a comédienne, and, by heaven, a heroine.

The high courage of the younger girl was cracking under the strain of that ordeal by bombs. Kitty saw how it was with her, and for five long hours she gave a recital of song, dialogue, and dance—most of it improvised—while the bombs fell and the anti-aircraft guns screamed. In all probability she saved the younger girl's reason.

When the last raider had dropped the last bomb, Kitty sank down, all but exhausted, and for long cried and laughed hysterically. Hers was not the least heroic part played upon that night.—*H. N., London, E.*

Samson, but Shorn

DURING the German attack near Zillebeke in June 1916 a diminutive Cockney, named Samson, oddly enough, received a scalp wound from a shell splinter which furrowed a neat path through his hair.

The fighting was rather hot at the time, and this great-hearted little Londoner carried on with the good work.

Some hours later came the order to fall back, and as the Cockney was making his way down the remains of a trench, dazed and staggering, a harassed sergeant, himself nearly " all in," ordered him to bear off a couple of rifles and a box of ammunition.

This was the last straw. " Strike, sergeant," he said, weakly, " I can't 'elp me name being Samson, but I've just 'ad me perishin' 'air cut ! "—*" Townie," R.A.F.*

" What's Bred in the Bone——! "

WHEN we were at Railway Wood, Ypres Salient, in 1916, " Muddy Lane," our only communication trench from the front line to the support line, had been reduced to shapelessness by innumerable " heavies." Progress in either direction entailed exposure to snipers in at least twelve different places, and runners and messengers were, as our sergeant put it, " tickled all the way."

In the support line one afternoon, hearing the familiar " Crack ! Crack ! Crack ! " I went to Muddy Lane junction to await the advertised visitor. He arrived—a wiry little Cockney Tommy, with his tin hat dented in two places and blood trickling from a bullet graze on the cheek.

In appreciation of the risk he had run I remarked, " Jerry seems to be watching that bit ! "

" Watching ! " he replied. " 'Struth ! I felt like I was walking darn Sarthend Pier naked ! "—*Vernon Sylvaine, late Somerset L.I., Grand Theatre, Croydon.*

A Very Human Concertina

IN March 1918, when Jerry was making his last great attack, I was in the neighbourhood of Petit Barisis when three enemy bombing planes appeared overhead and gave us their load. After all was clear I overheard this dialogue between two diminutive privates of the 7th Battalion, the London Regiment (" Shiny Seventh "), who were on guard duty at the Q.M. Stores :

" You all right, Bill ? "

" Yes, George ! "

" Where'd you get to, Bill, when he dropped his eggs ? "

" Made a blooming concertina of meself and got underneaf me blinkin' tin 'at ! "—*F. A. Newman, 8 Levett Gardens, Ilford, Ex-Q.M.S., 8th London (Post Office Rifles).*

A One-Man Army

THE 47th London Division were holding the line in the Bluff sector, near Ypres, early in 1917, and the 20th London Battalion were being relieved on a very wet evening, as I was going up to the front line with a working party.

Near Hell Fire Corner shells were coming over at about three-minute intervals. One of the 20th London Lewis gunners was passing in full fighting order, with fur coat, gum boots, etc., carrying his Lewis gun, several drums of ammunition, and the inevitable rum jar.

One of my working party, a typical Cockney, surveyed him and said : " Look ! Blimey, he only wants a field gun under each arm and he'd be a bally division."—*Lieut.-Col. J. H. Langton, D.S.O.*

" Nah, Mate ! Soufend ! "

DURING the heavy rains in the summer of 1917 our headquarters dug-out got flooded. So a fatigue party was detailed to bale it out.

" Long Bert " Smith was one of our baling squad. Because of his abnormal reach, he was stationed at the " crab-crawl," his job being to throw the water outside as we handed the buckets up to him.

It was a dangerous post. Jerry was pasting the whole area unmercifully and shell splinters pounded on the dug-out roof every few seconds.

Twenty minutes after we had started work Bert got badly hit, and it was some time before the stretcher-bearers could venture out to him. When they did so he seemed to be unconscious.

" Poor blighter ! " said one of the bearers. " Looks to be going West."

Bert, game to the last, opened his eyes and, seeing the canvas bucket still convulsively clutched in his right fist, " Nah, mate ! " he grunted— " Soufend ! "

But the stretcher-bearer was right.—*C. Vanon, 33 Frederick Street, W.C.1.*

"I Got 'Ole Nelson Beat!"

SEVERAL stretcher cases in the field dressing station at the foot of "Chocolate Hill," Gallipoli, awaited removal by ambulance, including a Cockney trooper in the dismounted Yeomanry.

He had a bandage round his head, only one eye was visible, and his left arm was bound to his breast with a sandbag.

His rapid-fire of Cockney witticisms had helped to keep our spirits up while waiting—he had a comment for everything. Suddenly a "strafe" started, and a shrapnel shell shot its load among us.

Confusion, shouts, and moans—then a half-hysterical, half-triumphant shout from the Cockney: "Lumme, one in the blinkin' leg this time. I got 'ole Nelson beat at last!"—*J. Coomer (late R.E.), 31 Hawthorn Avenue, Thornton Heath.*

Two Kinds of Fatalist

A GERMAN sniper was busy potting at our men in a front-line trench at Cambrai in March 1918. A Cockney "old sweat," observing a youngster gazing over the parapet, asked him if he were a fatalist.

The youngster replied "Yes."

"So am I," said the Cockney, "but I believes in duckin'."—*"Brownie," Kensal Rise, N.W.10.*

Double up, Beauty Chorus!

ONE summer afternoon in '15 some lads of the Rifle Brigade were bathing in the lake in the grounds of the château at Elverdinghe, a mile or so behind the line at Ypres, when German shells began to land uncomfortably near. The swimmers immediately made for the land, and, drawing only boots on their feet, dashed for the cellar in the château.

As they hurried into the shelter a Cockney sergeant bellowed, "Nah then, booty chorus: double up an' change for the next act!—*G. E. Roberts, M.C. (late Genl. List, att'd 21st Divn. Signal Co.), 28 Sunbury Gardens, Mill Hill, N.W.7.*

The Theatre of War

DURING the battle of Arras, Easter 1917, we were lying out in front of our wire in extended order waiting for our show to begin. Both our artillery and that of Fritz were bombarding as hard as they could. It was pouring with rain, and everybody was caked in mud.

Our platoon officer, finding he had a good supply of chocolate, and realising that rations might not be forthcoming for some time, crept along the line and gave us each a piece.

As he handed a packet to one cheerful Cockney he was asked, "Wot abaht a programme, sir?"—*W. B. Finch (late London Regiment), 155 High Road, Felixstowe.*

" It's the Skivvy's 'Arf Day Orf "

EASTER Monday, April 9, 1917. Night. Inches of snow and a weird silence everywhere after the turmoil of the day. Our battalion is held up in front of Monchy-le-Preux during the battle of Arras. I am sent out with a patrol to reconnoitre one of our tanks that is crippled and astride the German wire 300 yards out.

It is ticklish work, because the crew may be dead or wounded and

" I'll have to let yer in meself . . . it's the skivvy's 'arf day orf ! "

Fritz in occupation. Very warily we creep around the battered monster and presently I tap gingerly on one of the doors. No response. We crawl to the other side and repeat the tapping process. At last, through the eerie silence, comes a low, hoarse challenge.

"Oo are yer?"

"Fusiliers!" I reply, as I look up and see a tousled head sticking through a hole in the roof.

"Ho!" exclaims the voice above, "I'll 'ave ter come dahn and let yer in meself, it's the skivvy's 'arf day orf!"

The speaker proved to have a shattered arm—among other things— and was the sole survivor of the crew.—*D. K., Fulham, S.W.6.*

Cricket on the Somme

"SPIDER" WEBB was a Cockney—from Stepney, I believe—who was with us on the Somme in 1916. He was a splendid cricketer.

We had had a very stiff time for six or seven hours and were resting during a lull in the firing. Then suddenly Jerry sent over five shells. After a pause another shell came over and burst near to "Spider" and his two pals.

When the smoke cleared I went across to see what had happened. "Spider's" two pals were beyond help. The Cockney was propping himself up with his elbows surveying the scene.

"What's happened, Webb?" I said. "Blimey! What's happened?" was the reply. "One over—two bowled" (and, looking down at his leg)—"and I'm stumped." Then he fainted.—*George Franks, M.C. (late Lieut., Royal Artillery), Ilford, Essex.*

M'Lord, of Hoxton

WE called him "M'lord." He came from Hoxton—"That's where they make 'em," he used to say. He was a great asset to us, owing to the wonderful way in which he went out and "won" things.

One night, near Amiens, in 1916, "M'lord" said, "I'm going aht to see wot some uvver mob has got too much of." One or two of us offered to accompany him, but he refused, saying, "You bloomin' elephants 'ud be bahnd to give the gime away."

About three hours later, when we were beginning to get anxious, we saw him staggering in with a badly wounded German, who was smoking a cigarette.

Seeing us, and very much afraid of being thought soft-hearted, "M'lord" plumped old Fritz down on the fire-step and said very fiercely, "Don't you dare lean on me wif impunity, or wif a fag in your mouf."

Jerry told us later that he had lain badly wounded in a deserted farmhouse for over two days, and "M'lord" had almost carried him for over a mile.

"M'lord" was killed later on in the war. Our battalion was the 7th Batt. Royal Fusiliers (London Regt.)—*W. A., Windsor.*

The Tall Man's War

IN our platoon was a very tall chap who was always causing us great amusement because of his height. Naturally he showed his head above the parapet more often than the rest of us, and whenever he did so *ping* would come a bullet from a sniper and down our tall chum would drop in an indescribably funny acrobatic fashion.

The climax came at Delville Wood in August 1916, when, taking over the line, we found the trench knocked about in a way that made it most uncomfortable for all of us. Here our tall friend had to resort to his acrobatics more than ever : at times he would crawl on all fours to "dodge 'em." One shot, however, caused him to dive down more quickly than usual—right into a sump hole in the trench.

Recovering himself, he turned to us and, with an expression of unutterable disgust, exclaimed, "You blokes can laugh ; anybody 'ud fink I was the only blighter in this war."—*C. Bragg (late Rifle Brigade, 14th Division), 61 Hinton Road, Herne Hill, S.E.24.*

Germany Didn't Know This

ONE night in June 1916, on the Somme, we were ordered to leave our line and go over and dig an advance trench. We returned to our trench before dawn, and shortly afterwards my chum, "Pussy" Harris, said to me, "I have left my rifle in No Man's Land."

"Never mind," I said, "there are plenty more. Don't go over there : the snipers are sure to get you."

But my advice was all in vain ; he insisted on going. When I asked him why he wanted that particular rifle he said, "Well, the barrel is bent, *and it can shoot round corners.*"

He went over. . . .

That night I saw the regimental carpenter going along the trench with a roughly-made wooden cross inscribed "R.I.P. Pte. Harris."—*W. Ford, 613 Becontree Avenue, Chadwell Heath, Essex.*

Better than the Crystal Palace

ONE night, while going round the line at Loos, I was accompanied by Sergeant Winslow, who was a London coster before the war.

We were examining the field of fire of a Lewis gun, when the Germans opened up properly on our sector. Clouds of smoke rose from the surrounding trenches, crash after crash echoed around the old Loos crassier, and night was turned into day by Verey lights sent up by both sides.

Suddenly a lad of 18, just out, turned to Sergeant Winslow, and in a quivering voice said : "My God, sergeant, this is awful ! "

Sergeant Winslow replied : "Now, look 'ere, me lad, you'd have paid 'alf a dollar to take your best gal to see this at the Crystal Palace before the war. What are yer grousing abaht ? "—*A. E. Grant (late 17th Welch Regt.), 174 Broom Road, Teddington.*

A Short Week-end

ONE Saturday evening I was standing by my dug-out in Sausage Valley, near Fricourt, when a draft of the Middlesex Regt. halted for the guide to take them up to the front line where the battalion was. I had a chat with one of the lads, who told me he had left England on the Friday.

They moved off, and soon things got lively ; a raid and counter-raid started.

Later the casualties began to come down, and the poor chaps were ying around outside the 1st C.C.S. (which was next to my dug-out). On a stretcher was my friend of the draft. He was pretty badly hit. I gave him a cigarette and tried to cheer him by telling him he would soon be back in England. With a feeble smile he said, " Blimey, sir, this 'as been a short week-end, ain't it ? "—*Pope Stamper* (15th Durham L.I.), 188A *Upper Richmond Road, East Sheen, S.W.*14.

Simultaneous Chess

AT Aubers Ridge, near Fromelles, in October 1918, my chum and I were engrossed in a game of chess, our chessboard being a water-proof sheet with the squares painted on it, laid across a slab of concrete from a destroyed pillbox.

The Germans began to drop 5·9's with alarming regularity about 150 yards to our rear, temporarily distracting our attention from the game.

Returning to the game, I said to my chum, " Whose move, Joe ? "

Before he could reply a shell landed with a deafening roar within a few yards of us, but luckily did not explode (hence this story).

His reply was : " Ours "—and we promptly did.—*B. Greenfield, M.M. (late Cpl. R.F.A., 47th (London) Division), L.C.C. Parks Dept., Tooting Bec Common, S.W.*

Fire-step Philosophy

ON July 1, 1916, I happened to be among those concerned in the attack on the German line in front of Serre, near Beaumont Hamel. Our onslaught at that point was not conspicuously successful, but we managed to establish ourselves temporarily in what had been the Boche front line, to the unconcealed indignation of the previous tenants.

During a short lull in the subsequent proceedings I saw one of my company—an elderly private whose melancholy countenance and lank black moustache will ever remain engraved on my memory—seated tranquilly on the battered fire-step, engrossed in a certain humorous journal.

Meeting my astonished eye, he observed in a tone of mild resentment: " This 'ere's a dud, sir. 'S not a joke in it—not what *I* calls a joke, anyway."

So saying, he rose, pocketed the paper, and proceeded placidly to get on with the war.—*K. R. G. Browne,* 6B *Winchester Road, N.W.*3.

" Teddie " Gets the Last Word

SERGEANT "TEDDIE" was rather deaf, but I am inclined to think that this slight affliction enabled him to pull our legs on occasions.

Our company of the London Regiment had just taken over a part of the line known as the Paris Redoubt, and on the first evening in the sector the company commander, the second in command, Sergeant

" A quarter to seven, sir."

"Teddie," and myself had a stroll along the observation line, which was just forward of the front line, in order to visit the various posts.

Suddenly a salvo of shells came over and one burst perilously near us. Three of the party adopted the prone position in record time, but on our looking round "Teddie" was seen to be still standing and apparently quite unconcerned.

"Why the dickens didn't you get down?" said one of the party, turning to him. "It nearly had us that time."

"Time?" said "Teddie," looking at his watch. "A quarter to seven, sir."—*J. S. O. (late C.S.M., 15th London Regt.).*

" Nobbler's " Grouse

JUST before the battle of Messines we of the 23rd Londons were holding the Bluff sector to the right of Hill 60. "Stand down" was the order, and the sergeant was coming round with the rum.

"Nobbler," late of the Mile End Road, was watching him in joyful anticipation when . . . a whizz-bang burst on the parapet, hurling men in all directions. No one was hurt . . . but the precious rum jar was shattered.

"Nobbler," sitting up in the mud and moving his tin hat from his left eye the better to gaze upon the ruin, murmured bitterly: "Louvain—Rheims—the *Lusitania*—and now our perishin' rum issue. Jerry, you 'eathen, you gets worse and worse. But, my 'at, won't you cop it when 'Aig knows abaht this!"—*E. H. Oliver, Lanark House, Woodstock, Oxford.*

Dust in 'Indenburg's Sauerkraut!

TO all those thousands who remember Shrapnel Corner and the sign: "DRIVE SLOWLY! SPEED CAUSES DUST WHICH DRAWS THE ENEMY'S SHELL FIRE" this incident will appeal.

I had rounded the corner into Zillebeke Road with a load of ammunition, and had gone about 200 yards along the road, when Fritz let go with a few shells.

"Rum Ration" (my mate's nick-name) looked out of the lorry to observe where the shells were falling.

"Nah we're for it," he exclaimed, "our dust must 'ave gorn into ole 'Indenberg's blinkin' sauerkraut."—*J. H. Clarke, ex-Pte., M.T.A.S.C.*

A Valiant Son of London

CRACK! CRACK! CRACK!—and men falling with each crack. It is terrible; we are faced with mud, misery, and despair. A German machine-gun is taking its toll.

It seems impossible to get at the gunners, and we spend hours lying in wait. This waiting proves too much for one of us; single-handed he takes a chance and crawls away from my side. I keep him covered; minutes roll by; they seem hours, days; and, as he is now out of sight, I begin to give up hope for him, my Cockney pal.

Some instinct warns me to keep watch, and I am rewarded. I feel my eyes start from my head as I see the approaching procession—four Germans, hands above their heads, and my pal following, carrying the machine-gun across his shoulders. I marvel at his courage and wonder how it was done . . . but this I am never to know. As I leap from the trench to give him assistance I realise his number is nearly up. He is covered with blood.

I go to relieve him of his burden, and in that moment one of the Germans, sensing that my pal is almost out, turns on us with his revolver. We are held at the pistol-point and I know I must make a desperate bid to save my pal, who has done his best in an act which saved a portion of our line.

I drop the gun and, with a quick movement, I am able to trip the nearest German, but he is quick too and manages to stick me (and I still carry the mark of his bayonet in my side).

The realisation I am still able to carry on, that life is sweet, holds me up, and, with a pluck that showed his determination and Cockney courage, my pal throws himself into a position in which he can work the gun. *Crack!* and *Crack!* again: the remaining Germans are brought down.

I am weak with loss of blood, but I am still able to drag my pal with me, and, aided by his determination, we get through. It seems we are at peace with the world. But, alas, when only five yards from our trenches a shell bursts beside us ; I have a stinging pain in my shoulder and cannot move! Machine-guns and rifles are playing hell.

My pal, though mortally wounded, still tries to drag me to our trench. He reaches the parapet . . . *Zip* . . . *Zip*. The first has missed, but the second gets him. It is a fatal shot, and, though in the greatest agony, he manages to give me a message to his folks. . . .

He died at my side, unrewarded by man. The stretcher-bearer told me that he had five bullet-holes in him. He lies in France to-day, and I owe my life to him, and again I pay homage to his memory and to him as one of England's greatest heroes—a Valiant Son of London.—*John Batten (late Rifleman*, 13 *Bn., K.R.R.C.*), 50 *Sussex Gardens, Hyde Park, W*.2.

A Hint to the Brigadier

ALEC LANCASTER was a showman at the White City in pre-war days. Short in stature, he possessed a mighty heart, and in the ghastly days in front of Poelcapelle he made history as the sergeant who took command of a brigadier.

The brigadier had been on a visit to the front line to inspect a new belt of wire and, passing the —— headquarters, paused to look around.

Just then a few shells came over in quick succession and things looked nasty.

Alec Lancaster took command and guided the brigadier somewhat forcibly into a dug-out with the laconic, " Nah, then. We don't want any dead brigadiers rahnd 'ere."—*Geo. B. Fuller*, 146 *Rye Road, Hoddesdon, Herts.*

" Salvage ? Yus, Me ! "

ON the third day of the German offensive in March 1918 a certain brigade of the R.F.A. was retiring on Péronne.

A driver, hailing from London town, was in charge of the cook's cart, which contained officers' kits belonging to the headquarters' staff.

As he was making his way along a " pip-squeak " came over and burst practically beneath the vehicle and blew the whole issue to pieces. The driver had a miraculous escape.

When he recovered from the shock he ruefully surveyed the debris, and after deciding that nothing could be done, continued his journey on foot into Péronne.

Just outside that town he was met by the Adjutant, who said, " Hullo, driver, what's happened—where's cook's cart with the kits ? "

DRIVER : Blown up, sir.

ADJUTANT (*anxiously*) : Anything salved ?

DRIVER : Yus, sir, me !—*F. H. Seabright*, 12 *Broomhill Road, Good-mayes, Essex.*

Almost Self-inflicted

THE London (47th) Division, after a strenuous time on the Somme in September 1916, were sent to Ypres for a quiet (?) spell, the depleted ranks being made up by reserves from home who joined us *en route.*

The 18th Battalion (London Irish), were informed on taking the line that their opponents were men of the very same German regiment as they had opposed and vanquished at High Wood.

Soon after " stand down " the following morning Rifleman S—— mounted the fire-step and, cupping his hands to his mouth, shouted, " Compree 'Igh Wood, Fritz ? "

The words had hardly left his lips when *zip*, a sniper's bullet knocked his tin hat off his head and Rifleman S—— found himself lying on the duckboards with blood running down his face.

Picking himself up, he calmly gathered his souvenirs together and said as he made his way out, " Cheerio, boys, I've got a Blighty one, but don't tell the colonel it was self-inflicted."—*A. C. B., Ilford, Essex.*

Nobby's 1,000 to 1 Chance

OUR division (the Third) was on its way from the line for the long-looked-for rest. We were doing it by road in easy stages.

During a halt a pack animal (with its load of two boxes of " ·303 ") became restive and bolted. One box fell off and was being dragged by the lashing. Poor old Nobby Clarke, who had been out since Mons, stopped the box with his leg, which was broken below the knee.

As he was being carried away one of the stretcher-bearers said, " Well, Nobby, you've got a Blighty one at last."

" Yus," said Nobby ; " but it took a fousand rahnds to knock me over."—*H. Krepper (late 5th Fusiliers), 62 Anerley Road, Upper Nor-wood, S.E.19.*

That Derby Scheme

THE Commanding Officer of a Territorial battalion was wounded in both hands during the third battle of Gaza in 1917. He had much service to his credit, was a lieutenant-colonel of over two years' standing, had been wounded twice before, and held the D.S.O.

He pluckily remained with his unit for thirty-six hours. Then, worn out with lack of sleep, pain, and loss of blood, and filled with disappointment at having to leave his battalion still in the fight, he trudged back to the field ambulance.

His sufferings, which had aged his appearance, and the Tommy's tunic which he wore in action, apparently misled a party of 10th London men whom he passed. They looked sympathetically at him, and one said, " Poor old blighter, *'e ought never to 'ave been called up.*"—*Captain J. Finn, M.C., Constitutional Club, W.C.2.*

" Shoo-Shoo-Shooting "

THERE were no proper trenches in front of Armentières in early December 1914, and a machine gun section was doing its best to build an emplacement and cover. It was in the charge of a young Londoner who in times of excitement stuttered badly.

Not being satisfied with the position of one sandbag, he hopped over those already in place, and in full view of Jerry (it was daylight too), began to adjust the sandbag that displeased him.

Jerry immediately turned a machine gun on him, but the young officer finished his work, and then stood up.

Looking towards Jerry as the section yelled to him to come down, he stuttered angrily. " I b-b-be-lieve the bli-bli-blighters are shoo-shoo-shoo-shoo-ting at me." At that moment someone grabbed his legs and pulled him down. It was a fine example of cool nerve.—*T. D., Victoria, S.W.1.*

Ancient Britons ?—No !

IT happened late in 1917 in Tank Avenue, just on the left of Monchy-le-Preux. It was a foul night of rain, wind, sleet, and whizz-bangs.

My battalion had just been relieved, and we were making our way out as best we could down the miry communication trench. Every now and again we had to halt and press ourselves against the trench side to allow a straggling working party of the K.R.R.s to pass up into the line.

Shells were falling all over the place, and suddenly Fritz dropped one right into the trench a few bays away from where I was.

I hurried down and found two of the working party lying on the duck-boards. They were both wounded, and one of them had his tunic ripped off him by the force of the explosion. What with his tattered uniform—and what remained of it—and his face and bare chest smothered in mud, he was a comical though pathetic sight. He still clung to his bundle of pickets he had been carrying and he sat up and looked round with a puzzled expression.

One of our sergeants—a rather officious fellow—pushed himself forward.

" Who are you ? " he asked. " K.R.R.s ? "

" 'Course," retorted the half-naked Cockney. " Oo d'ye fink we was —Ancient Britons ? "—*E. Gordon Petrie (late Cameron Highlanders), " Hunky-Dory," Demesne Road, Wallington, Surrey.*

Desert Island—Near Bullecourt

BETWEEN Ecoust and Bullecourt in January 1918 my platoon was passing a mine crater which was half-full of water when suddenly Jerry sent one over. Six of our fellows were wounded, and one of them, a Bow Road Cockney, was hurled into the crater.

"Robinson Crusoe."

He struggled to his feet and staggered towards a pile of rubble that rose above the muddy water like an island. Arrived there, he sat down and looked round him in bewilderment.

Then : "Blimey," he muttered, "Robinson ruddy Crusoe ! "—*E. McQuaid* (*late R.S.F.*), 22 *Grove Road, S.W.*9.

" Tiger's " Little Trick

ON October 11–12, 1914, during the Mons retreat, a small party of 2nd Life Guards were told off as outpost on the main road, near Wyngene, Belgium. After we had tied our horses behind a farmhouse at the side of the road, we settled down to await the arrival of " Jerry."

Time went slowly, and one of our troopers suggested that we all put a half-franc into an empty " bully " tin, and the first one of us who shot a German was to take the lot. To this we all agreed.

It was about midnight when, suddenly, out of the shadows, rode a German Death's-head Hussar. We all raised our rifles as one man, but before we could shoot " Tiger " Smith, one of our real Cockney troopers, shouted, " Don't shoot! Don't shoot! " During our momentary hesitation " Tiger's " rifle rang out, and off rolled the German into the road.

Upon our indignant inquiry as to why he had shouted " Don't shoot," " Tiger " quietly said, " Nah, then, none of your old buck ; just hand over that tin of 'alf francs I've won."—*Fred Bruty (late Corporal of Horse, 2nd Life Guards), City of London Police Dwellings, No. 3, Ferndale Court, Ferndale Road, S.W.9.*

Raffle Draw To-night !

NEAR St. Quentin, in October 1918, I was in charge of a section that was detailed to cross a railway to establish communication with troops on the other side. Unfortunately we were spotted by a German machine gunner, who made things very hot for us, two men being quickly hit. We managed, however, to reach a small mound where, by lying quite flat, we were comparatively safe.

Glancing in the direction from which we had come, I saw a man whom I recognised as " Topper " Brown, our company runner, dashing as hard as he could for the cover where we had sheltered.

" How do, corp ? " he said when he came up. " Any of your blokes like to go in a raffle for this watch ? " (producing same). " 'Arf a franc a time ; draw to-night in St. Quentin."—*S. Hills (late Rifle Brigade), 213, Ripple Road, Barking.*

Exit the General's Dessert

IN the early part of the War we were dug in between the Marne and the Aisne with H.Q. situated in a trench along which were growing several fruit trees which the troops were forbidden to touch.

The Boche were shelling with what was then considered to be heavy stuff, and we were all more or less under cover, when a large one hit the back of the trench near H.Q.

After the mess staff had recovered from the shock it was noticed that apples were still falling from a tree just above, and the mess corporal, his ears and eyes still full of mud, was heard to say : " Thank 'eaven, I shan't have to climb that perishin' tree and get the old man's bloomin' dessert to-night."—*E. Adamson, Overseas Club, St. James's.*

" Try on this Coat, Sir "

IN September 1916, while with the 17th K.R.R.C., I lost my overcoat in a billet fire at Mailly-Maillet and indented for a new one, which, however, failed to turn up.

We moved to Hebuterne, where the line was very lively and the working parties used to be strafed with " Minnies " all night.

One night, while on patrol, with nerves on the jump, I was startled to hear a voice at my elbow say, " Try this on."

It was the Q.M.'s corporal with the overcoat !

I solemnly tried it on there and then in No Man's Land, about 300 yards in front of our front line and not very far from the German line.

The corporal quite casually explained that he had some difficulty in finding me out there in the dark, but he did not want the trouble of carrying stuff out of the line when we moved !—*S. W. Chuckerbutty*, (*L.R.B. and K.R.R.C.*), 3 *Maida Hill West, London, W.2.*

On the Kaiser's Birthday

IN the Brickstacks at Givenchy, 1916. The Germans were celebrating the Kaiser's birthday by putting a steady succession of " Minnies " into and around our front line trench.

Just when the strain was beginning to tell and nerves were getting jumpy, a little Cockney corporal jumped on the fire-step and, shaking his fist at the Germans forty yards away, bawled, " You wait till it's *my* ruddy birthday ! "

Fritz didn't wait two seconds, but the little corporal had got his laugh and wasn't taking a curtain.—" *Bison* " (*late R.W.F.*).

" Chuck us yer Name Plate ! "

IN June 1917 we were ordered to lay a line to the front line at " Plug Street." Fritz started to bombard us with whizz-bangs, and my pal and I took cover behind a heap of sandbags, noticing at the same time that all the infantrymen were getting away from the spot.

When things quietened down we heard a Cockney voice shouting, " Hi, mate ! Chuck us yer name plate (identification disc). Y're sitting up against our bomb store."—*S. Doust* (*late Signal Section, " F " Battery, R.H.A.*), 53 *Wendover Road, Well Hall, Eltham, S.E.9.*

To Hold His Hand

WHILE on our way to relieve the 1st R.W.F.s, who were trying their utmost to hold a position in front of Mametz Wood, it was necessary to cross a road, very much exposed to Jerry's machine guns.

A burst of firing greeted our attempt, and when we succeeded, a Cockney who had a flesh wound caused a smile by saying, " Go back ? Not me. Next time I crosses a road I wants a blinking copper ter 'old me 'and ? "—*G. Furnell*, 57*a Southwold Road, Upper Clapton, E.5.*

The New Landlord

DURING an advance on the Somme in 1916 my company was rushed up to the captured trenches to search the dug-outs and to bring in the prisoners.

My Cockney pal was evidently enjoying himself. As he went from one dug-out to another he was singing :

> "Orl that I want is lo-ove,
> Orl that I want is yew."

Entering one dug-out, however, his voice suddenly changed. In the dug-out were three Germans. Showing them the point of his bayonet, the Cockney roared : " Nah, then, aht of it ; 'op it. I'm lan'lord 'ere nah."—*C. Grimwade, 26 Rotherhithe New Road, Rotherhithe, S.E.16.*

" Out of Bounds " in the Line

ONE night in October '14, in the neighbourhood of Herlies, " Ginger," a reservist, was sent out to call in the men of a listening post.

Dawn came, but no " Ginger " returned, and as he did not turn up during the day he was given up for lost.

Soon after dusk, however, a very worn and fed-up " Ginger " returned. We gathered that he had suddenly found himself in the German lines, had had a " dust-up," had got away, and had lain out in No Man's Land until dusk allowed him to get back.

The company officer was inclined to be cross with him, and asked him,
But what made you go so far as the enemy position ? "

" Ginger " scratched his head, and then replied, " Well, sir, nobody said anyfink to me abaht it being aht o' bahnds."—*T. L. Barling (late Royal Fusiliers), 21 Lockhart Street, Bow, E.3.*

Epic of the Whistling Nine

ON May 14, 1917, the 2/2nd Battalion of the London Regiment occupied the support lines in front of Bullecourt. " A " company's position was a thousand yards behind the front line trenches. At 2 p.m. the enemy began to subject the whole area to an intense bombardment which lasted more than thirteen hours.

In the middle of the bombardment (which was described by the G.O.C.-in-Chief as " the most intense bombardment British troops had had to withstand "), No. 3 platoon of " A " company was ordered to proceed to the front line with bombs for the battalion holding it. The platoon consisted of 31 N.C.O.s and men and one officer.

.   .   .   .   .

The only means of communication between the support and front lines was a trench of an average depth of two feet. Along this trench the platoon proceeded, carrying between them forty boxes of Mills bombs. Every few yards there were deep shell holes to cross ; tangled telephone wires tripped the men ; M. G. bullets swept across the trench, and heavy shells obtained direct hits frequently, while shrapnel burst overhead without cessation.

A man was hit every few minutes; those nearest him rendered what aid was possible, unless he was already dead; his bombs were carried on by another.

.   .   .   .

Of the thirty-one who started, twenty-one were killed or wounded; the remainder, having taken an hour and a half to cover the 1,000 yards, reached the front line *with the forty boxes of bombs intact.*

They were ordered to remain, and thus found themselves assisting in repulsing an attack made by the 3rd Lehr Regiment of Prussian Guards, and two of the men succeeded in wounding and capturing the commanding officer of the attacking regiment.

Of the ten N.C.O.s and men who were left, a lance-corporal was blown to pieces in the trench; the remainder stayed in the front line until they were relieved four days later. On their way back, through Vaux Vraucourt, they picked clusters of May blossom, and with these in their equipment and rifle barrels, marched into the transport lines whistling.— *Captain, London Regiment.*

Tale of a Cook and a " Crump "

OUR cook was having the time of his life. The transition from trench warfare to more or less open warfare in late October 1918 brought with it a welcome change of diet in the form of pigs and poultry from the deserted farms, and cook had captured a nice young porker and two brace of birds.

From the pleasant aroma which reached us from the cottage as we lay on our backs watching a German aeroplane we knew that cook would soon be announcing the feast was ready.

Suddenly from the blue came a roar like that of an express train. We flung ourselves into the ditch. . . . *K-k-k-k-r-r-r-ump* !

When the smoke and dust cleared away the cottage was just a rubbish heap, but there was cook, most miraculously crawling out from beneath a debris of rafters, beams, and bricks !

" Ruddy 'orseplay ! " was the philosopher's comment.—*I. O.*, 19 *Burnell Road, Sutton, Surrey.*

" —— Returns the Penny "

WHEN my husband commanded the 41st Division in France he was much struck by the ready wit of a private of the Royal Fusiliers (City of London Regiment) in a tight corner.

A bomb landed in a crowded dug-out while the men were having a meal. Everyone stared aghast at this ball of death except one Tommy, who promptly picked it up and flung it outside saying: " Grite stren'th returns the penny, gentlemen ! " as he returned to his bully beef.—*Lady Lawford, London, S.W.*1.

"In Time for the Workman's ? "

A NIGHT wire-cutting party in the Arras sector had been surprised by daylight. All the members of the party (21st London Regiment) crawled back safely except one Cockney rifleman.

When we had reached the trenches and found that he was missing, we were a bit upset. Would he have to lie out in No Man's Land all day ? Would he be spotted by snipers ?

After a while our doubts were answered by a terrific burst from the German machine guns. Some of the bolder spirits peered over the top of the " bags " and saw our Cockney pal rushing, head down, towards our line while streams of death poured around him.

He reached our parapet, fell down amongst us in the mud, uninjured, and immediately jumped to his feet and said, " Am I in time for the workman's ? "—*D. F., Acton, W.3.*

A Lovely Record

THE TIME : March 1916.

THE SCENE : The Talus des Zouaves—a narrow valley running behind Vimy Ridge from Neuville St. Vaast through Souchez. The weather is bleak, and there is a sticky drizzle—it is towards dusk.

THE MAN : A native of " somewhere just awf the ' Bricklayers Arms '— you know where that is, sir." Height, just over 5 feet ; complexion, red ; hair, red and not over tidy ; appearance, awkward ; clothes don't seem to fit quite. Distinguishing marks—a drooping red moustache almost concealing a short clay pipe, stuck bowl sideways in the corner of the mouth. On the face there is a curious—whimsical—wistful, in fact, a Cockney expression.

THE OCCASION : The Boche is putting down his evening " strafe "— an intense and very accurate barrage laid like a curtain on the southern slope of the valley. Our hero, his hands closed round the stock of his rifle held between his knees, is squatting unconcernedly on the wet ground in the open on the northern side of the valley, where only a shell with a miraculous trajectory could have scored a direct hit, watching the shells burst almost every second not a great distance away. The din and pandemonium are almost unbearable. Fragments of H.E. and shrapnel are dropping very near.

THE REMARK : Removing his pipe to reveal the flicker of a smile, he remarked, in his inimitable manner : " *Lor' blimey, guv'nor, wouldn't this sahnd orl rite on a grammerphone ?* "—*Gordon Edwards, M.C. (Captain, late S.W.B.), " Fairholm," 48 Alexandra Road, Wimbledon, S.W.19.*

Logic in No Man's Land

FRITZ had been knocking our wire about, and a party of us were detailed to repair it. One of our party, a trifle more windy than the rest, kept ducking at the stray bullets that were whistling by. Finally,

'Erb, who was holding the coil of wire, said to him, " Can't yer stop that bobbin' abaht ? They won't 'urt yer unless they 'its yer."—*C. Green, 44 Monson Road, New Cross, S.E.14.*

Fousands . . . and Millions

IT was on the Mons-Condé Canal, on the afternoon of August 23, 1914. Our artillery had just opened up when a tiny Cockney trumpeter, who could not have been more than 15 years old, came galloping up to us with a message.

"They're coming on in millions."

" How are the gunners going on, boy ? " said my captain.

" Knocking 'em down in fousands, sir," replied the lad.

" Good," said the captain.

" Yus, and they're coming on in millions," replied the boy as he rode away to his battery.

A plucky kid, that.—*W. H. White, 29 Clive Road, Colliers Wood, S.W.19.*

Lost : A Front Line

TWO or three American officers were attached to our brigade H.Q. on the Somme front.

We were doing our usual four days in the front line when one morning an American officer emerged from the communication trench. Just then the Germans opened out with everything from a 5.9 to rifle grenade. We squeezed into funk-holes in the bottom of the trench. Presently there was a lull, and the American officer was heard to ask, " Say, boys, where is the front line in these parts ? "

" Tich," a little Cockney from Euston way, extracted himself from the earth, and exclaimed, " Strike ! j'ear that ? Wot jer fink this is—a blinkin' rifle range ? "—*W. Wheeler* (*late 23rd Battalion Royal Fusiliers*), 55 *Turney Road, Dulwich, S.E.*

" If Our Typist Could See Me Nah "

IMAGINE (if you can) the mud on the Somme at its worst. A Royal Marine Artilleryman (a very junior clerk from " Lambeff ") was struggling up the gentle slope behind Trones Wood with a petrol tin of precious water in either hand. A number of us were admiring his manly efforts from a distance when the sudden familiar shriek was heard, followed by the equally familiar bang.

We saw him thrown to the ground as the whizzbang burst but a few feet from him, and we rushed down, certain that he had " got his." Imagine our surprise on being greeted by an apparition that had struggled to a sitting posture, liberally plastered with mud, and a wound in the shoulder, who hoarsely chuckled and said : " If our typist could see me *nah* ! "—*C. H. F.* (*W/Opr. attached R.M.A. Heavy Brigade*).

Q ! Q ! Queue !

THE scene was an observation post in the top of a (late) colliery chimney, 130 ft. up, on the outskirts of Béthune, during the last German offensive of the War.

A great deal of heavy shelling was in progress in our immediate vicinity, and many of Fritz's " high-velocities " were screaming past our lofty pinnacle, which was swaying with the concussion. At any moment a direct hit was possible.

My Cockney mate had located a hostile battery, and after some difficulty with the field telephone was giving the bearing to headquarters.

Faults in the line seemed to prevent him from finishing his message, which consisted of giving the map square (Q 20) being " strafed." The " Q " simply would not reach the ears of the corporal at headquarters, and after many fruitless efforts, using " Q " words, I heard him burst out in exasperation : " Q ! Q ! Queue ! . . . Blimey ! you know—the blinkin' thing wot the pore blighters at home wite abaht for ' mawgarine ' in."—*B. W. Whayman* (*late F.S.C., R.E.*), 24 *Oxford Street, Boston, Lincolnshire.*

" Fine 'eads er Salery ! "

WE were in a deep railway cutting near Gouzeaucourt. Jerry's aeroplanes had found us and his artillery was trying to shift us.

On the third day we had run out of cigarettes, so the sergeant-major asked for a volunteer to go to a canteen four miles away.

Our Cockney, a costermonger well known in the East End, volunteered. He could neither read nor write, so we fixed him up with francs, a sandbag, and a list.

Hours passed, the strafe became particularly heavy, and we began to fear our old pal had been hit.

Suddenly during a lull in the shelling far away along the ravine we heard a voice shouting, " 'Ere's yer fine 'eads er salery 'orl white." He was winning through.—" *Sparks," Lowestoft, Suffolk.*

The Old Soldier Falls

AFTER my battalion had been almost wiped out in the 1918 retirement, I was transferred to the 1st Batt. Middlesex Regt. One old soldier, known to us as " Darky," who had been out since '14, reported at B.H.Q. that he wanted to go up the front line with his old mates instead of resting behind the line.

His wish was granted. He was detailed to escort a party of us to the front line.

All went well till we arrived at the support line, where we were told to be careful of snipers.

We had only gone 20 yards further when the old soldier fell back into my arms, shot through the head. He was dying when he opened his eyes and said to me, " Straight on, lad. You can find your way now."— *A. H. Walker, 59 Wilberforce Road, Finsbury Park, N.4.*

Not Meant For Him

AT the end of September 1917 my regiment (5th Seaforth Highlanders) were troubled by bombing raids by enemy aircraft at the unhealthy regularity of one raid per hour. We were under canvas at Siege Camp, in the Ypres sector, and being near to a battery of large guns we were on visiting terms with some of the gunners, who were for the most part London men.

A Lewisham man was writing a letter in our tent one day when we again had the tip that the Germans were flying towards us. So we all scattered.

After the raid we returned to our tent and were surprised to see our artillery friend still writing his letter. We asked him whether he had stayed there the whole time and in reply he read us the following passage from his letter which he had written during the raid :

" As I write this letter Jerry is bombing the Jocks, but although I am in their camp, being a Londoner, I suppose the raid is not meant for me, and I feel quite safe."—*W. A. Bull, M.M., 62 Norman Road, Ilford, Essex.*

An Extra Fast Bowler

DURING the defence of Antwerp in October 1914 my chum, who was wicket-keeper in the Corps cricket team, got hit in the head. I was with him when he came to, and asked him what happened.

"Extra fast one on the leg side," was his reply.—*J. Russell (late R.M.L.I.), 8 Northcote Road, Deal, Kent.*

"I'll Call a Taxi, Sir"

DURING an engagement in East Africa an officer was badly wounded. Bill, from Bermondsey, rode out to him on a mule. Whilst he was trying to get the officer away on his mule the animal bolted. Bill then said, "Me mule 'opped it, sir. 'E's a fousand miles from 'ere, so I'll giv yer a lift on my Bill and Jack (back)."

The officer was too heavy, so Bill put him gently on the ground saying, "Sorry, sir, I'll 'ave ter call a taxi." Bill then ran 500 yards under heavy machine-gun fire to where the armoured cars were under cover. He brought one out, and thereby saved the officer's life.

After the incident, Bill's attention was drawn to a bullet hole in his pith helmet. "Blimey," he said, "what a shot ! If he 'adn't a missed me 'e'd a 'it me." Bill was awarded the Distinguished Conduct Medal. —*W. B. Higgins, D.C.M. (late Corpl. Mounted Infantry), 46 Stanley Road, Ilford.*

Attack in "Birthday Clothes"

WE came out of the line on the night of June 14–15, 1917, to "bivvies" at Mory, after a hot time from both Fritz and weather at Bullecourt. When dawn broke we were astonished and delighted to see a "bath." Whilst we were in the line our Pioneers had a brain wave, dug a hole in the ground, lined it with a tarpaulin sheet, and filled it with water.

As our last bath was at Achiet-le-Petit six weeks before, there was a tremendous crowd waiting "mit nodings on," because there was "standing room only" for about twenty in the bath.

Whilst ablutions were in progress an aeroplane was heard, but no notice was taken because it was flying so low—"one of ours" everybody thought. When it came nearer there was a shout, "Strewth, it's a Jerry plane."

Baths were "off" for the moment and there was a stampede to the "bivvies" for rifles. It was the funniest thing in the world to see fellows running about in their "birthday suits" plus only tin hats, taking pot shots at the aeroplane.

Even Fritz seemed surprised, because it was some moments before he replied with his machine gun.

We watched him fly away back to his own lines and a voice broke the silence with, "Blinkin' fools to put on our tin 'ats. Uvverwise 'ole Fritz wouldn't a known but what we might be Germans."

I often wonder if any other battalion had the " honour " of " attacking the enemy " clad only in tin hats.—*G. M. Rampton (late 12th London Regt., " Rangers "), 43 Cromwell Road, Winchester.*

His Good-bye to the Q.M.

SCENE, Ypres, May 1915. The battalion to which I belonged had been heavily shelled for many hours, and among the casualties was " Topper " Brown, a Cockney, who was always in trouble for losing items of his kit. Taken to the dressing station to have a badly shattered foot amputated, he recovered consciousness to find the C.Q.M.S. standing by the stretcher on which he lay.

The C.Q.M.S., not knowing the extent of Brown's injury, inquired, " What's the trouble, Brown ? "

In a weak voice the Cockney replied, " Lost one boot and one sock again, Quarter."—*E. E. Daniels (late K.R.R.), 178 Caledonian Road, N.1.*

From Bow and Harrow

WE were in the line at Neuville St. Vaast in 1916. A raid had just been carried out. In the party were two inseparable chums, one from Bow and one from Harrow. (Of course they were known as Bow and Arrow.)

The bulk of the raiders had returned, but some were yet to come in. Some time later three forms were seen crawling towards our line. They were promptly helped in.

As their faces were blackened they were hard to recognise, and a corporal asked them who they were.

" Don't yer know us ? " said the chap from Bow. " We're Bow and Arrow." " Blimey ! " said another Cockney standing by. " And I suppose the other bloke's Robin 'ood, aint 'e."—*G. Holloway (late London Regt. and 180 M.G.C.), 179 Lewis Buildings, West Kensington, W.14.*

Piccadilly in the Front Line

TOWARDS the end of September 1918 I was one of a party of nine men and an officer taking part in a silent raid in the Ypres sector, a little in front of the well-known spot called Swan and Edgar's Corner. The raid was the outcome of an order from Headquarters demanding prisoners for information.

Everything had been nicely arranged. We were to approach the German line by stealth, surprise an outpost, and get back quickly to our own trenches with the prisoners.

Owing perhaps to the wretchedness of the night—it was pouring with rain, and intensely black—things did not work according to plan. Instead of reaching our objective, our party became divided, and the group that I was with got hopelessly lost. There were five of us, including " Ginger," a Cockney.

We trod warily for about an hour, when we suddenly came up against a barbed-wire entanglement, in the centre of which we could just make out the figure of a solitary German. After whispered consultation, we decided to take him prisoner, knowing that the German, having been stationary, had not lost sense of direction and could guide us back to our line. Noiselessly surmounting the barbed wire, we crept up to him and in a second Ginger was on him. Pointing his bayonet in Fritz's back, he said, " Nah, then, you blighter, show us the way 'ome."

Very coolly and without the slightest trace of fear, the German replied in perfect English, " I suppose you mean me to lead you to the British trenches."

" Oh ! " said Ginger, " so yer speak English, do yer ? "

" Yes," said the German, " I was a waiter at a restaurant in Piccadilly before the War."

" Piccadilly, eh ? You're just the feller we want. Take us as far as Swan and Edgar's Corner."—*R. Allen (late Middlesex Regt., 41st Division, 7 Moreland Street, Finsbury Park, N.4.*

" Wag's " Exhortation

ON a bitterly cold night, with a thick fog settling, the Middlesex Regt. set out on a raid on a large scale on the enemy's trenches. Fritz must have got wind of it, for when they were about half-way across the enemy guns opened fire and simply raked No Man's Land. The air was alive with shrapnel and nearly two-thirds of the raiders were casualties in no time.

Those that could tried to crawl back to our lines, but soon lost all direction in the fog. About half a dozen of them crawled into a shell-hole and lay there wounded or exhausted from their efforts, and afraid to move while the bombardment continued.

Meanwhile " Wag " Bennett, a Cockney, though badly wounded, had dragged himself out of a shell-hole, and was crawling towards what proved later to be the enemy lines when he saw the forms of the other fellows in the darkness. As he peered down upon them he called out, " Strike me pink ! Lyin' abaht dahn there as if you was at the 'Otel Cissle, while there's a ruddy war agoin' on. Come on up aht of it, else you'll git us all a bad name."

In a moment they were heartened, and they crawled out, following " Wag " on their hands and knees and eventually regained our lines. Poor " Wag " died soon afterwards from his wounds.—*H. Newing, 1 Park Cottages, Straightsmouth, Greenwich, S.E.10.*

Making a King of Him

OUR company of the Middlesex Regiment had captured a hill from Johnny Turk one evening, and at once prepared for the counter-attack on the morrow. My platoon was busy making a trench. On the parapet we placed large stones instead of sandbags.

During these operations we were greeted with machine-gun fire from

Johnny and, our numbers being small, we had to keep firing from different positions so as to give the impression that we were stronger than we really were.

It was while we were scrambling from one position to another that " Smudger " Smith, from Hammersmith, said : " Love us, Sarge, 'ow's this for a blinkin' game of draughts ? " The words were hardly out of his mouth when Johnny dropped a 5.9 about thirty yards away. The force of the explosion shook one of the stones from the parapet right on to " Smudger's " head, and he was knocked out.

When he came round his first words were : " Blimey, they must 'ave 'eard me to crown me like that."—*W. R. Mills (late Sergt., 2/10th Middlesex Regt.), 15 Canterbury Road, Colchester, Essex.*

" Peace ? Not wiv you 'ere ! "

TWO Cockney pals who were always trying to get the better of one another in a battle of words by greeting each other with such remarks as " Ain't you blinkin' well dead yet ? " earned for themselves the nicknames of Bill and Coo.

One evening they were sent to fetch water, and on the return journey the Germans started to shell rather heavily.

Coo ran more quickly than Bill and fell into a shell-hole. He scrambled out in time to see his pal blown sky high by what appeared to be a direct hit.

Coo was heard to remark : " I always told 'im 'e ought to be reported missing, and blimey if 'e ain't."

He then went to see if he could find the body : instead he found Bill alive, though badly wounded.

When finally Coo got his pal back to the trench, Bill opened his eyes. Seeing Coo bending over him, he said : " Lumme, I thought peace 'ad come at last, but it ain't—not wiv you 'ere."—*William Walker, 30 Park Road, Stopsley Road, Luton, Beds.*

An Expert on Shells

WE were billeted in the vaults of Ypres Post Office. Towards dusk of a summer's day in 1916 four of us were lounging at the top of the vault stairs, discussing the noise made by different shells. Jerry, a Cockney, was saying, " Yes, yer can always tell big 'uns—they shuffles," and went on to demonstrate with *Shsh-shsh-shsh*, when someone said " Listen ! "

There was the real sound, and coming straight for us. We dived or fell to the bottom of the stairs. Followed a terrific " crump " right in the entrance, which was completely blocked up.

Every candle and lamp was blown out ; we were choking with dust and showered with bricks and masonry.

There was a short silence, and Jerry's voice from the darkness said, " There y'are ; wot did I tell yer ? "—*H. W. Lake, London.*

A Camel " on the Waggon "

DURING the battle of Gaza in April 1917 camels were used for the conveyance of wounded. Each camel carried a stretcher on either side of its hump. Travelling in this manner was something akin to a rough Channel crossing.

I was wounded in the leg. My companion was severely wounded in

" I believe he was drunk before we set eyes on him."

both legs. Some very uncomplimentary remarks were passed between us concerning camels, particularly the one which was carrying us.

When we arrived at a field dressing-station a sergeant of the R.A.M.C. came along with liquid refreshments.

" Sergeant," said my chum, " if you give this bloke (indicating the camel) anything to drink I'm going to walk, 'cos I believe the blighter was drunk before we ever set eyes on him."—*Albert J. Fairall*, 43 *Melbourne Road, Leyton, E.*10.

Parting Presents

IT was on Passchendaele Ridge in 1917. Jerry had been giving us a hot time with his heavies. Just before daybreak our telephone line went west and we could not get through to our O.P.

I was detailed to go out and repair the line with a young Cockney from

Hackney. He had only been with us a few days and it was his first time up the line.

We had mended one break when shells dropped all round us. When I got to my feet, I saw my pal lying several feet away. I escaped with a few splinters and shock. I dragged my chum to a shell-hole which was full of water and found he was badly hit about the shoulder, chest, and leg. I dressed him as best I possibly could, when, *bang*, a shell seemed to drop right on us and something came hurtling into our hole with a splash.

It turned out to be a duckboard. I propped my chum against it to stop him slipping back into the water. After a few minutes he opened his eyes, and though in terrible pain, smiled and said, " Lummy, Jeff, old Jerry ain't so bad, after all. He has given me a nice souvenir to take to Blighty and now he has sent me a raft to cross the Pond on." Then he became unconscious.

It was now daybreak and quiet. I pulled him out of the hole and went and repaired the line. We got him away all right, but I never heard from him. I only hope he pulled through : he showed pluck.—*Signaller H. Jeffrey (late Royal Artillery), 13 Bright Road, Luton, Chatham, Kent.*

Bluebottles and Wopses

WE had just gone into the front line. Two of us had not been there before.

During a conversation with a Cockney comrade, an old hand, we told him of our dislike of bombs. He tried to re-assure us something like this : " Nah, don't let them worry you. You treat 'em just like blue-bottles, only different. With a blue-bottle you watch where it settles an' 'it it, but with bombs, you watch where they're goin' to settle and 'op it. It's quite simple."

A short time after a small German bomb came over and knocked out our adviser. My friend and I picked him up and tried to help him. He was seriously hurt. As we lifted him up my friend said to him, " You didn't get your blue-bottle that time, did you ? " He smiled back as he replied : " Twasn't a blue-bottle, mate ; must 'ave been a blinkin' wopse."—*C. Booth, 5 Creighton Road, N.W.6.*

The Cheerful " Card "

ON that June morning in 1917 when Messines Ridge went up, a young chap was brought in to our A.D.S. in Woodcote Farm. A piece of shell had torn a great gap in each thigh. Whilst the sergeant was applying the iodine by means of a spray the M.O. asked, " How are things going this morning ? " The lad was wearing a red heart as his battalion sign, and despite his great pain he answered : " O.K. sir. Hearts were trumps this morning."—*R. J. Graff, 3/5th L.F.A., 47th Division, 20 Lawrie Park Road, Sydenham.*

2*

Great Stuff This Shrapnel

DURING the retreat from Mons it was the cavalry's work to hold up the Germans as long as possible, to allow our infantry to get in position.

One day we had a good way to run to our horses, being closely pursued by the Germans. When we reached them we were all more or less out of breath. A little Cockney was so winded that he could hardly reach his stirrup, which kept slipping from under his foot.

Just then a shrapnel shell burst directly overhead, and the Cockney, without using his stirrup, vaulted clean into the saddle.

As we galloped off he gasped, " Blimey, don't they put new life in yer ? They're as good as Kruschens."—*E. H. (late R.H.G.), 87 Alpha Road, Surbiton, Surrey.*

Wot a War !

THREE of us were sitting on the high ground on the Gallipoli Beach watching shells dropping from the Turk positions.

A " G.S." wagon was proceeding slowly along below us, the driver huddled in his coat, for the air was chill.

Suddenly he jumped from the wagon and ran in our direction—he had heard the shell before we had.

The next moment the wagon was proceeding skywards in many directions, and the horses were departing at top speed in different directions.

The driver surveyed the scene for a moment and then in a very matter-of-fact voice said : " Blimey ! See that ? Now I suppose I've got to *walk* back, and me up all night—wot a war ! " And away he trudged !— *C. J. A., N.W.11.*

The Umpire

AFTER a retreat in May 1915 we saw, lying between our fresh position and the German lines, an English soldier whom we took to be dead.

Later, however, we advanced again, and discovered that the man was not dead, but badly wounded.

On being asked who he was, he replied in a very weak voice, " I fink I must be the blinkin' umpire."—*W. King (late Royal Fusiliers), 94 Manor Grove, Richmond, Surrey.*

" Don't Tell 'Aig "

LITTLE " Ginger " was the life and soul of our platoon until he was wounded on the Somme in 1918.

As he was carried off to the dressing-station he waved his hand feebly over the side of the stretcher and whispered, " Don't tell 'Aig ! He'd worry somethin' shockin'."—*G. E. Morris (late Royal Fusiliers), 368 Ivydale Road, Peckham Rye, S.E.15.*

" . . . In Love and War "

DURING a most unpleasant night bombing raid on the transport lines at Haillecourt the occupants of a Nissen hut were waiting for the next crash when out of the darkness and silence came the Cockney voice of a lorry driver saying to his mate, " ' Well,' I sez to 'er, I sez, ' You do as you like, and I can't say no fairer than that, can I ? ' "— *F. R. Jelley, Upland Road, Sutton, Surrey.*

" Afraid of Yer Own Shells "

I WAS on the Italian front in June 1918, and our battery was being strafed by the Austrians with huge armour-piercing shells, which made a noise like an express train coming at you, and exploded with a deafening roar.

An O.K. had just registered on one of our guns, blowing the wheels and masses of rock sky-high. A party of about twenty Austrian prisoners, in charge of a single Cockney, were passing our position at the time, and the effect of the explosion on the prisoners was startling. They scattered in all directions, vainly pursued by the Cockney, who reminded me of a sheep-dog trying to get his flock together.

At last he paused. " You windy lot o' blighters," he shouted as he spat on the ground in evident disgust, " afraid of yer own bloomin' shells ! "—*S. Curtis, 20 Palace Road, Upper Norwood, S.E.19.*

The Leader of the Blind

IN July 1918, at a casualty clearing station occupying temporary quarters in the old College of St. Vincent at ruined Senlis we dealt with 7,000 wounded in eight days. One night when we were more busy than usual an ambulance car brought up a load of gas-blinded men.

A little man whose voice proclaimed the city of his birth—arm broken and face blistered with mustard gas, though he alone of the party could see—jumped out, looked around, and then whispered in my ear, " All serene, guv'nor, leave 'em to me."

He turned towards the car and shouted inside, " Dalston Junction, change here for Hackney, Bow, and Poplar."

Then gently helping each man to alight, he placed them in a line with right hand on the shoulder of the man in front, took his position forward and led them all in, calling softly as he advanced, " Slow march, left, left, I had a good job and I *left* it."—*Henry T. Lowde (late 63rd C.C.S., R.A.M.C.), 101 Stanhope Gardens, Harringay, N.4.*

Pity the Poor Ducks

WE were in the Passchendaele sector in 1917, and all who were there know there were no trenches—just shell-holes half-filled with water.

Jerry had been strafing us for two days without a stop and of our platoon of twenty-three men only seven came out alive. As we were coming down the duckboard track after being relieved Jerry started to put over a barrage. We had to dive for the best cover we could get.

Three of us jumped into a large shell-hole, up to our necks in water. As the shells dropped around us we kept ducking our heads under the water.

Bert Norton, one of us—a Cockney—said : " Strike, we're like the little ducks in 'Yde Park—keep going under."

After another shell had burst and we had just come up to breathe Bert chimed in again with : " Blimey, mustn't it be awful to have to get your living by ducking ? "—*J. A. Wood, 185 Dalston Lane, E.8.*

Waiting Room Only

IT was in No Man's Land, and a party of New Zealand troops were making for shelter in a disabled British tank to avoid the downpour of shrapnel. They were about to swarm into the tank when the head of a London Tommy popped out of an aperture, and he exclaimed, " Blimey. Hop it ! This is a waiting room, not a blinkin' bee-hive."—*A. E. Wragg, 1 Downs Road, Beckenham, Kent.*

Not Yet Blasé

WE arrived at the Cambrai front in 1917—just a small bunch of Cockneys—and were attached to the Welsh Brigade of Artillery, being told to report to B.H.Q. up the sunken road in front of Bapaume.

En route our escort of Welshmen were telling us of the " terrible " shelling up the line. It was no leg pulling, for we quickly found out for ourselves that it was hot and furious.

Down we all went for cover as best we could, except one Cockney who stood as one spellbound watching the bursting of the shells. One of the Welshmen yelled out, " Drop down, Cockie ! " The Cockney turned round, to the wonderment and amusement of the rest, with the retort, " Blimey ! Get away with yer, you're windy. I've only just come out ! " —*Driver W. H. Allen (attached 1st Glamorgan R.H.A.), 8 Malden Crescent, Kentish Town, N.W.1.*

Paid with a Mills

DURING severe fighting in Delville Wood in August 1916 our regiment (the East Surreys) was cut off for about three days and was reduced to a mere handful of men, but still we kept up our joking and spirits.

A young Cockney, who was an adept at rhyming slang, rolled over, dead as I thought, for blood was streaming from his neck and head. But he sat up again and, wiping his hand across his forehead, exclaimed : " Strike me pink ! One on the top of my loaf of bread (head), and one in the bushel and peck (neck)." Then, slinging over a Mills bomb, he shouted : " 'Ere, Fritz, my thanks for a Blighty ticket."—*A. Dennis, 9 Somers Road, Brixton Hill, S.W.2.*

The Guns' Obligato

THE day after the Canadians attacked Vimy Ridge my battalion of the Royal Fusiliers advanced from Bully Grenay to a château on the outskirts of Lieven under heavy shell fire.

At the back of the château a street led to the main road to the town.

" Tipperary ! "

There, despite the bombardment, we found a Cockney Tommy of the Buffs playing " Tipperary " on a piano which had been blown out of a house into the road.

We joined in—until a shell took the top off the château, when we scattered !—*L. A. Utton*, 184 *Coteford Street, Tooting, S.W.*

In the Garden of Eden

WE had reached the district in " Mespot " reputed to be the Garden of Eden. One evening I was making my way with six men to relieve the guard on some ammunition barges lying by the bank of the Tigris.

We had approached to within about one hundred yards of these, when the Turks started sending over some " long-rangers." The sixth shell scored a direct hit on the centre barge, and within a few seconds the whole lot went up in what seemed like the greatest explosion of all time. Apart from being knocked over with the shock, we escaped injury, with the exception of a Cockney in our company.

Most of his clothing, except his boots, had been stripped from his body, and his back was bleeding. Slowly he struggled to his hands and knees, and surveying his nakedness, said : " Now where's that blinkin' fig tree ? " —*F. Dennis, 19 Crewdson Road, Brixton, S.W.*

Santa Claus in a Hurry

A FORWARD observation officer of the Artillery was on duty keeping watch on Watling Crater, Vimy Ridge, towards the end of 1916.

The observation post was the remains of a house, very much battered. The officer had to crawl up what had once been a large fireplace, where he had the protection of the only piece of wall that remained standing.

He was engrossed on his task when the arrival of a " Minnie " shook the foundations of the place, and down he came in a shower of bricks and mortar with his shrapnel helmet not at the regimental angle.

A couple of Cockney Tommies had also made a dive for the shelter of this pile of bricks and were crouching down, when the officer crawled from the fireplace. " Quick, Joe," said one of the Cockneys, " 'ang up yer socks—'ere comes ole Santa Claus ! "—*A. J. Robinson (late Sergeant, R.F.A.), 21 Clowders Road, Catford, S.E.6.*

What Paderewski was Missing

IT was on the night of October 27, 1917, at Passchendaele Ridge. Both sides were " letting it go hell for leather," and we were feeling none too comfortable crouching in shell-holes and taking what cover we could.

The ground fairly shook—and so did we for that matter—with the heavy explosions and the din was ear-splitting.

Just for something to say I called out to the chap in the next shell-hole —a Brentford lad he was : " What d'you think of it, Alf ? "

" Not much," he said, " I was just finkin' if Paderewski could get only this on 'is ol' jo-anner."—*M. Hooker, 325A Md. Qrs., Henlow Camp, Bedford.*

A Target, but No Offers

DURING the battle of the Somme, in September 1916, our Lewis gun post was in a little loop trench jutting out from the front line at a place called, I believe, Lone Tree, just before Combles. Jerry's front line was not many yards away, and it was a very warm spot.

Several casualties had occurred during the morning through sniping, and one enterprising chap had scored a bull's-eye on the top of our periscope.

Things quietened down a bit in the afternoon, and about 4 p.m. our captain, who already had the M.C., came along and said to our corporal, " I believe the Germans have gone."

A Cockney member of our team, overhearing this, said, " Well, it won't take long to find out," and jumping upon the fire-step exposed himself from the waist upwards above the parapet.

After a minute's breathless silence he turned to the captain and said, with a jerk of his thumb, " They've hopped it, sir."

That night we and our French friends entered Combles.—*M. Chittenden (late " C " Coy., 1/16th London Regt., Q.W.R.), 26 King Edward Road, Waltham Cross, Herts.*

Their own Lord Mayor's Show

IN April 1918 our unit was billeted near Amiens in a small village from which the inhabitants had been evacuated two days earlier, owing to the German advance.

On the second day of our stay there Jerry was shelling the steeple of the village church, and we had taken cover in the cellars under the village school. All at once we heard roars of laughter coming from the street, and wondering what on earth anyone could find to laugh at, we tumbled up to have a look.

The sight that met our eyes was this : Gravely walking down the middle of the street were two of the " Hackney Ghurkas," the foremost of whom was dressed in a frock coat and top hat, evidently the property of the village *maire*, and leading a decorated mule upon the head of which was tied the most gaudy " creation " which ever adorned a woman's head.

The second Cockney was clad in the full garb of a twenty-stone French peasant woman, hat and all, and was dragging at the end of a chain a stuffed fox, minus its glass case, but still fastened to its baseboard.

They solemnly paraded the whole length of the street and back again, and were heard to remark that the village was having at least one Lord Mayor's Show before Jerry captured it !

And this happened at the darkest time of the war, when our backs were to the wall.—*A. C. P. (late 58th London Division), Fulham, S.W.6.*

Pill-Box Crown and Anchor

IN the fighting around Westhoek in August 1917 the 56th Division were engaged in a series of attacks on the Nonne Boschen Wood, and owing to the boggy nature of the ground the position was rather obscure.

A platoon of one of the London battalions was holding a pill-box which had been taken from the Germans during the day. In the night a counter-attack was made in the immediate vicinity of the pill-box, which left some doubt as to whether it had again fallen to the enemy.

A patrol was sent out to investigate. After cautiously approaching the position and being challenged in a Cockney tongue, they entered the pill-box, and were astonished to see the occupants playing crown and anchor.

The isolated and dangerous position was explained to the sergeant in charge, but he nonchalantly replied, " Yes, I know all abaht that ; but, yer see, wot's the use of frightenin' the boys any more ? There's been enough row rahnd 'ere all night as it is."—*N. Butcher (late 3rd Londons)*, 43 *Tankerville Drive, Leigh-on-Sea.*

" C.O.'s Paid 'is Phone Bill "

ON the Somme, during the big push of 1916, we had a section of Signallers attached to our regiment to keep the communications during the advance. Of the two attached to our company, one was a Cockney. He had kept in touch with the " powers that be " without a hitch until his wire was cut by a shell. He followed his wire back and made the necessary repair. Three times he made the same journey for the same reason. His mate was killed by a shrapnel shell and he himself had his left arm shattered : but to him only one thing mattered, and that was to " keep in touch." So he stuck to his job.

The wire was broken a fourth time, and as he was about to follow it back, a runner came up from the C.O. wanting to know why the signaller was not in communication. He started back along his wire and as he went he said, " Tell 'im to pay 'is last account, an' maybe the telephone will be re-connected."

A permanent line was fixed before he allowed the stretcher-bearers to take him away. My chum had taken his post at the end of the wire, and as the signaller was being carried away he called out feebly, " You're in touch with H.Q. C.O.'s paid 'is bill, an' we'll win the war yet."— *L. N. Loder, M.C. (late Indian Army), Streatham.*

The " Garden Party Crasher "

IN April 1917 two companies of our battalion were ordered to make a big raid opposite the sugar refineries at 14 Bis, near Loos. Two lines of enemy trenches had to be taken and the raiding party, when finished, were to go back to billets at Mazingarbe while the Durhams took over our trenches.

My batman Beedles had instructions to go back to billets with all my kit, and wait there for my return. I was in charge of the right half of the first wave of the raid, and after a bit of a scrap we got into the German front line.

Having completed our job of blowing up concrete emplacements and dug-outs, we were waiting for the signal to return to our lines when, to my surprise, Beedles came strolling through the German wire. When he saw me he called out above the row going on : " I 'opes yer don't mind me 'aving come to the garden party wivout an invertition, sir ? "

The intrepid fellow had taken all my kit back to billets some four miles, made the return journey, and come across No Man's Land to find me, and see me safely back ; an act which might easily have cost him his life.—*L. W. Lees (Lieut.), late 11th Batt. Essex Regt., " Meadow Croft," Stoke Poges, Bucks.*

Those Big Wasps

SALONIKA, 1918, a perfect summer's day. The 2/17th London Regiment are marching along a dusty road up to the Dorian Lake. Suddenly, out of the blue, three bombing planes appear. The order is given to scatter.

Meanwhile, up comes an anti-aircraft gun, complete with crew on lorry. Soon shells are speeding up, and little small puffs of white smoke appear as they burst ; but the planes are too high for them. A Cockney of the regiment puts his hands to his mouth and shouts to the crew : " Hi, don't hunch 'em ; let 'em settle."—*A. G. Sullings (late 2/17th London Regiment)*, 130 *Cann Hall Road, Leytonstone, E.11.*

Why he Looked for Help

ON July 1, 1916, the 56th (London) Division attacked at Hebuterne, and during the morning I was engaged (as a lineman) in repairing our telephone lines between Battalion and Brigade H.Q. I had just been temporarily knocked out by a flat piece of shell and had been attended by a stretcher-bearer, who then left me and proceeded on his way back to a dressing station I had previously passed, whilst I went farther on down the trench to get on with my job.

I had not gone many yards when I met a very young private of the 12th Londons (the Rangers). One of his arms was hanging limp and was, I should think, broken in two or three places. He was cut and bleeding about the face, and was altogether in a sorry plight.

He stopped and asked me, " Is there a dressing station down there, mate ? " pointing along the way I had come, and I replied, " Yes, keep straight on down the trench. It's a good way down. But," I added, " there's a stretcher-bearer only just gone along. Shall I see if I can get him for you ? "

His reply I shall never forget : " Oh, I don't want him for *me*. I want someone to come back with me to get my mate. *He's hurt!* "—*Wm. R. Smith*, 231 *Halley Road, Manor Park, E.12.*

The Winkle Shell

ABOVE the entrance to a certain dug-out somewhere in Flanders some wit had fixed a board upon which was roughly painted, " The Winkle Shell."

The ebb and tide of battle left the dug-out in German hands, but one day during an advance the British infantry recaptured the trench in which " The Winkle Shell " was situated.

Along the trench came a Cockney with his rifle ready and his bayonet fixed. Hearing voices coming from the dug-out he halted, looked reflectively at the notice-board, and then cautiously poking his bayonet into the dug-out called out, " Nah, then, come on aht of it afore I gits me blinkin' ' pin ' busy."—*Sidney A. Wood (late C/275 Battery, R.F.A.)*, 32 *Lucas Avenue, Upton Park, E.13.*

Forgot his Dancing Pumps

WE were in a trench in front of Carnoy on the Somme when the Germans made a raid on us. It was all over in a few minutes, and we were minus eight men—taken away by the raiders.

Shortly afterwards I was standing in a bay feeling rather shaky when a face suddenly appeared over the top. I challenged, and was answered with these words:

"It's orl right. It's me. They was a-takin' us to a dance over there, but I abaht-turned 'arfway acrorst an' crawled back fer me pumps."—*E. Smith (late Middlesex Regt.), 2 Barrack Road, Aldershot.*

Lift Out of Order

ONE day in 1916 I was sitting with some pals in a German dug-out in High Wood. Like others of its kind, it had a steep, deep shaft. Suddenly a shell burst right in the mouth of the shaft above, and the next instant "Nobby," a Cockney stretcher-bearer, landed plump on his back in our midst. He was livid and bleeding, but his first words were: "Strike! I thought the lift were outer order!"—*J. E., Vauxhall, S.W.8.*

Lost : A Fly Whisk

DURING the very hot summer of 1916 in Egypt it was necessary, while eating, to keep on flicking one hand to keep the flies away from one's mouth.

One day a heavy shell came over and knocked down my Cockney chum, Tubby White. He got up, holding his wrist, and started looking round.

I said: "What have you lost, Tubby?"

"Blimey," he said, "can't you see I've lost me blooming fly whisk?" It was then I noticed he had lost his hand.—*J. T. Marshall (Middlesex Regiment), 17 Evandale Road, Brixton, S.W.9.*

Change at Wapping

WHEN Regina Trench was taken in 1916 it was in a terrible state, being half full of thick liquid mud. Some of the fellows, sooner than wade through this, were getting up and walking along the top, although in view of the Germans.

The Cockney signaller who was with me at the time, after slithering along the trench for a time, said: "I've 'ad enough er this," and scrambled out of the trench.

He had no sooner got on top when—*zipp*—and down he came with a bullet through his thigh.

While bandaging his wound I said: "We're going to have a job to get you out of here, but we'll have a good try."

"That's all right," said the Cockney, "you carry on an' leave me. I'll wait for a blinkin' barge and change at Wapping."—*H. Redford (late R.F.A.), 49 Anselm Road, Fulham.*

" The Canary's Flowed Away ! "

I WAS in charge of a party carrying material from the dump to the Engineers in the front line. One of the party, a man from Camberwell, was allotted a bulky roll of barbed wire.

After a desperate struggle through the muddy and narrow support trenches, we reached the front line. There was still another 400 yards to go, and our Cockney decided to continue the journey along the parapet.

He had not gone far before the German machine guns began to spit and he fell in a heap into the bottom of the trench with the coil of barbed wire on top of him.

Thinking he was wounded, I went back to him and inquired if he was hit.

" 'It ? 'It be blowed," he said, " but if somebody was to take this blinkin' birdcage orf me chest I might be able to get up."

The journey was completed through the trench, our friend being a sorry sight of mud and cut fingers and face.

On arriving at our destination he dropped the wire at the feet of the waiting corporal with the remark, " 'Ere you are, mate ; sorry the canary's flowed away."—*A. S. G. (47th Division), Kent.*

" Go it, Applegarf ! I'll time yer ! "

OUR battalion was making a counter-attack at Albert on March 29, 1918, against a veritable hail of lead. Wounded in the thigh, I tumbled into a huge shell hole, already occupied by two officers of the Fusiliers (Fusiliers had been on our left), a lance-corporal of my own battalion, and three other men (badly wounded).

Whilst I was being dressed by the lance-corporal another man jumped in. He had a bullet in the chest. It didn't need an M.O. to see that he was " all in," and he knew it.

He proved to be the most heroic Cockney I have ever seen. He had only minutes to live, and he told us not to waste valuable bandages on him.

Thereupon one of the officers advised me to try to crawl back before my leg got stiff, as I would stand a poor chance of a stretcher later with so many badly-wounded men about. If I got back safe I was to direct stretcher-bearers to the shell hole.

I told the officer that our battalion stretcher-bearers were behind ridge only about 100 yards in the rear, and as my wound had not troubled me yet I would make a sprint for it, as the firing was still too heavy to be healthy.

On hearing my remarks this heroic Cockney, who must also have been a thorough sportsman, grinned up at me and, with death written on his face, panted : " Go it, Applegarf, an' I'll time yer." [Applegarth was the professional sprint champion of the world.] The Cockney was dead when I left the shell hole.—*F. W. Brown (late 7th Suffolks), 247 Balls Pond Road, Dalston, N.*

That Other Sort of Rain

WE were out doing a spot of wiring near Ypres, and the Germans evidently got to know about it. A few " stars " went up, and then the *rat-tat-tat* of machine guns told us more than we wanted to know.

" 'Ope it don't rain ; I'd get me 'ead wet."

We dived for shell holes. Anybody who knows the place will realise we did not have far to dive. I found myself beside a man who, in the middle of a somewhat unhealthy period, found time to soliloquise :

" Knocked a bit right aht me tin 'at. Thought I'd copped it that time. Look, I can get me little finger through the 'ole. Blimey, 'ope it don't rain, I shall git me 'ead all wet."—*H. C. Augustus*, 67 *Paragon Road, E.*9.

Better Job for Him

I WAS at Vimy Ridge in 1916. On the night I am writing about we were taking a well-earned few minutes' rest during a temporary lull. We were under one of the roughly-built shelters erected against the Ridge, and our only light was the quivering glimmer from a couple of candles. A shell screeched overhead and " busted " rather near to us—and out went the candles.

" Smith, light up those candles," cried the sergeant-major to his batman. " Smithy," who stuttered, was rather shaken and took some time to strike a match and hold it steadily to the candles. But no sooner were the candles alight than another " whopper " put them out again.

" Light up those ruddy candles ! " cried the S.M. again, " and don't dawdle about it ! "

"Smithy," muttering terrible things to himself, was fumbling for the matches when the order came that a bombing party was required to clear "Jerry" out of a deep shell-hole.

"'Ere!" said "Smithy" in his rich Cockney voice. "J-just m-my m-mark. I'd r-rather f-frow 'eggs' t-than light c-c-candles!"—*W. C. Roberts, 5 Crampton Street, S.E.17.*

Sentry's Sudden Relief

I WAS the next turn on guard at a battery position in Armentières one evening in the summer of 1917. A Cockney chum, whom I was going to relieve, was patrolling the position when suddenly over came a 5·9, which blew him about four yards away.

As he scrambled to his feet our sergeant of the guard came along, and my chum's first words were, "Sorry, sergeant, for deserting me post."—*T. F. Smithers (late R.F.A.), 14 Hilda Road, Brixton, S.W.9.*

The World Kept Turnin'

THE Poperinghe-Ypres road. A large shell had just pitched. Among the wounded was a Cockney who was noted for his rendering on every possible occasion of that well-known song, "Let the Great Big World Keep Turning."

He was lying on the roadway severely hurt. Another Cockney went up to him and said "'Ello, matey, 'urt? Why ain't yer singin' 'Let the Great Big World Keep Turnin',' eh?"

The reply came: "I *was* a singin' on it, Bill, but I never thought it would fly up and 'it me."—*Albert M. Morsley (late 85th Siege Battery Am. Col.), 198 Kempton Road, East Ham, E.6.*

That Blinkin' "Money-box"

I WAS limping back with a wounded knee after the taking of Monchy-le-Preux on April 11, 1917, when a perky little Cockney of the 13th Royal Fusiliers who had a bandaged head caught me up with a cheery, "Tike me Chalk Farm (arm), old dear, and we'll soon be 'ome."

I was glad to accept his kindly offer, but our journey, to say the least, was a hazardous one, for the German guns, firing with open sights from the ridge in front of the Bois du Sart, were putting diagonal barrages across the road (down which, incidentally, the Dragoon Guards were coming magnificently out of action, with saddles emptying here and there as they swept through that deadly zone on that bleak afternoon).

Presently we took refuge in a sandbag shelter on the side of the road, and were just congratulating ourselves on the snugness of our retreat, when a tank stopped outside. Its arrival brought fresh gunfire on us, and before long a whizz-bang made a direct hit on our shelter.

When we recovered from the shock, we found part of our roof missing, and my little pal, poking his bandaged head through the hole, thus addressed one of the crew of the tank who was just visible through a gun slit :

" Oi, why don't yer tike yer money-box 'ome ?   This ain't a pull-up fer carmen ! "

The spirit that little Cockney imbued into me that day indirectly saved me the loss of a limb, for without him I do not think I would have reached the advance dressing station in time.—*D. Stuart (late Sergeant, 10th R.F., 37th Division) 103 St. Asaph Road, Brockley, S.E.4.*

" Oo, You Naughty Boy ! "

IN front of Kut Al-'Amarah, April 1916, the third and last attack on the Sannaiyat position, on the day before General Townshend capitulated. Days of rain had rendered the ground a quagmire, and lack of rations, ammunition, and shelter had disheartened the relief force.

The infantry advanced without adequate artillery support, and were swept by heavy machine-gun fire from the entrenched Turks. One fellow tripped over a strand of loose barbed wire, fell down, and in rising ripped the seat nearly off his shorts. Cursing, he rejoined the slowly moving line of advancing men.

Suddenly one sensed one of those fateful moments when men in the mass are near to breaking point. Stealthy looks to right and left were given, and fear was in the men's hearts. The relentless tat-tat-tat of machine guns, the " singing " of the driven bullets, and the dropping of men seemed as if it never would end.

A Cockney voice broke the fear-spell and restored manhood to men. " Oo, 'Erbert, you naughty boy ! " it said. " Look at what you've done to yer nice trahsers ! ' Quarter ' won't 'arf be cross. He said we wasn't to play rough games and tear our trahsers."—*L. W. Whiting (late 7th Meerut Division), 21 Dale Park Avenue, Carshalton, Surrey.*

Cool as a Cucumber

EARLY in 1917 at Ypres I was in charge of part of the advance party taking over some trenches from another London battalion. After this task had been completed I was told of a funny incident of the previous night.

It appeared that the battalion we were due to relieve had been surprised by a small party of the enemy seeking "information." During the mêlée in the trench a German " under-officer " had calmly walked over and picked up a Lewis gun which had been placed on a tripod on top of the trench some little distance from its usual emplacement. (This was done frequently when firing at night was necessary so as to avoid betraying the regular gun position.)

A boyish-looking sentry of the battalion on the left jumped out of the trench and went after the Jerry who was on his way " home " with the gun in his arms. Placing his bayonet in dangerous proximity to the

" under-officer's " back, the young Cockney exclaimed, " Hi ! Where the 'ell are yer goin' wiv that gun ? Just you put the ' coocumber ' back on the ' barrer ' and shove yer blinkin' 'ands up ! "

The " under-officer " lost his prize and his liberty, and I understand the young sentry received the M.M.—*R. McMuldroch (late 15th London Regt., Civil Service Rifles), 13 Meadway, Bush Hill Park, Enfield.*

The Sergeant's Tears

ONE afternoon on the Somme our battery received a severe strafe from 5·9's and tear-gas shells. There was no particular " stunt " on, so we took cover in a trench behind the guns.

When the strafe had finished, we found our gun resting on one wheel, with sights and shield smashed by a direct hit. There was tear gas hanging about, too, and we all felt anything but cheerful.

Myself and detachment were solemnly standing around looking at the smashed gun, and as I was wiping tears from my eyes, Smithy, our bright Walworth lad, said : " Don't cry, Sarg'nt, they're bahnd ter give us anuvver."—*E. Rutson (late Sergeant, R.F.A., 47th London Division), 43a Wardo Avenue, S.W.6.*

" But yer carn't 'elp Laughin' "

THERE were a bunch of us Cockneys in our platoon, and we had just taken over some supports. It being a quiet sector, we were mooning and scrounging around, some on the parapet, some in the trenches, and some at the rear.

All at once a shower of whizz-bangs and gas shells came over ; our platoon " sub." started yelling " Gas." We dived for the dug-outs.

Eight of us tried to scramble through a narrow opening at once, and we landed in a wriggling mass on the floor. Some were kneeling and some were sitting, all with serious faces, until one fellow said : " Phew, it's 'ell of a war, but yer carn't 'elp laughin', can yer ? "—*B. J. Berry (late 9th Norfolk Regt.), 11 Rosemont Avenue, N. Finchley, N.12.*

" Only an Orphan "

HE came to the battalion about three weeks before going overseas, and fell straight into trouble. But his Cockney wit got him out of trouble as well as into it.

He never received a parcel or letter, but still was always the life of our company. He never seemed to have a care.

We had been in France about a fortnight when we were ordered to the front line and over the top. He was one of the first over, shouting " Where's the blighters." They brought him in riddled with bullets.

When I asked if I could do anything for him, he said : " Are there many hurt ? " " Not many," I replied. " Thank Heaven for that," he replied. " Nobody 'll worry over me. I'm only a blinkin' orphan."—*W. Blundell (late N.C.O., 2nd East Surreys), Cranworth Gardens, S.W.9.*

Joking at the Last

IT was after the attack by the 2nd Londons on the village of Aubigny au Bac. I was hit by shell splinters, and whilst I was looking for someone to dress my wounds I came across one of the lads lying by the roadside mortally wounded.

As I bent over him to give him a drink he noticed my blood-streaked face and gasped: " Crikey ! Your barber was blinkin' clumsy this morning." So passed a gallant 2nd London man.—*E. C. Easts* (*M.M.*), *Eliot Place, Blackheath, S.E.*3.

Everybody's War

DURING the general advance on the Somme in August 1918 our platoon became isolated from the rest of the company.

We had been under heavy shell-fire for about three hours, and when at last things seemed to have quietened down, a German plane came over. We immediately jumped for cover and were concealed from view.

The plane had only circled round a couple of times when a Cockney private, unable to resist the temptation any longer, jumped up and had a pot at it.

He had fired three rounds when the N.C.O. pulled him down and called him a fool for giving away our position.

The Cockney turned round and replied, " Blimey, ain't I in this blinkin' war as well as 'im ? "—*E. Purcell* (*late 9th Royal Fusiliers*), 4 *Lyndhurst Grove, Peckham, S.E.*15.

Orders is Orders

WHEN I was with the 6th Dorsets at Hooge, a party of us under a Cockney lance-jack were sent down the Menin Road to draw rations. It seemed as though the Germans knew we were waiting at the corner, for they were dropping shells all around us.

After a while a voice in the darkness cried : " Don't stay there, you chaps ; that's Hell Fire Corner ! "

" Can't 'elp it, guv'nor," replied our lance-jack. " 'Ell Fire Corner or 'Eaven's Delight, we gotta stop 'ere till our rations comes up."— *H. W. Butler* (*late 6th Dorsets*), 2 *Flint Cottages, Stone, Kent.*

Leaving the Picture

AS we were going " over " at Passchendaele a big one dropped just behind our company runner and myself. Our runner gave a shout and stumbling on a little way, with his hand on his side, said : " Every picture tells a story "—and went down.

I just stopped to look at him, and I am sorry to say his war had finished. He came from Bow.—*G. Hayward* (*late Rifle Brigade*), *Montague Street, W.C.*1.

Ginger's Gun Stopped

I WAS in a Lewis gun section, and our sergeant got on our nerves while we were learning the gun by always drumming in our ears about the different stoppages of the gun when in action. My mate, Ginger Bryant, who lived at Stepney, could never remember the stops, and our sergeant was always rousing poor old Ginger.

Well, we found ourselves one day in the front line and Jerry had started an attack. Ginger was No. 1 on the gun and I was lying beside him as No. 2. We were giving Jerry beans with our gun when a bomb hit it direct and blew Ginger and myself yards away.

Ginger had his hand blown off, but crawled back to the gun, which was smashed to pieces. He gave one look at it and shouted to me : " Nah go and ask that blinkin' sergeant what number stoppage he calls this one ! " Next thing he fainted.—*Edward Newson (late 1st West Surrey)*, 61 *Moneyer Street, Hoxton, N.1.*

A Careless Fellow

AN officer with our lot was a regular dare-devil. He always boasted that the German bullet had not yet been made which could find him.

One day, regardless of his own safety, he was on the parapet, and though many shots came over he seemed to bear a charmed life.

One of the men happened to put his head just out of the trench when a bullet immediately struck his " tin hat " sending him backwards into the trench.

The officer, from the parapet, looked down and said, " You *are* a fool, I told you not to show yourself."—*A. Smith (Cameronians)*, 40 *White-chapel Road, E.1.*

Standing Up to the Turk

IN the second attempt to capture Gaza we were making our advance in face of heavy machine-gun fire. In covering the ground we crouched as much as possible, the Turks directed their fire accordingly, and casualties were numerous, so our Cockney humorist shouted : " Stand up, boys. It's best to be hit in yer props (legs) than in yer blinkin' office (head)."— *W. Reed (late 7th Battn., Essex Regiment)*, 3 *Shenfield Road, Woodford Green, Essex.*

Lodging with the Bombs

I WAS driving a lorry along the road from Dickebusch to Ypres when the Germans started shelling with shrapnel and high explosive.

By the side of the road was a cottage, partly ruined, with the window-space boarded up : and, with some idea of seeking protection from the flying fragments, I leaned up against one of the walls.

I hadn't been there long when a face appeared at a gap in the boards, and a voice said : " Do yer fink y're safe there, mate, cos we're chock full o' bombs in 'ere."—*Edward Tracey, c/o Cowley Cottage, Cowley, Middlesex.*

In Fine Feather

WHILE on the Somme in 1916 my battery was sent to rest in a village behind the line. The billet allotted to us had been an hotel, and all the furniture, including bedsteads and feather mattresses, had been stored in the room which did duty as an orderly room.

"They must 'ave 'it a blinkin' sparrer."

Returning one day from exercise, we saw a flight of enemy 'planes coming over, and as we approached the billet a bomb was dropped straight through the roof of our building, the sole occupant of which at the time was a Cockney signaller on duty, in touch with Brigade Headquarters.

We hurried forward, expecting to find that our signaller had been killed. The orderly room was a scene of indescribable chaos. Papers were everywhere. Files and returns were mixed up with " iron rations," while in a corner of the room was a pile of feathers about 4 feet deep— all that remained of the feather mattresses. Of our signaller there was no sign.

As we looked around, however, his head appeared from beneath the feather pile. His face was streaming with blood, and he looked more dead than alive, but as he surveyed his temporary resting-place, a grin spread over his features, and he picked up a handful of feathers.

" Blimey ! " he observed, " they must 'ave 'it a blinkin' sparrer."— " *Gunner," Oxford Street, W*.1.

All the Fun of the Fair

AT Neuve Eglise, March 1918, we were suddenly attacked by Jerry, but drove him back. Every now and again we spotted Germans dodging across a gap in a hedge. At once a competition started as to who could catch a German with a bullet as he ran across the gap.

" Reminds me of shooting at the bottles and fings at the fair," said my pal, another Cockney Highlander.

A second later a piece of shrapnel caught him in the hand. " Blimey, I always said broken glass was dangerous," he remarked as he gazed sadly at the wound.—*F. Adams (late H.L.I.), 64 Homestead Road, Becontree, Essex.*

Teacup in a Storm

WE were in support trenches near Havrincourt Wood in September 1917. At midday it was exceptionally quiet there as a rule.

Titch, our little Cockney cook, proceeded one day to make us some tea by the aid of four candles in a funk-hole. To aid this fire he added the usual bit of oily " waste," and thereby caused a thin trail of smoke to rise. The water was just on the boil when Jerry spotted our smoke and let fly in its direction everything he had handy.

Our trench was battered flat. . . . We threw ourselves into a couple of old communication trenches. Looking around presently for our cook we found him sitting beneath a waterproof sheet calmly enjoying his sergeant-major's tea. " Ain't none of you blokes firsty ? " was his greeting.—*R. J. Richards (late 61st Trench Mortar Battery, 20th London Division), 15 London Street, W.2.*

Jack's Unwelcome Present

OUR company were holding the line, or what *was* a line of trenches a short time before, when Jerry opened out with all kinds of loud-speakers and musical instruments that go to make war real.

We were knocked about and nearly blinded with smoke and flying sandbags. The best we could do was to grope our way about with arms outstretched to feel just where we were.

Eventually someone clutched me, saying, " Is that you, Charlie—are you all right ? "

" Yes, Jack," I answer, " are you all right ? "

" Well, I don't know fer sure," he says as he dives his hand through his tunic to his chest and holds on to me with the other. I had a soft place in my heart for Jack, for nobody ever sent him a parcel, so what was mine was Jack's. But not the piece of shrapnel that came out when he withdrew his hand from inside his tunic !

" The only thing that ever I had sent me—and that from Jerry ! " says Jack. " We was always taught to love our enemies ! ".

They sure loved us, for shortly after I received my little gift of love, which put me to by-by for several months. But that Cockney lad from East London never grumbled at his hard lot. He looked at me, his corporal, and no wonder he clung round my neck, for he has told me since the war that he was only sixteen then. A brave lad !—*D. C. Maskell* (*late 20th Battn. Middlesex Regt.*), 25 *Lindley Road, Leyton, E.*10.

Goalie Lets One Through

IN September 1916 we landed in a portion of German trench and I was given orders to hang on. Shells were bursting all around us, so we decided to have a smoke.

My two Cockney pals—Nobby and Harry, who were a goalie and centre-forward respectively—were noted for their zeal in keeping us alive.

Nobby was eager to see what was going on over the top, so he had a peep—and for his pains got shot through the ear. He fell back in a heap and exclaimed, " Well saved, goalie ! Couldn't been better if I'd tried."

" Garn," said Harry, bending over him, " it's blinkin' well gorn right frew, mate."—*Patrick Beckwith,* 5 *Duke Road, Chiswick, W.*4.

A Good Samaritan Foiled

I WAS rather badly wounded near Bullecourt, on the Arras front, and was lying on a stretcher outside the dressing station.

Nearby stood a burly Cockney with one arm heavily bandaged. In the other hand he held his ration of hot coffee.

Noticing my distress, he offered me his drink, saying, " 'Ere y'are, mate, 'ave a swig at this." One of the stretcher-bearers cried : " Take that away ! He mustn't have it ! "

The Cockney slunk off.

" All right, ugly," he said. " Take the food aht of a poor bloke's mouf, would yer ? "

Afterwards I learned the stretcher-bearer, by his action, had saved my life. Still, I shan't forget my Cockney friend's generosity.—*A. P. S.* (*late 5th London Regiment*), *Ilford.*

Proof of Marksmanship

POPERINGHE : a pitch-black night. We were resting when a party of the West Indian Labour Company came marching past. Jerry sent one over. Luckily, only one of the party was hit.

A voice from the darkness : " Alf ! keep low, mate. Jerry 'as got his eye in—'e's 'it a nigger in the dark ! "—*C. Jakeman* (*late 4/4th City of London Royal Fusiliers*), 5 *Hembridge Place, St. John's Wood, N.W.*8.

" Well, He Ain't Done In, See ! "

DURING the great German offensive in March 1918 our company was trying to hold the enemy at Albert. My platoon was in an old trench in front of Albert station, and was in rather a tight corner, the casualties being pretty heavy. A runner managed to get through to us with a message. He asked our sergeant to send a man to another platoon with the message.

One of my pals, named Gordon, shouted, " Give it to me ; I'll go."

He crept out of the trench and up a steep incline and over the other side, and was apparently being peppered by machine-gun fire all the way. We had little hope of him ever getting there. About a couple of hours later another Cockney cried : " Blimey ! He's coming back ! "

We could see him now, crawling towards us. He got within a dozen yards of our trench, and then a Jerry " coalbox " arrived. It knocked us into the mud at the bottom of our trench and seemed to blow Gordon, together with a ton or so of earth, twenty feet in the air, and he came down in the trench.

" That's done the poor blighter in," said the other Cockney as we rushed to him. To our surprise Gordon spoke :

" Well, he ain't done in—see ! "

He had got the message to the other platoon, and was little the worse for his experience of being blown skyward. I think that brave fellow's deed was one of many that had to go unrewarded.—*H. Nachbaur (late 7th Suffolks), 4 Burnham Road, St. Albans, Herts.*

" Baby's Fell Aht er Bed ! "

THE day before our division (38th Welch) captured Mametz Wood on the Somme, in July 1916, our platoon occupied a recently captured German trench. We were examining in a very deep dug-out some of Jerry's black bread when a heavy shell landed almost at the entrance with a tremendous crash. Earth, filled sand-bags, etc., came thundering down the steps, and my thoughts were of being buried alive about forty feet underground. But amid all the din, Sam (from Walworth) amused us with his cry : " Muvver ! Baby's fell aht er bed ! "—*P. Carter (late 1st London Welch), 6 Amhurst Terrace, Hackney, E.8.*

Stamp Edging Wanted

DURING severe fighting in Cambrai in 1917 we were taking up position in the front line when suddenly over came a " present " from Jerry, scattering our men in all directions and causing a few casualties.

Among the unfortunate ones was a Cockney whose right hand was completely blown off.

In a sitting position he calmly turned to the private next to him and exclaimed " Blimey, they've blown me blinkin' German band (hand) off. Got a bit of stamp edging, mate ? "—*T. Evans, 24 Russell Road, Wood End Green, Northolt, Greenford.*

" Oo's 'It—You or Me ? "

IT was our fifth day in the front line in a sector of the Arras front.   In the afternoon, after a terrible barrage, Jerry came over the top on our left, leaving our immediate front severely alone.

Our platoon Lewis gun was manned at that time by " Cooty," a Cockney, he being " Number One " on the gun.   We were blazing away at the advancing tide when a shell exploded close to the gun.

" Cooty " was seen to go rigid for a moment, and then he quickly rolled to one side to make way for " Number Two " to take his place. He took " Number Two's " position beside the gun.

The new " Number One " saw that " Cooty " had lost three fingers, and told him to retire.   " Cooty " would not have that, but calmly began to refill an empty magazine.   " Number One " again requested him to leave, and a sharp tiff occurred between them.

" Cooty " was heard to say, " Look 'ere, oo's '*it*—you or me ? "   " You are," said " Number One."

" Then mind your own blinkin' business," said " Cooty," " and get on with shelling these peas."

Poor " Cooty," who had lost his left foot as well, passed out shortly after, was a Guardsman at one time.—*D. S. T., Kilburn, N.W.*

The Stocking Bomb

WE were a desert mobile column, half-way across the Sinai Peninsula from Kantara to Gaza.   Turkish aeroplanes paid us a daily visit and pelted us with home-made " stocking-bombs " (old socks filled with nails, old iron, and explosives).

On this particular day we were being bombed and a direct hit on one gunner's shoulder knocked him to the ground, but failed to explode.

Sitting up in pain he blinked at the stocking-bomb and then at the plane and shouted: " Nah chuck us yer blinkin' boots dahn ! "   He then fainted and we helped him, but could not resist a broad smile.— *A. Crose, 77 Caistor Park Road, West Ham, E.15.*

Not an Acrobat

IN a communication trench on the Somme, near Guillemont, in August 1916, we were halted for a " blow " on our way up when Jerry opened with shrapnel.

Private Reynolds, from Marylebone, had his right hand cut off at the wrist.   We bound his arm as best we could, and whilst doing so one man said to him, " A sure Blighty one, mate—and don't forget when you get home, drop us a line to let's know how you are getting on in hospital."

" Yus ! I'll write all right," said Reynolds, and then, suddenly, " 'Ere, wot d'yer fink I am, a blinkin' acrobat ?   'Ow can I write wivout a right arm ter write wiv ? "—*A. Sharman (late 12th Royal Fusiliers), 177 Grenville Road, N.W.2.*

Story Without an Ending

OUR gun position lay just behind the Ancre, and Fritz generally strafed us for an hour or two each day, starting about the same time. When the first shell came over we used to take cover in a disused trench.

One day, when the strafe began, I grabbed two story magazines just before we went to the trench, and, arrived there, handed one to my Cockney pal.

We had both been reading for some time when a shell burst uncomfortably near, and a splinter hit my pal's book and shot it right out of his hand. At which he exclaimed: " Fritz, yer blighter, I'll never know nah whether he was goin' to marry the girl or cut 'er bloomin' froat."—*G. W. Wicheloe (late 138th Heavy Battery, R.G.A.), 162 Stevens Road, Chadwell Heath, Essex.*

Cause and Effect

A 5.9 had burst on the parados of our trench, and caused—as 5.9's usually did—a bit of a mess.

A brand-new officer came around the trench, saw the damage, and asked: " Whatever caused this mess ? "

Without the slightest suspicion of a smile a Cockney private answered : " An explosive bullet, sir !"—*C. T. Coates, 46 Hillingdon Street, London, S.E.17.*

" . . . an explosive bullet, sir ! "

The Cockney and the Cop

DURING the final push near Cambrai Jerry had just been driven from a very elaborate observation post—a steel-constructed tower. Of course, we soon occupied it to enable us to see Jerry's hasty retreat.

No sooner had we got settled when, crash, Jerry had a battery of pip-squeaks trained on us, firing gas shells. A direct hit brought the building down.

By the time we had sorted ourselves out our eyes began to grow dim, and soon we were temporarily blind. So we took each other's hands, an ex-policeman leading.

After a few moments a Cockney friend chimed out, " Say, Cop, do you think you can find the lock-up now, or had you better blow your whistle ? "—*H. Rainford (late R.F.A.), 219 The Grove, Hammersmith, W.6.*

In the Drorin' Room

IT was on " W " Beach, Gallipoli, some months after the historic landing.   It was fairly safe to picnic here, but for the attentions of " Beachy Bill," a big Turkish gun.   I was with six other R.F.A. details in a dug-out which was labelled, or rather libelled, " The Ritz."

" Smiler " Smith gave it that name, and always referred to this verminous hovel in terms of respect.   Chalked notices such as " Wait for the Lift," " Card Room," " Buffet," were his work.

A dull thud in the distance—the familiar scream—and *plomp* came one from " Bill," a few yards from the Ritz.   Only " Smiler " was really hurt.   He received a piece of shell on his arm.   As they carried him away, he called faintly for his tobacco tin.

" Where did you leave it, ' Smiler ' ? "

" In the drorin' room on the grand pianner," said " Smiler " faintly.— *Gunner W. (late 29th Division, R.F.A.).*

Getting His Goat

SANDY was one of those whom nature seemed to have intended for a girl.   Sandy by colour, pale and small of features, and without the sparkling wit of his Cockney comrades, he was the butt of many a joke.

One dark and dirty night we trailed out of the line at Vermelles and were billeted in a barn.   The farm-house still sheltered its owner and the remainder of his live-stock, including a goat in a small shed.

" Happy " Day, having discovered the goat, called out, " Hi, Sandy ! There's some Maconochie rations in that 'ere shed.   Fetch 'em in, mate."

Off went Sandy, to return hastily with a face whiter than usual, and saying in his high treble : " 'Appy, I can't fetch them.   There's two awful eyes in that shed."

Subsequently Jerry practically obliterated the farm, and when we returned to the line " Happy " Day appropriated the goat as a mascot.

We had only been in the line a few hours when we had the worst bombardment I remember.   Sandy and the goat seemed kindred spirits in their misery and terror.

" Happy " had joined the great majority.   The goat, having wearied of trench life and army service, had gone over the top on his own account. The next thing we knew was that Sandy was " over " after him, shells dropping around them. Then the goat and "Sandy Greatheart " disappeared behind a cloud of black and yellow smoke.—*S. G. Bushell (late Royal Berks), 21 Moore Buildings, Gilbert Street, W.*

Jennie the Flier

IT was my job for about two months, somewhere in the summer of 1917, to take Jennie the mule up to the trenches twice a day with rations, or shells, for the 35th Trench Mortar Battery, to which I was attached.   We had to cover about 5 kilos. from the Q.M. stores at Rouville,

Arras, to the line. When Jerry put a few over our way it was a job to get Jennie forward.

One night we arrived with a full load, and the officer warned me to get unloaded quick as there was to be a big bombardment. No sooner had I finished than over came the first shell—and away went Jennie, bowling over two or three gunners.

Someone caught her and I mounted for the return journey. Then the bombardment began in earnest.

You ought to have seen her go! Talk about a racehorse! I kept saying, " Gee up, Jennie, old girl, don't get the wind up, we shall soon get back to Rouville! "

I looked round and could see the flashes of the guns. That was the way to make Jennie go. She never thought of stopping till we got home.
—*W. Holmes (9th Essex Regiment), 72 Fleet Road, Hampstead, N.W.*

A Mission Fulfilled

ON August 28, 1916, we were told to take over a series of food dumps which had been formed in the front and support lines at Hamel, on the Ancre, before a general attack came off.

On the following night Corporal W——, a true and gallant Cockney who was in charge of a party going back to fetch rations, came to my dug-out to know if there were anything special I wished him to bring.

I asked him to bring me a tin of cigarettes. On the return journey, as the party was crossing a road which cut through one of the communicating trenches, a shell struck the road, killing two privates and fatally wounding Corporal W——.

Without a word the corporal put his hand into his pocket and, producing a tin, held it out to an uninjured member of the party.

I got my smokes.—*L. J. Morgan (late Capt., The Royal Sussex Regiment), 1 Nevern Square, S.W.5.*

He Saved the Tea

ON the night before our big attack on July 1, 1916, on the Somme, eight of us were in a dug-out getting a little rest. Jerry must have found some extra shells for he was strafing pretty heavily.

Two Cockney pals from Stratford were busy down on their hands and knees with some lighted grease and pieces of dry sand-bag, trying to boil a mess-tin of water to make some tea.

The water was nearly on the boil when Jerry dropped a " big 'un " right into the side of our dug-out.

The smoke and dust had hardly cleared, when one of the Stratfordites exclaimed, looking down at the overturned mess-tin, " Blimey, that's caused it." Almost immediately his pal (lying on his back, his face covered with blood and dirt, and his right hand clasped tightly) answered : " 'S'all right. I ain't put the tea and sugar in."—*J. Russ (Cpl., late 6th Battn. Royal Berkshire Regt.), 309 Ilford Lane, Ilford, Essex.*

Old Dutch Unlucky

AFTER a week in Ypres Salient in February 1915 we were back at a place called Vlamertinghe " resting," i.e. providing the usual working parties at night. Going out with one of these parties, well loaded with barbed wire, poles, etc., our rifles slung on our shoulders, things in general were fairly quiet. A stray bullet struck the piling swivel of the rifle of " Darkie," the man in front of me. " Missed my head by the skin of its teeth," said " Darkie." " Good job the old Dutch wasn't here. She reckons she's been unlucky ever since she set eyes on me—and there's another pension for life gone beggin'."—*B. Wiseman* (*late Oxford and Bucks L.I.*), 12 *Ursula Street, Battersea, S.W.*11.

A Long Streak of Misery

DUSK was falling on the second day of the battle of Loos. I was pottering about looking for the other end of our line at the entrance to Orchard Street trench. A voice hailed me : " 'Ere, mate ! Is this the way aht ? "

It came from a little Cockney, a so-called " walking " wounded case. Immediately behind him there hobbled painfully six feet of complete abjection.

I gave them directions, and told them that in two or three hundred yards they should be out of danger. Then Jerry dropped a " crump." It tortured the sorely-tried nerves of the long fellow, and when the bricks and dust had settled, he declared, with sudden conviction : " We're going to lose this blinkin' war, we are ! "

His companion gave him a look of contempt.

" You ain't 'arf a long streak of misery," he said. " If I fort that I'd go back nah an' 'ave another shot at 'em—even if you 'ad to carry me back."—" *Lines*," (33 (S) *Bty*), 24 *Clifton Road, Maida Vale, W.*9.

" Smudger's " Tattoo

" SMUDGER " SMITH, from Hoxton, had just returned off leave, and joined us at Frankton Camp, near Ypres. Not long after his arrival " Jerry " started strafing us with his long-range guns, but " Smudger " was more concerned with the tattooing which he had had done on his arms on leave.

I said they were very disfiguring, and advised him to have them removed, giving him an address to go to when he was again in London, and telling him the probable price.

Not very long after our conversation " Jerry " landed a shell about forty yards away from us and made us part company for a while. When I pulled myself together and looked for " Smudger " he was half-buried with earth and looked in much pain.

I went over to him and began to dig him out. Whilst I was thus engaged he said to me in a weak voice, but with a smile on his face :

" How much did yer say it would corst to take them tattoos orf ? "
And when I told him he replied : " I fink I can get 'em done at harf-
price nah."

When I dug him out I found he had lost one arm.—*E. R. Wilson (late
East Lancs Regt.)*, 22 *Brindley Street, Shardeloes Road, New Cross, S.E.*14.

Importance of a " Miss "

SOON after the capture of Hill 70 an artillery observation post was
established near the new front line.   A telephone line was laid to it,
but owing to persistent shelling the wire soon became a mere succession
of knots and joints.   Communication was established at rare intervals,
and repairing the line was a full-time job. A Cockney signaller and I went
out at daybreak one morning to add more joints to the collection, and
after using every scrap of spare wire available made another temporary
job of it.

Returning, however, we found at a cross-over that the wire had fallen
from a short piece of board that had been stuck in the parapet to keep it
clear of the trench.   As my pal reached up to replace it his head caught
the eye of a sniper, whose bullet, missing by a fraction, struck and knocked
down the piece of wood.

The signaller's exclamation was : " Blimey, mate, it's lucky he ain't
broke the blinkin' line again ! "—*J. Hudson (late R.G.A.)*, 6 *Ventnor Road,
New Cross, S.E.*14.

" In the Midst of War—— "

A BATTALION of a London regiment was in reserve in Rivière-
Grosville, a small village just behind the line, in March 1917.
Towards midnight we were ordered to fall in in fighting order as it was
believed that the Germans had retired.

Our mission was to reconnoitre the German position, and we were
cautioned that absolute silence must be preserved.

All went well until we reached the German barbed wire entanglements,
that had to be negotiated by narrow paths, through which we proceeded
softly and slowly, and with the wind " well up."

Suddenly the air was rent by a stream of blistering invective, and a
Cockney Tommy turned round on his pal, who had tripped and accidentally prodded him with the point of his bayonet, and at the top of
his voice said :

" Hi, wot's the blinkin' gime, Charlie ?   Do that again and I'll knock
yer ruddy 'ead off."

Charlie raised his voice to the level of the other's and said he'd like
to see him do it, and while we flattened ourselves on the ground expecting
a storm of bullets and bombs at any moment, the two pals dropped their
rifles and had it out with their fists.

Fortunately, rumour was correct, the Germans had retired.—*H. T
Scillitoe, 77 Stanmore Road, Stevenage, Herts.*

A Case for the Ordnance

A PITCH dark night on the Salonika front in 1917. I was in charge of an advanced detachment near a railhead.

A general and a staff officer were travelling by rail-motor towards the front line when in the darkness the rail-motor crashed into some stationary freight trucks, completely wrecking the vehicle and instantly killing the driver.

I rushed with a stretcher party to render help. The general and his staff officer were unconscious amid the wreckage.

Feverishly we worked to remove the debris which pinned them down. Two of us caught the general beneath the shoulders, and one was raising his legs when to his horror one leg came away in his hand.

When the general regained his senses, seeing our concern, he quickly reassured us. The leg turned out to be a wooden one! He had lost the original at Hill 60.

The tension over, one of the stretcher-bearers, a Cockney from Mile End, whispered into my ear, " We can't take 'im to the 'orspital, sarge, he wants to go dahn to the Ordnance ! "—*Sgt. T. C. Jones, M.S.M.,* 15 *Bushey Mill Lane, Watford.*

Dismal Jimmy's Prisoner

OUT of the ebb and flow, the mud and blood, the din and confusion of a two days' strafe on the Somme in September 1917 my particular chum, Private James X., otherwise known as " Dismal Jimmy," emerged with a German prisoner who was somewhat below the usual stature and considerably the worse for the wear and tear of his encounter with the Cockney soldier.

" Jimmy," although obviously proud of his captive, was, as usual, " fed up " with the war, the strafe, and everything else. To make matters worse, on his way to the support trenches he was caught in the head by a sniper's bullet.

His pet grievance, however, did not come from this particular misfortune, but from the fact that the prisoner had not taken advantage of the opportunity to " 'Op it ! " when the incident occurred. " Wot yer fink ov 'im, mate ? " he queried. " Followed me all rahnd the blinkin' trenches, 'e did ! Thinks I got a bit o' tripe on a skewer, maybe, th' dirty dog ! " " Jimmy " muttered. Then he came under the orders of a Higher Command.—*H. J. R.,* 1 *Central Buildings, Westminster, S.W.*1.

That Creepy Feeling

IN the brick-fields at La Bassée, 1915, there was a pump about five yards from our front line which we dare not approach in daylight. At night it was equally dangerous as it squeaked and so drew the sniper's fire.

We gave up trying to use it after a few of our fellows had been sniped in their attempts, until Nobby Clarke said *he* would get the water, adding : " That blinkin' sniper hasn't my name on any of his ruddy bullets."

After he had gone we heard the usual squeak of the pump, followed by the inevitable *ping ! . . . ping !* We waited. No Nobby returned.

Two of us crawled out to where he lay to bring him in. " Strewth, Bill," he cried when my mate touched him, " you didn't 'arf put the blinkin' wind up me, *creepin' aht like that !* "

There he lay, on his back, with a piece of rope tied to the handle of the pump. We always got our water after that.—*F. J. Pike (late 2nd Grenadier Guards), 4 Hilldrop Road, Bromley, Kent.*

" Toot-Sweet," the Runner

SCENE : Before Combles in the front line.
Position : Acute.

Several runners had been despatched from the forward position with urgent messages for Headquarters, and all had suffered the common fate of these intrepid fellows. One Cockney named Sweet, and known as " Toot-Sweet " for obvious reasons, had distinguished himself upon various occasions in acting as a runner.

A volunteer runner was called for to cover a particularly dangerous piece of ground, and our old friend was to the fore as usual. " But," said the company officer, " I can't send you again—someone else must go."

Imagine his astonishment when " Toot-Sweet " said, " Giv' us this charnce, sir. I've got two mentions in dispatches now, an' I only want annuvver to git a medal."

He went, but he did not get a medal.—*E. V. S. (late Middlesex Regt.), London, N.W.2.*

Applying the Moral

BEFORE we made an attack on " The Mound of Death," St. Eloi, in the early part of 1916, our Brigadier-General addressed the battalion and impressed upon us the importance of taking our objective.

He told us the tale of two mice which fell into a basin of milk. The faint-hearted one gave up and was drowned. The other churned away with his legs until the milk turned into butter and he could walk away ! He hoped that we would show the same determination in our attack.

We blew up part of the German front line, which had been mined, and attacked each side of the crater, and took the position, though with heavy losses.

On the following day one of my platoon fell into the crater, which, of course, was very muddy. As he plunged about in it he shouted " When I've churned this ruddy mud into concrete I'm 'opping aht of it."

This was the action in which our gallant chaplain, Captain the Rev. Noel Mellish, won the V.C.—*" Reg. Bomber," 4th Royal Fusiliers, 3rd Division.*

Spelling v. Shelling

AN attack was to be made by our battalion at Givenchy in 1915. The Germans must have learned of the intention, for two hours before it was due to begin they sent up a strong barrage, causing many casualties.

Letters and cards, which might be their last, were being sent home by our men, and a Cockney at the other end of our dug-out shouted to his mate, " 'Arry, 'ow d'yer spell 'delightful' ? " —*H. W. Mason (late 23rd London Regt.), 26 Prairie Street, Battersea, S.W.*

" 'Ow d'yer spell ' delightful ' ? "

Too Much Hot Water

WE were taking a much-needed bath and change in the Brewery vats at Poperinghe, when Jerry started a mad five minutes' " strafe " with, as it seemed, the old Brewery as a target.

Above the din of explosions, falling bricks, and general " wind-up " the aggrieved voice of Sammy Wilkes from Poplar, who was still in the vat, was heard :

" Lumme, and I only asked for a little drop more 'ot water."—*Albert Girardot (late K.R.R.), 250 Cornwall Road, Ladbroke Grove, W.11.*

" Ducks and Drakes ! Ducks and Drakes ! "

AFTER the evacuation of the Dardanelles the " Drakes " of the Royal
Naval Division were ordered to France. Amongst them was Jack
(his real name was John). A young Soccer player, swift of foot, he was
chosen as a " runner."

One day he tumbled into a shell hole. And just as he had recovered
his wits in came Colonel Freyberg, V.C., somewhat wounded. Seeing
Jack, he told him he was just the boy he wanted—the lad had run away
from home to join up before he was seventeen—and scribbling a note
the colonel handed it to him.

The boy was told if he delivered it safely he could help the colonel
to take Beaucourt. Jack began to scramble out. It was none too inviting,
for shells were bursting in all directions, and it was much more comfortable inside. With a wide vocabulary from the Old Kent Road, he timely
remembered that his father was a clergyman, and muttering to himself,
" Ducks and drakes, ducks and drakes," he reached the top and went
on his way.

The sequel was that the message was delivered, reinforcements came
up, led by the boy to the colonel, and Beaucourt was taken.—*Father
Hughes, 60 Hainault Avenue, Westcliff-on-Sea.*

You Must have Discipline

ON September 14, 1916, at Angle Wood on the Somme, the 168th
(London) Brigade Signals were unloading a limber on a slope, on
top of which was a battery which Jerry was trying to find. One of his
shells found us, knocking all of us over and wounding nine or ten of us
(one fatally).

As the smoke and dust cleared, our Cockney sergeant (an old soldier
whose slogan was " You must have discipline ") gradually rose to a
sitting position, and, whipping out his notebook and pencil, called
" Nah, then, oo's wounded ? " and calmly proceeded to write down
names.—*Wm. R. Smith (late R.E. Signals), 231 Halley Road, Manor
Park, E.12.*

L.B.W. in Mespot

AT a certain period during the operations in Mesopotamia so dependent
were both the British and the Turks on the supply of water from
the Tigris that it became an unwritten law that water-carriers from both
sides were not to be sniped at.

This went on until a fresh British regiment, not having had the position
explained, fired on a party of Turks as they were returning from the
river. The next time we went down to get water the Turks, of course,
returned the compliment ; so from then onwards all water carrying had
to be done under cover of darkness.

On one of these occasions a Turkish sniper peppered our water party
as they were returning to our lines. They all got back, however ; but

one, a man from Limehouse, was seen to be struggling with his water container only half full, and at the same time it was noticed that his trousers and boots were saturated.

" Hi ! " shouted the sergeant, " you've lost half the water. Did that sniper get your bucket ? "

" Not 'im," replied the Cockney, " I saw to that. 'E only got me leg."

What, in the darkness, appeared to be water spilt from the bucket was really the result of a nasty flesh wound.—*J. M. Rendle (Lieut., I.A.R.O.), White Cottage, St. Leonard's Gardens, Hove, Sussex.*

Trench-er Work

WE were attacking Messines Ridge. The ground was a mass of flooded shell-holes. Hearing a splash and some cursing in a familiar voice, I called out, " Are you all right, Tubby ? "

The reply came, as he crawled out of a miniature mine crater, " Yus, but I've lorst me 'ipe (rifle)."

I asked what he was going to do, and he replied, " You dig them German sausages out with yer baynit and I'll eat 'em."

So saying, he pulled out his knife and fork and proceeded towards the enemy trenches.—*" Pip Don " (London Regt.), 22 Ingram Road, Thornton Heath.*

" The Best Man—Goes Fust "

IN the second battle of Arras, 1917, our regiment was held up near Gavrelle and was occupying a line of shell-holes. The earth was heaving all around us with the heavy barrage. Peeping over the top of my shell-hole I found my neighbours, " Shorty " (of Barnes) and " Tiny " (of Kent) arguing about who was the best man.

All of a sudden over came one of Jerry's five-nines. It burst too close to " Shorty," who got the worst of it, and was nearly done for. But he finished his argument, for he said to " Tiny " in a weak voice, " That shows you who's the best man. My ole muvver always says as the best goes fust."—*J. Saxby, Paddington, W.2.*

When Clemenceau Kissed the Sergeant

ABOUT Christmas of 1917 I was on the Somme with one of the most Cockney of the many battalions of the Royal Fusiliers. As we sheltered in dug-outs from the " gale " Fritz was putting over, to our surprise we heard a voice greet us in French, " Allons, mes enfants : Ça va toujours."

Looking up we beheld an old man in shabby suit and battered hat who seemed the typical French peasant. " Well, of all the old idiots," called out the sergeant. " Shut yer face an' 'ook it, ye blamed old fool." For answer the old man gave the sergeant the surprise of his life by seizing him in a grip of iron and planting a resounding kiss on each cheek, French fashion.

Just at that moment some brass hats came along and the mystery was explained. The " old fool " was the late Georges Clemenceau, then French War Minister, who had come to see for himself what it was like in our sector and had lost his guides.

" An' to think that 'e kissed me just like I was a kid, after I'd told 'im to 'ook it," commented the sergeant afterwards. " Wonder wot 'e'd 'a done 'ad I told 'im to go to 'ell, as I'd 'alf a mind to."

Years later I was one of a party of the British Legion received in Paris by " The Tiger," and I recalled the incident. " Père La Victoire " laughed heartily. " That Cockney sergeant was right," he said, " I was an old fool to go about like that in the line, but then somebody has got to play the fool in war-time, so that there may be no follies left for the wise heads to indulge in."—*H. Stockman, Hôtel Terminus, Rue St. Lazare, Paris, VIIIème, France.*

Poet and—Prophet

I WAS sitting with my pal in the trenches of the front line waiting for the next move when I heard our Cockney break into the chorus of a home-made song :

> " 'Twas moonlight in the trenches,
> The sky was royal blue,
> When Jerry let his popgun go,
> And up the 'ole 'ouse flew."

The last words were drowned in a terrific crash. There was sudden quiet afterwards, and then a voice said, " There y'are, wot did I tell yer ? "—*T. E. Crouch, 28 Eleanor Road, Hackney, E.8.*

Pub that Opened Punctually

IT was at the village of Zudkerque, where Fritz had bombed and blown up a dump in 1916. My pal and I were standing outside a café, the windows of which were shuttered, when the blast of a terrific explosion blew out the shutters. They hit my pal and me on the head and knocked us into the roadway.

My pal picked himself up, and, shaking bits of broken glass off him and holding a badly gashed head, said : " Lumme, Ginger, they don't 'arf open up quick 'ere. Let's go an 'ave one."—*J. March (late R.E.), London, S.E.*

That Precious Tiny Tot

WE had paraded for the rum issue at Frankton Camp, near Ypres, when the enemy opened fire with long-range guns. A Cockney came forward with his mug, drew his issue, and moved off to drink it under cover and at leisure. Suddenly a large shell whooped over and burst about 40 yards away. With a casual glance at the fountain of earth which soared up, the man calmly removed his shrapnel helmet and held it over his mug until the rain of earth and stones ceased.—" *Skipper,*" *D.L.I., London, W.2.*

3*

Cigs and Cough Drops

CIGARETTES we knew not ; food was scarce, so was ammunition. Consequently I was detailed on the eve of the retreat from Serbia to collect boxes of S.A.A. lying near the front line.

On the way to report my arrival to the infantry officer I found a Cockney Tommy badly wounded in the chest. " It's me chest, ain't it, mate ? " he asked. I nodded in reply. " Then I'll want corf drops, not them," and with that he handed me a packet of cigarettes. How he got them and secretly saved them up so long is a mystery.

I believe he knew that he would not require either cough drops or cigarettes, and I took a vow to keep the empty packet to remind me of the gallant fellow.—*H. R. (late R.F.A.), 10th Division, London, N.3.*

" Smiler " to the End

WHEN Passchendaele started on July 31, 1917, we who were holding ground captured in the Messines stunt of June 7 carried out a " dummy " attack.

One of the walking wounded coming back from this affair of bluff, I struck a hot passage, for Jerry was shelling the back areas with terrific pertinacity. Making my way to the corduroy road by Mount Kemmel, I struck a stretcher party. Their burden was a rifleman of the R.B.'s, whose body was a mass of bandages. Seeing me ducking and dodging every time a salvo burst near he called out :

" Keep wiv me, mate, 'cos two shells never busts in the same 'ole— and if I ain't a shell 'ole 'oo is ? "

Sheer grit kept him alive until after we reached Lord Derby's War Hospital outside Warrington, and the nickname of " Smiler " fitted him to the last.—*W. G. C., 2 Avonly Road, S.E.14.*

" The Bishop " and the Bright Side

A FULLY-QUALIFIED chartered accountant in the City, my pal, " The Bishop "—so called because of his dignified manner—was promoted company-clerk in the Irish Rifles at Messines in 1917.

Company headquarters were in a dark and dismal barn where the Company Commander and " The Bishop " were writing under difficulties one fine morning—listening acutely to the shriek and crash of Jerry's whizz-bangs just outside the ramshackle door.

The betting was about fifty to one on a direct hit at any moment. The skipper had a wary eye on " The Bishop "—oldish, shortish, stoutish, rather comical card in his Tommy's kit. Both were studiously pre- serving an air of outward calm.

Then the direct hit came—high up, bang through the rafters, and blew off the roof. " The Bishop " looked up at the sky, still clutching his fountain-pen.

" Ah, that's better, sir," he said. " Now we can see what we are doing." —*P. J. K., Westbourne Grove, W.2.*

" Chuck yer Blinkin' 'Aggis at 'im ! "

THE Cockney inhabitants of " Brick Alley," at Carnoy, on the Somme in 1916, had endured considerable attention from a German whizz-bang battery situated a mile or so away behind Trones Wood.

During a lull in the proceedings a fatigue party of " Jocks," each carrying a 40-lb. sphere, the business end of a " toffee-apple " (trench mortar bomb), made their appearance, and were nicely strung out in the trench when Jerry opened out again.

The chances of a direct hit made matters doubly unpleasant.

The tension became a little too much for one of the regular billetees, and from a funk-hole in the side of the trench a reproachful voice addressed the nearest Highlander : " For the luv o' Mike, Jock, get up and chuck yer blinkin' 'aggis at 'em."—*J. C. Whiting (late 8th Royal Sussex Pioneers), 36 Hamlet Gardens, W.6.*

Back to Childhood

I HAD been given a lift in an A.S.C. lorry going to Jonchery on May 27, 1918, when it was suddenly attacked by a German plane. On getting a burst of machine-gun bullets through the wind-screen the driver, a stout man of about forty, pulled up, and we both clambered down.

The plane came lower and re-opened fire, and as there was no other shelter we were obliged to crawl underneath the lorry and dodge from one side to the other in order to avoid the bullets.

" Fancy a bloke my age playin' 'ide an' seek "

After one hurried " pot " at the plane, and as we dived for the other side, my companion gasped : " Lumme ! Fancy a bloke my age a-playin' 'ide an' seek ! "—*H. G. E. Woods, " The Willows," Bridge Street, Maidenhead.*

The Altruist

ONE afternoon in July 1917 our battalion was lying by a roadside on the Ypres front waiting for night to fall so that we could proceed to the front line trenches.

" Smiffy " was in the bombing section of his platoon and had a bag of Mills grenades to carry.

Fritz began to get busy, and soon we had shrapnel bursting overhead.

"Smiffy" immediately spread his body over his bag of bombs like a hen over a clutch of eggs.

"What the 'ell are you sprawling over them bombs for?" asked the sergeant.

"Well," replied Smiffy, "it's like this 'ere, sergeant. I wouldn't mind a little Blighty one meself, but I'd jest 'ate for any of these bombs ter get wounded while I'm wiv 'em."—*T. E. M.* (*late London Regt.*), *Colliers Wood, S.W.*19.

"Minnie's Stepped on my Toe!"

WE were lying in front of Bapaume in August 1918 awaiting rein- forcements. They came from Doullens, and among them was a Cockney straight from England. He greeted our sergeant with the words, "Wot time does the dance start?" The sergeant, an old-timer, replied, "The dance starts right now."

So over the top we went, but had not gone far when the Cockney was bowled over by a piece from a minnenwerfer, which took half of one foot away.

I was rendering first aid when the sergeant came along. He looked down and said, "Hello, my lad, soon got tired of the dance, eh?"

The little Cockney looked up and despite his pain he smiled and said, "On wiv the dance, sergeant! I'm sitting' this one aht, fer Minnie has stepped on my toe."—*E. C. Hobbs* (*late 1st Royal Marine Battn.*), 103 *Moore Park Road, Fulham, S.W.*

In the Dim Dawn

JERRY had made a surprise raid on our trenches one morning just as it was getting light. He got very much the worst of it, but when everything was over Cockney Simmonds was missing.

We hunted everywhere, but couldn't find him. Suddenly we saw him approaching with a hefty looking German whom he had evidently taken prisoner.

"Where did you get him from, Simmonds?" we asked.

"Well, d'yer see that shell-'ole over there 'alf full o' water?"

"Yes," we said, all craning our necks to look.

"Well, this 'ere Fritz didn't."—*L. Digby* (*12th East Surreys*), 10 *Windsor Road, Holloway, N.*7.

Beau Brummell's Puttees

MARCH 1918. Just before the big German offensive. One night I was out with a reconnoitring patrol in "No Man's Land." We had good reason to believe that Jerry also had a patrol in the near vicinity.

Suddenly a burst of machine-gun fire in our direction seemed to indicate that we had been spotted. We dived for shell-holes and any available cover, breathlessly watching the bullets knock sparks off the barbed wire. When the firing ceased and we attempted to re-form our little party, a Cockney known as " Posh " Wilks was missing.

Fearing the worst, we peered into the darkness. Just then a Verey light illuminated the scene, and we saw the form of " Posh " Wilks some little distance away. I went over to see what was wrong, and to my astonishment he was kneeling down carefully rewinding one of his puttees. " Can't get these ruddy things right anyhow to-day," he said.—*H. W. White (late Royal Sussex Regt.), 18 Airthrie Road, Goodmayes, Essex.*

Plenty of Room on Top

ON December 4, 1917, we made a surprise attack on the enemy in the Jabal Hamrin range in Northern Mesopotamia.

We wore our winter clothing (the same as in Europe), with tin hats complete. After stumbling over the rocks in extended order for some time, the platoon on my left, who were on higher ground, sighted a Turkish camp fire on the right.

We swung round in that direction, to find ourselves up against an almost blank wall of rock, about 20 ft. high, the enemy being somewhere on top.

At last we found a place at which to scale it, one at a time. We began to mount, in breathless silence, expecting the first man to come tumbling down on top of all the rest.

I was the second, and just as I started to climb I felt two sharp tugs at my entrenching tool and a hoarse Cockney voice whispered, " Full up inside ; plenty o' room on top." I was annoyed at the time, but I have often laughed over it since.—*P. V. Harris, 89 Sherwood Park Road, S.W.16.*

Nearly Lost His Washing-Bowl

IN March 1917 we held the front line trenches opposite a sugar refinery held by the Germans. We got the order to stand to as our engineers were going to blow up a mine on the German position.

Up went the mine. Then Fritz started shelling us. Shells were bursting above and around us. A piece of shrapnel hit a Cockney, a lad from Paddington, on his tin hat.

When things calmed down another Cockney bawled out, " Lumme, that was a near one, Bill." " Blimey, not arf," was the reply. " If I 'adn't got my chin-strap dahn I'd 'ave lost my blooming washing-bowl."—*E. Rickard (late Middlesex Regt.), 65 Apsley End, Hemel Hempstead, Herts.*

Bath Night

THE trenches on the Somme were very deep and up to our knees in mud, and we were a pretty fine sight after being in the front line several days over our time.

I shall never forget the night we passed out of the trenches—like a lot of mud-larks. The O.C., seeing the state we were in, ordered us to have a bath. We stopped at an old barn, where the R.E.'s had our water ready in wooden tubs. Imagine the state of the water when, six to a tub, we had to skim the mud off after one another !

Just as we were enjoying the treat, Jerry started sending over some of his big stuff, and one shell took the back part of the barn off.

Everybody began getting out of the tubs, except a Cockney, who sat up in his tub and shouted out, " Blimey, Jerry, play the blinkin' game. Wait till I've washed me back. I've lorst me soap."—*C. Ralph (late Royal Welch Fusiliers), 153d Guinness Buildings, Hammersmith, W.6.*

Back to the Shack

WHILST on the Somme in October 1916 my pal Mac (from Notting Hill) and myself were sent forward to a sunken road just behind Les Bœufs to assist at a forward telephone post which was in communication with battalion H.Q. by wire and with the companies in the trenches by runner.

During the night a false " S O S " was sent up, and our guns opened out—and, of course, so did the German guns—and smashed our telephone wire.

It being " Mac's " turn out, he picked up his 'phone and went up the dug-out steps. When he had almost reached the top a big shell burst right in the dug-out entrance and blew " Mac " back down the stairs to the bottom, bruised, but otherwise unhurt.

Picking himself up slowly he removed his hat, placed his hand over his heart, and said, gazing round, " Back to the old 'ome agin—and it ain't changed a bit."—*A. J. West (late Corpl., Signals), 1/13th London Regt.), 212 Third Avenue, Paddington, W.10.*

His Last Gamble

ONE night in July 1917, as darkness came along, my battalion moved up and relieved a battalion in the front line.

Next morning as dawn was breaking Jerry started a violent strafe. My platoon occupied three fire-bays, and we in the centre one could shout to those in the bays on either side, although we could not see them.

In one of the end bays was " Monte Carlo " Teddy, a true lad from London, a " bookie's tick-tack " before the war. He was called " Monte Carlo " because he would gamble on anything. As a shell exploded anywhere near us Teddy would shout, " Are you all right, sarge ? " until this kind of got on my nerves, so I crawled into his bay to inquire why he had suddenly taken such an interest in my welfare. He explained, " I gets up a draw larst night, sarge, a franc a time, as to which of us in this lot stopped a packet first, and you're my gee-gee."

I had hardly left them when a shell exploded in their bay. The only one to stop a packet was Teddy, and we carried him into the next bay to await the stretcher-bearers. I could see he would never reach the dressing station.

Within five minutes I had stopped a lovely Blighty, and they put me alongside Teddy. When he noticed who it was he said, " Well I'm blowed, just my blinkin' luck ; licked a short head and I shan't last long enough to see if there's a' objection."

Thus he died, as he always said he would, with his boots on, and my company could never replace him. Wherever two men of my old mob meet you can bet your boots that one or the other is sure to say, " Remember ' Monte Carlo ' Ted ? "—*E. J. Clark (late Sergeant, Lincoln Regt.), c/o Sir Thomas Lipton, Bart., K.C.V.O., Osidge, Southgate, N.14.*

That Infernal Drip-Drip-Drip !

WE were trying to sleep in half a dug-out that was roofed with a waterproof sheet—Whale and I. It was a dark, wet night. I had hung a mess tin on a nail to catch the water that dripped through, partly to keep it off my head, also to provide water for an easy shave in the morning.

A strafe began. The night was illuminated by hundreds of vivid flashes, and shells of all kinds burst about us. The dug-out shook with the concussions. Trench mortars, rifle grenades, and machine-gun fire contributed to the din.

Whale, who never had the wind up, was shifting his position and turning from one side to the other.

" What's the matter ? " I asked my chum. " Can't you sleep ? "

" Sleep ! 'Ow the 'ell can a bloke sleep with that infernal *drip-drip-drip* goin' on ? "—*P. T. Hughes (late 21st London Regiment, 47th Division), 12 Shalimar Gardens, Acton, W.*

" A Blinkin' Vanity Box "

AFTER the terrific upheaval of June 7, 1917, my brigade (the 111th) held the line beyond Wytschaete Ridge for some weeks. While my company was in support one day my corporal and I managed to scrounge into a pill-box away from the awful mud. We could not escape the water because the explosion of the mines on June 7 had cracked the foundation of our retreat and water was nearly two feet deep on the floor.

Just before dusk on this rainy July evening I was shaving before a metal mirror in the top bunk in the pill-box, while the corporal washed in a mess-tin in the bunk below. Just then Jerry started a severe strafe and a much-muddied runner of the 13th Royal Fusiliers appeared in the unscreened doorway.

" Come in and shelter, old man," I said. So he stepped on to an ammunition box that just failed to keep his feet clear of the water.

He had watched our ablutions in silence for a minute or so, when a shell burst almost in the doorway and flung him into the water below our bunks, where he sat with his right arm red and rent, sagging at his side.

" Call this a shelter ? " he said. " Blimey, it's a blinkin' vanity box ! "
—*Sgt., 10th R.F., East Sheen, S.W.14.*

Playing at Statues

WE were making our way to a detached post just on the left of Vimy, and Jerry was sending up Verey lights as we were going along. Every time one went up we halted, and kept quite still in case we should be seen.

"Playin' at statchoos."

It was funny indeed to see how some of the men halted when a light went up. Some had one foot down and one raised, and others were in a crouching position. "My missus orta see me nah playing at blinkin' statchoos," said one old Cockney. —*T. Kelly* (*late 17th London Regt.*), 43 *Ocean Street, Stepney, E.I.*

Bo Peep— 1915 Version

IN 1915 at Fricourt "Copper" Kingsland of our regiment, the 7th Royal West Surreys, was on sentry on the fire-step in the front line. At this period of the war steel helmets were not in use. Our cap badge was in the form of a lamb.

A Fritz sniper registered a hit through Kingsland's hat, cutting the tail portion of the lamb away. After he had pulled himself together "Copper" surveyed his cap badge and remarked : "On the larst kit inspection I reported to the sargint that yer was lorst, and nah I shall 'ave ter tell 'im that when Bo Peep fahnd yer, yer wagged yer bloomin' tail off in gratitood."—*"Spot," Haifu, Farley Road, Selsdon, Surrey.*

Jerry's Dip in the Fat

WE were out at rest in an open field on the Somme front when one morning, about 5 a.m., our cook, Alf, of Battersea, was preparing the company's breakfast. There was bacon, but no bread. I was standing beside the cooker soaking one of my biscuits in the fat.

Suddenly a Jerry airman dived down towards the cooker, firing his machine gun. I got under the cooker, Alf fell over the side of it, striking his head on the ground. I thought he was hit. But he sat up, rubbing his head and looking up at Jerry, who was then flying away.

"'Ere !" he shouted, "next time yer wants a dip in the fat, don't be so rough."—*H. A. Redford (late 24th London Regt.), 31 Charrington Street, N.W.1.*

Carried Unanimously

SOME recently captured trenches had to be cleared of the enemy, and in the company told off for the job was a Cockney youth. Proceeding along the trench with a Mills bomb in his hand, he came upon a number of the enemy hiding in a dug-out.

" Nah then," he shouted, holding up the bomb in readiness to throw it if necessary, " all them as votes for coming along wiv me 'old up your 'ands."

All hands were held up, with the cry " Kamerad ! Kamerad ! " Upon which the Cockney shouted, " Look, mates, it's carried unanermously."— *H. Morgan (late 4th Telegraph Construction Co., R.E. Signals), 26 Ranelagh Road, Wembley.*

A Very Hot Bath

DURING the retreat of the remnants of the Fifth Army in March 1918 two of the six-inch howitzers of the Honourable Artillery Company were in action in some deserted horse-lines outside Péronne.

During a lull Gunner A——, a Londoner, like the rest of us, went " scrounging " in some nearby cottages recently abandoned by their inhabitants. He reappeared carrying a large zinc bath, and after filling it with water from the horse pond he made a huge bonfire with broken tables and other furniture, and set the bath on the fire.

Just when the water had been heated Fritz opened out with 5.9's. As we were not firing just then we all took cover, with the exception of Gunner A——, who calmly set his bath of hot water down by one of the guns, undressed, and got into the bath. A minute later a large piece of shell also entered the bath, passed through the bottom of it and into the ground.

The gunner watched the precious water running out, then he slowly rose and, beginning to dress, remarked, " Very well, Fritz, have it your way. I may not be godly, but I *did* want to be clean."—*Edward Boaden (late H.A.C., 309 Siege Battery), 17 Connaught Gardens, Muswell Hill, N.10.*

In Lieu of ——

DURING a winter's night on the Somme a party of us were drawing rations just behind the front line trenches. A Cockney chum of mine was disgusted to hear the Q.M. say he was issuing hot soup in lieu of rum.

" Coo ! What next ? " he grumbled. " Soup in lieu of rum, biscuits in lieu of bread, jam in lieu——" While he spoke Jerry sent over two whizz-bangs which scattered us and the rations and inflicted several casualties.

My chum was hit badly. As he was being carried past the Q.M. he smiled and said, " Someone will have to be in lieu of me now, Quarter ! " —*T. Allen (late Plymouth Battn., R.N.D.), 21 Sydney Street, S.W.*

Putting the Hatt on It

TWO brothers named Hatt were serving together in France. The elder was always saying that he would never be hit, as the Germans, not being able to spell his name correctly, could not put it on any of their shells or bullets. (It was a common saying among the soldiers, of course, that a shell or bullet which hit a man had the victim's name on it.)

The younger brother was taken prisoner, and two days later the elder brother was shot through the finger. Turning to his mates he exclaimed, " Blimey, me brother's been an' split on me."—*W. J. Bowes, 224 Devon's Road, Bow, E.3.*

Tangible Evidence

WE were at Levantie in 1915, just before the Battle of Loos, and the rumour was about that the Germans were running short of ammunition. It was very quiet in our sector, as we were opposite the Saxons, and we strolled about at ease.

A party of us was told off to get water just behind the trenches in an old farmhouse which had a pump. We filled all the water bottles and rum jars and then had a look round the ruins to see what we could scrounge, when suddenly Fritz sent a shell over. It hit the wall and sent bricks flying all over the place. One of the bricks hit my mate on the head and knocked him out. When we had revived him he looked up and said, " Strewth, it's right they ain't got no ' ammo.' ; they're slinging bricks. It shows yer we've got 'em all beat to a frazzle, don't it ? "—*J. Delderfield, 54 Hampden Street, Paddington.*

What the Cornwalls' Motto Meant

A PLATOON of my regiment, the Duke of Cornwall's Light Infantry, was engaged in carrying screens to a point about 200 yards behind the front line. The screens were to be set up to shield a road from German observation balloons, and they were made of brushwood bound together with wire. They were rolled up for convenience of transport, and when rolled they looked like big bundles of pea-sticks about ten feet long. They were very heavy.

Three men were told off to carry each screen. One of the parties of three was composed of two Cornishmen (who happened to be at the ends of the screen) and their Cockney pal (in the middle), the screen being carried on their shoulders.

When they had nearly reached the point in the communication trench where it was to be dumped, Jerry sent over a salvo of whizz-bangs. His range was good, and consequently the carrying party momentarily became disorganised. The Cornishman at the front end of the screen dashed towards the front line, whilst the man at the other end made a hurried move backwards.

This left the Cockney with the whole of the weight of the screen on his shoulder. The excitement was over in a few seconds and the Cornishmen returned to find the Cockney lying on the duck-boards, where he had subsided under the weight of his burden, trying to get up. He stopped struggling when he saw them and said very bitterly, " Yus : One and All's yer blinkin' motter ; *one* under the blinkin' screen and *all* the rest 'op it."

" One and All," I should mention, is the Cornwalls' motto.— *" Cornwall," Greenford, Middlesex.*

Atlas—On the Somme

DURING the Somme offensive we were holding the line at Delville Wood, and a Cockney corporal fresh from England came to our company.

He was told to take charge of a very advanced post, and our company officer gave him all important instructions as to bomb stores, ammunition, rifle grenades, emergency rations, S O S rockets, gas, and all the other numerous and important orders for an advanced post.

After the officer asked him if he understood it all, he said, " Blimey, sir, 'as 'Aig gone on leave ? "—*Ex-Sergt. Geary, D.C.M. (East Surrey Regt.*), 57 *Longley Road, Tooting.*

Putting the Lid on It

ON the Struma Front, Salonika, in September 1916, I was detailed to take a party of Bulgar prisoners behind the lines.

Two Bulgars, one of them a huge, bald-headed man, were carrying a stretcher in which was reposing " Ginger " Hart, of Deptford, who was shot through the leg.

The white bursts of shrapnel continued in our vicinity as we proceeded. One shell burst immediately in front of us, and we halted.

It was at this juncture that I saw " Ginger " leave his stretcher and hop away on one leg. Having picked up a tin hat, he hopped back to the big Bulgar prisoner and put the hat on his bald head, saying, " Abaht time we put the lid on the sooit puddin', corp : that's the fifth shot they've fired at that target."—*G. Findlay, M.M. (late 81st Infantry Brigade, 27th Division*), 3a *Effie Place, Fulham, S.W.6.*

Taffy was a—German !

IN the confused fighting round Gueudecourt in 1916 a machine-gun section occupied a position in a maze of trenches, some of which led towards the German line. The divisional pioneer battalion was the Monmouthshire Regiment, all of whose men were Welsh and for the most part spoke Welsh.

A ration party of the M.G.C. had gone back one night and had been absent some time when two members rushed into the position, gasping : " We took the wrong turning ! Walked into Jerry's line ! They've got Smiffy—and the rations ! "

We had hardly got over the shock of this news when Smiffy came staggering up, dragging the rations and mopping a bleeding face, at the same time cursing the rest of the ration party.

" Luv us, Smiffy, how did you get away ? We thought the Germans had got you for sure ! "

" Germans," gasped Smiffy. " GERMANS ! *I thought they was the Monmouths !* "—*S. W. Baxter (late 86th M.G.C.), 110 Bishopsgate, E.C.2.*

A Tea-time Story

AT the Battle of Cambrai in November 1917 my regiment, the London Irish Rifles, was undergoing a terrific bombardment in Bourlon Wood.

The Germans had been plastering us for about 12 hours with " all calibres," to say nothing of continual gassing.

As we had been wearing gas-masks almost all day without respite, we were nearly " all in " as the afternoon wore on.

I was attending to a man with a smashed foot, when I felt a touch on my shoulder, and, blinking up through my sweat-covered mask, I saw our mess-orderly with his hand over a mess-tin (to keep the gas out, as he said).

I could hardly believe my eyes, but when I heard him say, " Tea is ready, Sarg. Blimey, what a strafe ! " I lifted my mask and drank deeply.

From that day till this it has been a wonder to me how he made it. —*S. Gibbons, 130 Buckhold Road, Southfields, S.W.18.*

A Tip to a Prisoner

THE object of our raiding party near Gouzeaucourt in 1917 was to obtain a prisoner.

One plucky, but very much undersized, German machine gunner blazed away at us until actually pounced upon. A Cockney who was well among the leaders jumped down beside him, and heaving him up said :

" Come on, old mate, you're too blinkin' good for this side ! "—and then, noticing his lack of inches, " and if yer wants ter make the ' old man ' larf tell him you're a ' Prussian Guard.' "—*Walter S. Johnson (late R.W.F.), 29 Southwold Road, Upper Clapton, E.5.*

Cockney Logic

EARLY in the war aeroplanes were not so common as they were later on, and trench " strafing " from the air was practically unheard of. One day two privates of the Middlesex Regiment were engaged in clearing a section of front line trench near the La Bassée road when a

. . . and they both went on digging.

German plane came along and sprayed the trenches with machine-gun bullets.

One of the men (both were typical Cockneys) looked up from his digging and said : " Strike, there's a blinkin' aeroplane."

The other took no notice but went on digging.

By-and-by the machine came back, still firing, whereupon the speaker again looked up, spat, and said : " Blimey, there's annuver of 'em."

" No, 'tain't," was the reply, " it's the same blighter again."

" Blimey," said the first man, " so 'tis." And both went on digging.—
W. P. (late Middlesex Regt. and R.A.F.), Bucks.

" Penalty, Ref ! "

IT was a warm corner on the Givenchy front, with whizz-bangs dealing out death and destruction. But it was necessary that communication be maintained between the various H.Q.'s, and in this particular sector " Alf," from Bow, and myself were detailed to keep the " lines " intact.

Suddenly a whizz-bang burst above us as we were repairing some shattered lines. We ducked instinctively, but friend " Alf " caught a bit of the shell and was thrown to the bottom of the slushy trench.

Being a football enthusiast he at once raised his arm in appeal, and, with the spirit that wins wars, shouted, " Penalty, ref ! "

He was dazed, but unhurt.—*W. G. Harris (late Sergt., R.E.)*, 34 *Denmark Street, Watford.*

An Appointment with his Medical Adviser

DURING the battle of the Ancre in November 1916 the 51st Division were going over the top on our left while our battalion kept Jerry engaged with a raid. Every inch of the rain-sodden landscape seemed to be heaving beneath the combined barrages of the opposing forces.

My sergeant, a D.C.M., had been lying in the trench badly wounded for some hours waiting for things to ease up before he could be got down to the dressing-station. Presently our raiding party returned with six prisoners, among them an insignificant-looking German officer (who, waving a map about, and jabbering wildly, seemed to be blaming his capture to the faulty tactics of his High Command).

The wounded sergeant watched these antics for a while with a grin, driving the pain-bred puckers from his face, and then called out, " Oi, 'Indenburg ! Never mind abaht ye map o' London ; wot time does this 'ere war end, 'cos I've got an appointment wiv my medical adviser ! "

Dear, brave old chap. His appointment was never kept.—*S.T. (late 37th Div.), Fulham, S.W.6.*

One Up, and Two to Go

ON the Struma front in 1917 a bombing plane was being put back into its hangar. Suddenly there was a terrific bang. A dozen of us ran up to see what had happened, but a Cockney voice from inside the hangar cried out, " Don't come in. There's two more bombs to go off, and I can't find 'em."—*A. Dickinson, Brixton.*

On the Parados

DAWN of a very hot day in September 1916 on the Balkan front. We were in the enemy trenches at " Machine Gun Hill," a position hitherto occupied by the Prussian Guards, who were there to encourage the Bulgars.

We had taken the position the previous evening with very little loss.

As the day broke we discovered that we were enfiladed on all sides and overlooked by the Prussians not more than forty yards away. It was impossible to evacuate wounded and prisoners or for reserves to approach with food, water, and ammunition. The enemy counter-attacked in overwhelming numbers; shells rained on us; our own were falling short; it was suicide to show one's head. Towards noon, casualties lying about. The sun merciless. Survivors thoroughly exhausted. Up jumped a Cockney bomber. "Blimey, I can't stick this," and perched himself on the parados. "I can see 'em; chuck some 'Mills' up." And as fast as they were handed to him he pitched bombs into the Prussians' midst, creating havoc. He lasted about three minutes, then fell, riddled with bullets. He had stemmed the tide.

Shortly afterwards we retired. His pluck was never recorded or recognised, but his feat will never be forgotten by at least one of the few who got through.—*George McCann, 50 Guilford Street, London, W.*

Not Croquet

WE were occupying a support line, early in 1918, and a party of us was detailed to repair the barbed wire during the night.

A Cockney found himself holding a stake while a Cornish comrade drove it home with a mallet.

Suddenly a shell exploded a few yards from the pair and both were very badly wounded.

When the Cockney recovered consciousness he was heard to remark to his comrade in misfortune, "Blimey, yer wants to be more careful wiv that there mallet; yer nearly 'it my 'and wiv it when that there firework exploded."—*A. A. Homer, 16 Grove Place, Enfield Wash, Middlesex.*

Sausages and Mashed

AT the end of 1914 we were in the trenches in the Ypres Salient. As we were only about 30 yards from the enemy lines, bombing went on all day. The German bombs, shaped like a long sausage, could be seen coming through the air. Our sentries, on the look-out for these, would shout: "Sausage right!" or "Sausage left!" as they came over.

One night we were strengthened by reinforcements, including several Cockneys. The next morning one of our sentries saw a bomb coming over and shouted "Sausage right!" There followed an explosion which smothered two of our new comrades in mud and shreds of sandbag. One of the two got up, with sackcloth twisted all round his neck and pack. "'Ere, Bill, wot was that?" he asked one of our men.

"Why, one of those sausages," Bill replied.

"Lumme," said the new man, as he freed himself from the sacking, "I don't mind the sausages, but," he added as he wiped the mud from his eyes and face, "I don't like the mash."—*H. Millard (late East Surrey Regt.), 3 Nevill Road, Stoke Newington, N.*

Cheery to the End

WE were lining up to go over in the Battle of Arras on April 9, 1917. Ours being a Lancashire regiment, there were only two of us Cockneys in our platoon. We were standing easy, waiting for the rum issue, and Tom, my pal (we both came from Stratford), came over to me singing " Let's all go down the Strand . . ."

Most of the Lancashire lads were looking a bit glum, but it cheered them up, and they all began to sing. I was feeling a bit gloomy myself, and Tom, seeing this, said : " What's the matter with you, Jimmy ? "

" I suppose I'll see you in London Hospital next week, Tom," I said.

" Oh, shut up," says he. " If Jerry sends one over and it's got our names on it, why worry ? And if we get a bad Blighty one, then I hopes they buries us at Manor Park. Here, Jim, tie this disc round me neck."

Then the rum came up, and he started them singing, " And another little drink wouldn't do us any harm ! "

Off we went—and only ten minutes later he was gone. He was buried at Blany, Arras, not Manor Park.—*J. Pugh (late 1st King's Own Royal Lancasters), 27 Lizban Street, Blackheath, S.E.5.*

Souvenirs First

THE following incident took place during the Battle of Loos, September 1915. I had been to Battalion H.Q. with a message and whilst awaiting a reply stood with others on " Harrow Road " watching our wounded go by.

We frequently recognised wounded pals on the stretchers and inquired as to the nature of their wounds. The usual form of inquiry was : " Hullo —— what have you got ? " In reply to this query one wounded man of our battalion, ignoring his wound as being of lesser importance, proudly answered : " Two Jerry helmets and an Iron Cross ! "—*A. H. Bell (late Private, 15th London Regt., T.F.), 31 Raeburn Avenue, Surbiton, Surrey.*

Seven Shies a Tanner !

IT was near Hebuterne and very early in the morning of July 1, 1916. A terrific bombardment by both the Germans and ourselves was in progress just prior to the launching of our Somme offensive. We were in assembly trenches waiting for the dread zero hour.

Away on our right some German guns were letting us have it pretty hot, and in consequence the " troops " were not feeling in the best of spirits.

With us was a very popular Cockney corporal. He took his tin hat from off his head when the tension was high and, banging on it with his bayonet, cried : " Roll up, me lucky lads ! Seven shies a tanner ! Who'll 'ave a go ! " That bit of nonsense relieved the tension and enabled us to pull ourselves together.—*A. V. B. (late 9th Londons), Guildford.*

Bill Hawkins Fights Them All

WHILST on the Ypres front during the fighting in 1918 we made an early-morning attack across the railway line in front of Dickebusch. After going about fifty yards across No Man's Land my Cockney pal (Bill Hawkins, from Stepney), who was running beside me, got a slight wound in the arm, and before he had gone another two yards he got another wound in the left leg.

Suddenly he stopped, lifted his uninjured arm at the Germans and shouted, "Blimey, wot yer all firing at me for ? Am I the only blinkin' man in this war ? "—*S. Stevens (late Middlesex Regt., 2nd Battn.), 7 Blenheim Street, Chelsea, S.W.*

Hide and Seek with Jerry

TO get information before the Somme offensive, the new idea of making daylight raids on the German trenches was adopted. It fell to our battalion to make the first big raid.

Our objective was the " brickfields " at Beaurains, near Arras, and our orders were to take as many prisoners as possible, hold the trench for half an hour, do as much damage as we could, and then return. A covering barrage was put down, and over we went, one hundred strong.

We got into Jerry's trench all right, but, owing to the many dug-outs and tunnels, we could only find a few Germans, and these, having no time to bolt underground, got out of the trench and ran to take cover behind the kilns and brick-stacks.

And then the fun began. While the main party of us got to work in the trench, a few made after the men who had run into the brickfields, and it was a case of hide and seek, round and round and in and out of the kilns and brick-stacks.

Despite the seriousness of the situation, one chap, a Cockney, entered so thoroughly into the spirit of the thing that when, after a lengthy chase, he at last clapped a German on the shoulder, he shouted, " You're 'e ! "—*E. W. Fellows, M.M. (late 6th D.C.L.I.), 35 Dunlace Road, Clapton, E.5.*

Too Much for his Imagination

IN the platoon of cyclists I was posted to on the outbreak of war was a Cockney—a " Charlie Chaplin " without the funny feet. If there was a funny side to a thing, he saw it.

One day, on the advance, just before the battle of the Marne, our platoon was acting as part of the left flank guard when a number of enemy cavalry were seen advancing over a ridge, some distance away. We were ordered to dismount and extend. We numbered about sixteen, so our line was not a long one.

A prominent object was pointed out to us, judged at about 150 yards away, and orders were given not to fire until the enemy reached that spot.

We could see that we were greatly outnumbered, and having to wait for them to reach that spot seemed to double the suspense. Our leader was giving commands one second and talking like a father the next. He said, " Keep cool ; each take a target ; show them you are British. You have as good a chance as they, and although they are superior in numbers they have no other superior quality. I want you just to imagine that you are on the range again, firing for your pay." Then our Cockney Charlie chimed in with : " Yes, but we ain't got no bloomin' markers."—*S. Leggs (late Rifle Brigade and Cyclists)*, 33 *New Road, Grays, Essex.*

" Currants " for Bunn

AFTER we had taken part in the advance on the Somme in August 1916 my battalion was ordered to rest at Bazentin.

We had only been there a day or so when we were ordered to relieve the Tyneside Scottish who were badly knocked about. Hardly had we reached the front lines, when a little Cockney named Bunn (we never knew how he carried his pack, he was so small) got hit. We called for stretcher-bearers.

When they put him on the stretcher and were carrying him down the line, a doctor asked him his name. The Cockney looked up with a smile and answered : " Bunn, sir, and the blighters have put some currants into me this time." This gallant Cockney died afterwards.—*J. E. Cully (late 13th King's Royal Rifles), 76 Milkwood Road, S.E.24.*

The Driver to his Horse

THE artillery driver's affection for his own particular pair of horses is well known. Our battery, in a particularly unhealthy spot in front of Zillebeke, in the Salient, had run out of ammunition, and the terrible state of the ground thereabout in the autumn of 1917 necessitated the use of pack-horses to " deliver the goods," and even then it was accomplished with difficulty.

A little Cockney driver with a pair named Polly and Bill had loaded up and was struggling through the mire. Three times Bill had dragged him on to his knees and up to his waist in the slush when a big Fritz shell dropped uncomfortably near. Polly, with a mighty rear, threw the Cockney on to his back and, descending, struck him with a hoof.

Fed up to the teeth and desperate, he struggled to his feet, covered from head to feet in slime, and, clenching his fist, struck at the trembling and frightened horse, unloading a brief but very vivid description of its pedigree and probable future.

Then, cooling off, he began to pacify the mare, apologised, and pardoned her vice by saying, " Never mind, ole gal—I didn't mean ter bash yer ! I fought the uvver one was hot stuff, but, strike me pink, you don't seem 'ooman ! "—*G. Newell (ex-Sergt., R.F.A.), 22 Queen Road, St. Albans.*

Two Kinds of " Shorts "

AUGUST 1916, Delville Wood. We had been brought specially from rest camp to take the remainder of the wood, which was being stoutly contested by the Germans and was holding up our advance. The usual barrage, and over we went, and were met by the Germans standing on top of their trenches. A fierce bombing fight began. The scrap lasted a long time, but at last we charged and captured the trench.

" Yus, yer needn't stare—I'm real."

One of our men, quite a small Cockney, captured a German about twice his own size. The German was so surprised at being captured by a person so insignificant looking that he stood and stared. Our Cockney, seeing his amazement, said : " Yus, yer needn't stare, I'm real, and wot's more, I got a good mind ter punch yer under the blinkin' ear fer spoiling me rest ! "—*F. M. Fellows, M.M. (late Corporal, 6th Batt. D.C.L.I.)*, 33 *Dunlace Road, Clapton, E.*5.

Mespot—On 99 Years' Lease

I WAS in Mesopotamia from 1916 till 1920, and after the Armistice was signed there was still considerable trouble with the Arabs.

In the summer of 1919 I, with a party of 23 other R.A.S.C. men, was surrounded by the Arabs at an outpost that was like a small fort. We had taken up supplies for troops stationed there. There were about 100 Indian soldiers, and a few British N.C.O.'s in charge.

It was no use "running the gauntlet." We were on a hill and kept the Arabs at bay all day, also the next night.

The next day all was quiet again, but in the afternoon an Arab rode into the camp on horseback with a message, which he gave to the first Tommy he saw. It happened to be one of our fellows, a proper Cockney. He read the message—written in English—requesting us to surrender.

Our Cockney pal said a few kind words to the Arab, and decided to send a message back.

He wrote this on the back of the paper : " Sorry, Mr. Shake. We have only just taken the place, and we have got it on 99 years' lease. Yours faithfully, Old Bill and Co., Ltd., London."—*W. Thurgood (late R.A.S.C., M.T.), 46 Maldon Road, Southend-on-Sea, Essex.*

" Fro Something at Them ! "

THERE was a certain divisional commander in France who enjoyed a popularity that was almost unique. He was quite imperturbable, whatever the situation.

Unfortunately, he had an impediment in his speech, and when first one met him he was difficult to understand. But heaven help anyone who asked him to repeat anything. A light would come into his eye, and he would seize hold of his victim by the shoulder-strap and heave and tug till it came off.

" You'll understand me," he would say, " when I tell you your shoulder-strap is undone ! "

The Division he commanded had just put up a wonderful fight just south of Arras in the March '18 show, and, having suffered very heavy casualties, were taken out of the line and put into a cushy front next door to the Portuguese.

The morning after they took over the Germans launched a heavy attack on the Portuguese, who withdrew somewhat hurriedly, so that the whole flank of the British division was open.

The general was sitting eating his breakfast—he had been roused at six by the bombardment—when an excited orderly came into the room and reported that the Germans had got right in behind the Division and were now actually in the garden of the general's château.

The general finished drinking his cup of coffee, the orderly still standing to attention, waiting instructions.

" Then you had better ' fro ' something at them—or shoo them away," said the general.—*F. A. P., Cavalry Club, Piccadilly, W.*

Missed his Mouth-organ

DURING the Battle of the Somme our trench-mortar battery was going back after a few days' rest. It was very dark and raining. As we neared our destination it appeared that Jerry and our chaps were having a real argument.

We were going up a road called " Queen's Hollow." Jerry was enfilading us on both sides, and a rare bombing fight was going on at the farther end of the Hollow—seventy or a hundred yards in front of us. We were expecting to feel the smack of a bullet any moment, and there was a terrible screeching and bursting of shells, with a few " Minnies " thrown in. We were in a fine pickle, and I had just about had enough when my pal (a lad from " The Smoke ") nearly put me on my back by stopping suddenly.

" I don't like this, Bomb," he said.

" What's wrong with you ? Get on," I replied, " or we'll all be blown sky high."

" Oh, all right," he said, " but I wish I'd brought me mouf orgin. I could then have livened fings up a bit."—" *Bombardier* " (*R.A.*), *late T.M.B., 7th Division.*

Water-cooled

THERE must be at least six men still alive who remember a certain affair at Kemmel. During the latter part of April 1918 our machine gunners had been having a bad time, and one old Cockney sergeant found himself and his party isolated miles in front of our line.

The cool way in which he gave orders, as he told his men to make their way back—lying down for a bit, then making a run for another shelter—would have been humorous if conditions had not been so terrifying.

He himself kept his gun working to protect their retreat, and when he saw they had reached a place of safety he picked up his gun and rejoined them unhurt.

One of his men, describing the action afterwards, said, " Carried his gun three miles—wouldn't part with it—and the first thing he did when he was able to settle down quietly was to start cleaning the blessed thing ! "—*H. R. Tanner, " Romsdal," Newton Ferrers, S. Devon.*

Top-hatted Piper of Mons

DURING the retreat from Mons it was a case of " going while the going was good " until called upon to make a stand to harass the enemy's advance.

After the stand at Le Cateau, bad and blistered feet caused many to stop by the wayside. Among these, in passing with my little squad, I noticed a piper belonging to a Scottish regiment sitting with his blistered feet exposed and his pipes lying beside him. Staff officers were continually riding back and urging the parties of stragglers to make an effort to push on before they were overtaken.

In the late afternoon of this same day, having myself come up with my unit, I was resting on the roadside when I heard the skirl of bagpipes. Before long there came into sight, marching with a fair swing, too, as motley a throng as one ever saw in the King's uniform. Headed by a staff officer were about 150 men of all regiments with that same piper, hatless and with one stocking, in front.

Beside him was a Cockney of the Middlesex Regiment, with a silk hat on his head, whose cheeks threatened to burst as he churned out the strains of " Alexander's Rag-time Band " on the bagpipes. Being a bit of a piper himself, he was giving " Jock " a lift and was incidentally the means of fetching this little band away from the clutches of the enemy.—" Buster " Brown (late Bedfordshire Regt.), Hertford.

Two Heads and a Bullet

EARLY in 1916 ten of us were going up with rations—chiefly bread and water. In one part of the trench there were no duck-boards and the vile mud was thigh-deep.

Here we abandoned the trench and stumbled along, tripping over barbed wire and falling headlong into shell-holes half-full of icy water.

A German sniper was at work. Suddenly a bullet pinged midway between the last two of the party.

" Hear that ? " said No. 9. " Right behind my neck ! "

" Yes," replied No. 10, " right in front of my bloomin' nose ! "— C. A. Davies (late 23rd R. Fusiliers), 85 Saxton Street, Gillingham, Kent.

Spoiling the Story

WE were billeted in the upper room of a corner house north of Albert, and were listening to " Spoofer's " memories of days " dahn Walworf way."

" Yus," he said, " I ses to the gal, ' Two doorsteps an' a bloater.' "

At that moment a " coal-box " caught the corner of the house, bringing down the angle of the wall and three-parts of the floor on which we had squatted.

Except for bruises, none of us was injured, and when the dust subsided we saw " Spoofer " looking down at us from a bit of the flooring that remained intact.

" Yus," he continued, as though nothing had happened, " as I was saying, I'd just called fer the bloater . . ."

Came another " coal-box," which shook down the remainder of the floor and with it " Spoofer."

Struggling to his hands and knees, he said, " Blimey, the blinkin' bloater's cold nah."—F. Lates, 62 St. Ervan's Road, North Kensington.

Afraid of Dogs

TOWARDS the end of October 1918 I was out on patrol in front of Tournai on a dark, windy night. I had a Cockney private with me, and we were some distance from our lines when we heard a dog barking. All at once, before I could stop him, the Cockney whistled it.

I threw the Cockney down and dropped myself. A German Verey light went up—followed by a hail of machine-gun bullets in our direction. As the light spread out, we saw the dog fastened to a German machine-gun ! We lay very still, and presently, when things had quietened down, we slid cautiously backwards until it was safe to get up.

All the Cockney said was, "Crikey, corp, I had the wind up. A blinkin' good job that there dawg was chained up. Why ? 'Cause 'e might 'ave bitten us. I allus was afeard o' dawgs."—*J. Milsun (late 1/5th Battn., The King's Own 55th Div.), 31 Collingwood Road, Lexden, Colchester.*

The Song of Battle

AT the first Gaza battle we had to advance 1,700 yards across a plain in full view of the Turks, who hurled a terrific barrage at us. We were in artillery formation, and we marched up until within rifle range. With machine guns and artillery the Turks were depleting our ranks, so that less than half of us were still marching on at 500 yards range.

In my section was the Cockney "funny man" of the company. When things were bad, and we were all wondering how long we would survive, he began singing lustily a song which someone had sung at our last concert party behind the lines, the refrain of which was "I've never heard of anybody dying from kissing, have you ? "

Before he had started on the second line nearly everyone was singing with him, and men were killed singing that song. To the remainder of us it acted like a tonic.

Good old Jack, when he was wounded later he must have been in terrible pain, yet he joked so that at first we would not believe he was seriously hit. He shouted, "Where is 'e ?—let me get at 'im."—*J. T. Jones (late 54th Division), 37 Whittaker Road, East Ham, E.6.*

Stalls at " Richthofen's Circus "

A NEW ZEALANDER was piloting an old F.E. 2B (pusher) 'plane up and down over the lines, observing for the artillery, when he got caught by " Richthofen's Circus."

The petrol tank behind the pilot's seat was set on fire and burning oil poured past him into the observer's cockpit ahead and the clothes of both men started to sizzle.

They were indeed in a warm situation, their one hope being to dive into Zillebeke Lake, which the New Zealander noticed below. By the time they splashed into the water machine and men were in flames ;

and, moreover, when they came up the surface surrounding them was aflame with the burning oil.

Treading water desperately and ridding themselves of their heavy sodden flying coats, they made a last bid for life by swimming under water, that flaming water, and at last, half-dead, reached the bank.

There a strong arm gripped the New Zealander by the scruff of the neck and he was hauled to safety, dimly aware of a hoarse voice complaining bitterly, " Ours is the best hid battery in this sector, the only unspotted battery. You *would* choose just 'ere to land, wouldn't yer, and give the bloomin' show away ? "

Our Cockney battery sergeant-major had, no doubt, never heard of Hobson or his choice.—*E. H. Orton,* 9 *High Grove, Welwyn Garden City, Herts.*

" Butter-Fingers ! "

A COCKNEY infantryman of the 47th Division was on the fire-step on the night preceding the attack at Loos. He was huddled up in a ground-sheet trying to keep cheerful in the drizzle.

Suddenly a British 12-in. shell passed over him, and as he heard its slow rumble he muttered, " Catch that one, you blighters."

Just then it burst, and with a chuckle he added, " Oh, butter-fingers, yer dropped it ! "—*Henry J. Tuck (late Lt., R.G.A.).*

Getting into Hot Water

W E were in the front line, and one evening a Battersea lad and myself were ordered to go and fetch tea for the company from the cookhouse, which was in Bluff Trench. It was about a mile from

" D'yer fink we wants ter be scalded ter death ? "

the line down a " beautiful " duckboard track.

With the boiling tea strapped to our backs in big containers, both of which leaked at the nozzles, we started for the line. Then Jerry started sniping at us. There came from the line a sergeant, who shouted, " Why don't you lads duck ? " " That's right," replied my chum. " D'yer fink we wants ter be scalded to death ? "—*H. G. Harrap (23rd London Regiment),* 25 *Renfrew Road, S.E.*

2. LULL

Rate of Exchange—on Berlin

WITH four Cockney comrades of the Rifle Brigade, during 1915 at Fleurbaix, I was indulging in a *quiet* game of nap in the front line.

One man dropped out, "broke to the wide." Being an enthusiastic card player, he offered various articles for sale, but could find no buyers. At last he offered to *find* a Jerry prisoner and sell him for a franc.

He was absent for some time, but eventually turned up with his hostage, and, the agreement being duly honoured, he recommenced his game with his fresh capital.

All the players came through alive, their names being J. Cullison, F. Bones, A. White, W. Deer (the first-named playing leading part), and myself.—*F. J. Chapman (late* 11th *Batt. Rifle Brigade)*, 110 Beckton Road, Victoria Docks, E.16.

A Hen Coup

DURING the retreat from Mons strict orders were issued against looting. One day an officer, coming round a corner, discovered a stalwart Cockney Tommy in the act of wringing the neck of an inoffensive-looking chicken. The moment the Tommy caught sight of his officer he was heard to murmur to the chicken, "Would yer, yer brute!" Quite obviously, therefore, the deed had been done in self-defence.—*The Rev. T. K. Lowdell, Church of St. Augustine, Lillie Road, Fulham, S.W.6.*

A " Baa-Lamb " in the Trenches

THE " dug-out " was really a hole scraped in the side of a trench leading up to the front line and some 50 yards from it. It was October '16 on the Somme, after the weather had broken. The trench was about two feet deep in liquid mud—a delightful thoroughfare for runners and other unfortunate ones who had to use it.

The officer in the dug-out heard the *splosh—splosh—splosh* . . . of a single passenger coming up the trench. As the splosher drew abreast the dug-out the officer heard him declaiming to himself: " Baa! baa! I'm a blinkin' lamb lorst in the ruddy wilderness. Baa! baa! . . . "

And when the bleating died away the *splosh—splosh—splosh* . . . grew fainter too, as the " lamb " was lost in the night.—*L. W. Martinnant*, 64 *Thornsbeach Road, Catford, S.E.6.*

4

He Coloured

WHEN serving with the Artists' Rifles in France we went into the line to relieve the " Nelsons " of the 63rd (Royal Naval) Division.

As I was passing one of their men, a regular " Ole Bill," who was seated on the fire-step, I heard him say, " Artists' Rifles, eh ; I wonder if any of you chaps would *paint* me a plate of 'am and eggs ! "—*R. C. Toogood, 43 Richmond Park Avenue, Bournemouth.*

Why the Fat Man Laughed

DURING the winter of 1914–15 the trenches were just like canals of sloppy mud, and dug-outs were always falling in. To repair the dug-outs pit-props were used, but they often had to be carried great distances up communication trenches, and were very difficult to handle. The most popular way to carry a prop was to rest one end on the left shoulder of one man and the other end on the right shoulder of the man behind.

On one occasion the leading man was short and fat, and the rear man was tall and thin. Suddenly the front man slipped and the prop fell down in the mud and splashed the thin man from head to foot. To add to his discomfort the little fat man gave a hearty laugh.

" Can't see anything to larf at, mate," said the mud-splashed hero, looking down at himself.

" I'm larfing," said the little fat Cockney, " 'cos I've just remembered that I tipped the recruiting sergeant a bloomin' tanner to put me name down fust on his list so as I'd get out here quick."—*A. L. Churchill (late Sergt., Worcs. Regt.), 6 Long Lane, Blackheath, Staffs.*

He Met Shackleton !

THE troops in North Russia, in the winter of 1918–19, were equipped with certain additional articles of clothing designed on the same principles as those used on Antarctic expeditions. Among these were what were known as " Shackleton boots," large canvas boots with thick leather soles. These boots were not at all suitable for walking on hard snow, being very clumsy, and they were very unpopular with everyone.

The late Sir Ernest Shackleton was sent out by the War Office to give advice on matters of clothing, equipment, and so on. When he arrived at Archangel he went up to a sentry whose beat was in front of a warehouse about three steps up from the road, and said to him, " Well, my man, what do you think of the Shackleton boot ? "

To this the sentry replied : " If I could only meet the perishing blighter wot invented them I'd very soon show—— "

Before he could complete the sentence his feet, clad in the ungainly boots, slipped on the frozen snow, and slithering down the steps on his back, he shot into Sir Ernest and the two of them completed the discussion on Shackleton boots rolling over in the snow !—*K. D., Elham, near Canterbury.*

Domestic Scene : Scene, Béthune

NEAR the front line at Béthune in 1917 was a farm which had been evacuated by the tenants, but there were still some cattle and other things on it. We were, of course, forbidden to touch them.

One day we missed one of our fellows, a Cockney, for about two hours, and guessed he was on the " scrounge " somewhere or other.

Eventually he was seen coming down the road pushing an old-fashioned

"... only taking the kid and the dawg for a bit of a blow."

pram loaded with cabbages, and round his waist there was a length of rope, to the other end of which was tied an old cow.

You can imagine what a comical sight it was, but the climax came when he was challenged by the corporal, " Where the devil have you been ? " " Me ? " he replied innocently. " I only bin takin' the kid and the dawg for a bit of a blow."—*A. Rush (late 4th Batt. R. Fus.), 27 Milton Road, Wimbledon.*

Getting Their Bearings

IT was on the Loos front. One night a party of us were told off for reconnoitring. On turning back about six of us, with our young officer, missed our way and, after creeping about for some 15 minutes, a message came down, " Keep very quiet, we are nearly in the German lines."

I passed on the message to the chap behind me, who answered in anything but a whisper, " Thank 'eaven we know where we are at last."— *H. Hutton (late 16th Lancers, attached Engineers), Marlborough Road, Upper Holloway.*

High Tea

DURING the winter of 1917–18 I was serving with my battery of Field Artillery in Italy. We had posted to us a draft of drivers just out from home, and one of them, seeing an observation balloon for the first time, asked an old driver what it was.

" Oh, that," replied the old hand, who hailed from Hackney—" that is the Air Force canteen ! "—*M. H. Cooke (late " B " Battery, 72nd Brigade, R.F.A.), Regency Street, Westminster.*

Lots in a Name

SALONIKA, mid-autumn, and torrents of rain. The battalion, changing over to another front, had trekked all through the night. An hour before dawn a halt was called to bivouac on the reverse slope of a hill until the journey could be completed in the darkness of the following night.

Orderlies from each platoon were collecting blankets from their company pack mules. Last of them all was a diminutive Cockney, who staggered off in the darkness with his load perched on his head. Slowly and laboriously, slipping backwards at almost every step, he stumbled and slithered up hill in the ankle-deep mud. Presently he paused for breath, and took advantage of the opportunity to relieve his feelings in these well-chosen words : " All I can say is, the bloke as christened this 'ere perishin' place Greece was about blinking well right."—*P. H. T. (26th Division).*

Gunga Din the Second

AFTER the battle of Shaikh Sa'Ad in Mesopotamia in January 1916 more than 300 wounded were being transported down the Tigris to Basra in a steamer and on open barges lashed on either side of it. Many suffered from dysentery as well as wounds—and it was raining.

There appeared to be only one Indian bhisti (water-carrier), an old man over 60 years of age, to attend to all. He was nearly demented in trying to serve everyone at once. When my severely wounded neighbour —from Camberwell, he said—saw the bhisti, his welcome made us smile through our miseries.

" Coo ! If it ain't old Gunga Din ! Wherever 'ave yer bin, me old brown son ? Does yer muvver know yer aht ? "—*A. S. Edwardes (late C.S.M., 1st Seaforth Highlanders), West Gate, Royal Hospital, Chelsea, S.W.3.*

A Fag fer an 'Orse

LATE one afternoon towards the end of 1917, on the Cambrai sector, enemy counter-attacks had caused confusion behind our lines, and as I was walking along a road I met a disconsolate-looking little Cockney

" Give us a fag and I'll give yer an 'orse."

infantryman leading a large-size horse. He stopped me and said, " Give us a fag, mate, and I'll give yer an 'orse."

I gathered that he had found the horse going spare and was taking it along with him for company's sake.—*H. J. Batt (late Royal Fusiliers)*, 21 *Whitehall Park Road, W* 4.

Put to Graze

IT was at the siege of Kut, when the 13th (" Iron ") Division was trying to relieve that gallant but hard-pressed body of men under General Townshend. Rations had been very low for days, and the battery had been digging gun-pits in several positions, till at last we had a change of position and " dug in " to stay a bit. What with bad water, digging in, and hardly any food, the men were getting fed up generally. An order came out to the effect that " A certain bunchy grass (detailed explanation) if picked and boiled would make a very nourishing meal." One hefty Cockney, " Dusty " Miller, caused a laugh when he vented his feelings with " 'Struth, and nah we got ter be blinking sheep. Baa-Baa ! "— *E. J. Bates (late R.F.A.), 37 Ulverscroft Road, E. Dulwich.*

Smith's Feather Pillow

THE boys had " rescued " a few hens from a deserted farm. The morning was windy and feathers were scattered in the mud.

Picquet officer (appearing from a corner of the trench) : " What's the meaning of all these feathers, Brown ? "

Brown : " Why, sir, Smiff wrote 'ome sayin' 'e missed 'is 'ome comforts, an' 'is ma sent 'im a fevver piller ; an' 'e's so mad at our kiddin' that 'e's in that dug-out tearin' it to bits."—*John W. Martin, 16 Eccles Road, Lavender Hill, S.W.11.*

Bombs and Arithmetic

WE were in the trenches in front of Armentières in the late summer of 1916. It was a fine, quiet day, with " nothing doing." I was convinced that a working party was busy in a section of the German trenches right opposite.

Just then " O. C. Stokes " came along with his crew and their little trench gun. I told him of my " target," and suggested that he should try a shot with his Stokes mortar. Glad of something definite to do, he willingly complied.

The Stokes gun was set down on the floor of the trench just behind my back, as I stood on the firestep to observe the shoot.

I gave the range. The gun was loaded. There was a faint pop, a slight hiss—then silence. Was the bomb going to burst in the gun and blow us all to bits ? I glanced round apprehensively. A perfectly calm Cockney voice from one of the crew reassured me :

" It's orl right, sir ! If it don't go off while yer counts five—*you'll know it's a dud !* "—*Capt. T. W. C. Curd (late 20th Northumberland Fusiliers), 72 Victoria Street, S.W.1.*

Help from Hindenburg

I WAS serving with the M.G.C. at Ecoust. Two men of the Middlesex Regiment had been busy for a week digging a sump hole in the exposed hollow in front of the village and had excavated to a depth of about eight feet. A bombardment which had continued all night became so severe about noon of the next day that orders were given for all to take what cover was available. It was noticed that the two men were still calmly at work in the hole, and I was sent to warn them to take shelter. They climbed out, and as we ran over the hundred yards which separated us from the trench a high explosive shell landed right in the hole we had just left, converting it into a huge crater. One of the men turned to me and said, " Lumme, mate, if old Hindenburg ain't been and gone and finished the blooming job for us ! "—*J. S. F., Barnet, Herts.*

Raised his Voice—And the Dust

IN the early part of 1917, while the Germans were falling back to the Hindenburg line on the Somme, trench warfare was replaced by advanced outposts for the time being. Rations were taken up to the company headquarters on mules.

" S'sh. For 'eaven's sake be quiet."

Another C.Q.M.S. and I were going up with mules one night and lost our way. We wandered on until a voice from a shell-hole challenged us. *We had passed the company headquarters and landed among the advanced outposts.*

The chap implored us to be quiet, and just as we turned back one of the mules chose to give the Germans a sample of his vocal abilities.

The outpost fellow told us what he thought of us. The transport chap leading the mule pulled and tugged, using kind, gentle words as drivers do.

And in the midst of it all my C.Q.M.S. friend walked up to the mule, holding his hands up, and whispered : " S-sh ! For 'eaven's sake be quiet."—*F. W. Piper (ex-Sherwood Foresters), 30 The Crescent, Watford, Herts.*

Mademoiselle from—Palestine

AFTER the fall of Gaza our battalion, on occupying a Jewish colony in the coastal sector which had just been evacuated by the Turks, received a great ovation from the overjoyed inhabitants.

One of our lads, born well within hearing of Bow Bells, was effusively

"Mademoiselle from Ah-my-Tears."

greeted by a Hebrew lady of uncertain age, who warmly embraced him and kissed him on each cheek.

Freeing himself, and gesticulating in the approved manner, he turned to us and said : " Strike me pink ! Mademoiselle from Ah-my-tears."— *Edward Powell*, 80 *Cavendish Road, Kentish Town, N.W.*

" Ally Toot Sweet "

AT the latter end of September 1914 the 5th Division was moving from the Aisne to La Bassée and a halt was made in the region of Crépy-en-Valois, where a large enemy shell was found (dud).

A Cockney private was posted to keep souvenir hunters from tampering with it. When he received his dinner he sat straddle-legged on the shell,

" Ally toot sweet. If this shell goes orf . . . "

admired by a few French children, whom he proceeded to address as follows: " Ally ! Toot sweet, or you'll get blown to 'ell if this blinkin' shell goes orf."—*E. P. Ferguson, " Brecon," Fellows Road, S. Farnborough, Hants.*

Luckier than the Prince

IN the autumn of 1916, while attending to the loading of ammunition at Minden Post, a driver suddenly exclaimed, " 'Struth, Quarter ; who's the boy officer with all the ribbons up ? "

Glancing up, I recognised the Prince of Wales, quite unattended, pushing a bicycle through the mud.

When I told the driver who the officer really was, the reply came

A*

quickly : " Blimey, I'm better off than he is ; they *have* given me a horse to ride."—*H. J. Adams (ex.-B.Q.M.S., R.F.A.), Highclare, Station Road, Hayes, Middlesex.*

A Jerry he *Couldn't* Kill

DURING a patrol in No Man's Land at Flesquières we were between a German patrol and their front line, but eventually we were able to get back. I went to our Lewis gun post and told them Jerry had a patrol out. I was told : " One German came dahn 'ere last night—full marchin' order." " Didn't you ask him in ? " I said. " No. Told him to get out of it. You can't put a Lewis gun on one man going on leave," was the reply.—*C. G. Welch, 109 Sayer Street, S.E.17.*

" Q " for Quinine

IN the autumn of 1917, on the Salonika front, we were very often short of bread, sugar, etc., the reason, we were told by the Quartermaster-Sergeant, being that the boats were continually sunk.

At this time the " quinine parade " was strictly enforced, because of malaria, which was very prevalent.

One day we were lined up for our daily dose, which was a very strong and unpleasant one, when one of our drivers, a bit of a wag, was heard to say to the M.O. : " Blimey ! the bread boat goes dahn, the beef boat goes dahn, the rum and sugar boat goes dahn, but the perishin' quinine boat always gets 'ere."—*R. Ore (100 Brigade, R.F.A.), 40 Lansdowne Road, Tottenham, N.17.*

Blinkin' Descendant of Nebuchadnezzar

WHILE stationed at Pozières in 1917 I was mate to our Cockney cook, who, according to Army standards, was something of an expert in the culinary art.

One day a brass hat from H.Q., who was visiting the unit, entered the mess to inquire about the food served to the troops.

" They 'as stew, roast, or boiled, wiv spuds and pudden to follow," said cook, bursting with pride.

" Do you give them any vegetables ? " asked the officer.

" No, sir, there ain't none issued in the rations."

" No vegetables ! What do you mean ?—there are tons growing about here waiting to be picked. Look at all those dandelions—they make splendid greens. See that some are put in the stew to-morrow." With which illuminating information he retired.

Followed a few moments' dead silence. Then the Cockney recovered from the shock.

" Lumme, mate, what did 'e say ? Dandelions ? 'E must be a blinkin' descendant of Nebuchadnezzar ! "—*R. J. Tiney (late Sapper, R.E. Signals, 10th Corps), 327 Green Lanes, Finsbury Park, N.*

Well-Cut Tailoring

BACK from a spell behind Ypres in 1915, a few of us decided to scrounge round for a hair-cut. We found a shop which we thought was a barber's, but it turned out to be a tailor's. We found out afterwards !

" My old girl will swear I bin in fer a stretch . . . "

Still, the old Frenchman made a good job of it—just as though someone had shaved our heads. My Cockney pal, when he discovered the truth, exclaimed : " Strike, if I go 'ome like this my old girl will swear I bin in fer a stretch."—*F. G. Webb (late Corpl., Middlesex Regiment),* 38 *Andover Road, Twickenham.*

Evacuating " Darby and Joan "

THINGS were going badly with the town of Albert, and all day the inhabitants had been streaming from the town. On horse, on foot, and in all manner of conveyances they hastened onwards. . . .

Towards evening, when the bombardment was at its height and the roads were being plastered with shells, an old man tottered into sight pulling a crazy four-wheeled cart in which, perched amidst a pile of household goods, sat a tiny, withered lady of considerable age. As the couple reached the point where I was standing, the old man's strength gave out and he collapsed between the shafts.

It seemed all up with them, as the guns were already registering on the only exit from the town when, thundering round a bend in the road, came a transport limber with driver and spare man. On seeing the plight of the old people, the driver pulled up, dismounted and, together with his partner, surveyed the situation.

" What are we going to do with Darby and Joan ? " asked the driver. " We can't get them and all their clobber in the limber and, if I know 'em, they won't be parted from their belongings."

" 'Ook 'em on the back," replied the spare man. Sure enough, the old man was lifted into the limber and the old lady's four-wheeler tied on the back.

Off they went at the gallop, the old lady's conveyance dragging like a canoe in the wake of the *Mauretania*. The heroic Cockney driver, forcing his team through the din and debris of the bombardment, was now oblivious to the wails of distress ; his mind was back on his duty ; he had given the old people a chance of living a little longer—that was all he could do : and so he turned a deaf ear to the squeals and lamentations that each fresh jolt and swerve wrung from the terrified antiquity he was towing.

Shells dropped all around them on their career through the town until it seemed that they must " go under." However, they appeared again and again, after each cloud cleared, and in the end I saw the little cavalcade out of the town and danger.—*N. E. Crawshaw (late 15th London Regt.), 4 Mapleton Road, Southfields, S.W.18.*

" Why ain't the Band Playing ? "

I SERVED with the 11th London Regiment in Palestine. One day our officer paid us a visit at dinner-time to find out if there were any complaints. While we were endeavouring to find the meat at the bottom of the spoilt water we heard a voice say : " Any complaints ? " One of the platoon, not seeing the officer, thought the remark was a joke, so he replied, " Yes, why ain't the band playing ? " On realising it was an official request he immediately corrected himself and said : " Sorry, sir, no complaints."

I rather think the officer enjoyed the remark.—*F. G. Palmer, 29 Dumbarton Road, Brixton, S.W.2.*

His Deduction

OUR battalion, fresh from home, all nicely groomed and with new kit, stepped out whistling " Tipperary." We were on the road to Loos. Presently towards us came a pathetic procession of wounded men struggling back, some using their rifles as crutches.

Our whistling had ceased ; some faces had paled. Not a word was spoken for quite a while, until my Cockney pal broke the silence, remarking, " Lumme, I reckon there's been a bit of a row somewhere."— *Charles Phillips (late Middlesex Regt.), 108 Grosvenor Road, Ilford.*

Peter in the Pool

WE had advanced beyond the German first line in the big push of '18. The rain was heavy, the mud was deep ; we had not quite dug in beyond " shallow," and rations had not come up—altogether a most dismal prospect.

Quite near to us was a small pool of water which we all attempted to avoid when passing to and fro. Suddenly there was a yell and much cursing—the Cockney of the company, complete with his equipment, had fallen into the pool.

After recovering dry ground he gazed at the pool in disgust and said, " Fancy a fing like that trying to drahn a bloke wiv a name like Peter."— *J. Carlton, Bayswater Court, St. Stephen's Court, W.2.*

Where " Movie " Shows Cost Soap

WE landed in North Russia in June 1918. We were piloted in on the *City of Marseilles* to a jetty. We did not know the name of the place. On the jetty we saw from the boat a British marine on sentry duty. We shouted down to him, " Where are we, mate ? " He answered " Murmansk."

We asked, " What sort of place," and he shouted, " Lumme, you've come to a blighted 'ole 'ere. They 'ave one picture palace and the price of admission is a bar of soap."—*M. C. Oliver (late Corporal R.A.F.), 99, Lealand Road, Stamford Hill, N.16.*

Sherlock Holmes in the Desert

IN the autumn of 1917, when training for the attack on Beersheba, in Palestine, we were encamped in bivouacs in the desert.

The chief meal of the day was served in the cool of the evening and more often than not consisted of bully beef stew.

One evening the Orderly Officer approached the dixie, looked into it, and seeing it half full of the usual concoction, remarked, " H'm, stew this evening."

At once there came a voice, that of a Cockney tailor, from the nearest bivouac—" My dear Watson ! "—*R. S. H. (late 16th County of London Q.W.R.), Purley, Surrey.*

The Army "Loops the Loop"

THE road from Jerusalem to Jericho was very bad, and if you went too close to the edge you were likely to go over the precipice; indeed, many lives were lost in this way.

One day a lorry toppled over and fell at least a hundred feet. When the rescuers got down to it, expecting to find a mangled corpse, they were

" I'll bet I'm the first bloke to loop the loop in a lorry."

surprised to hear a well-known Cockney voice from under the debris, exclaiming: "Blimey, I'll bet I'm the first bloke in the whole Army wot's looped the loop in a motor-lorry."—*Sidney H. Rothschild, York Buildings, Adelphi, W.C.2.*

Repartee on the Ridge

WHILE on the Vimy Ridge sector I was going one dark night across the valley towards the front line when I lost my way among the mud and shell-holes. Hearing voices, I shouted an inquiry as to the whereabouts of Gabriel Trench. Back came the reply: "Lummie, mate, I ain't the blinkin' harbourmaster!"—*T. Gillespie (late Mining Company, R.E.), London.*

A New Kind of " Missing "

A BATTALION of the 47th London Division was making its first journey to the front line at Givenchy.

As we were proceeding from Béthune by the La Bassée Canal we passed another crowd of the same Division who had just been relieved. We were naturally anxious to know what it was like " up there," and the following conversation took place in passing :

" What's it like, mate ? "

" All right."

" Had any casualties ? "

" Yes, mate, two wounded, and a bloke lost 'is 'at."—*F. G. Nawton, (ex-Major 15th Batt. M.G.C., 2 Kenton Park Road, Kenton, Middlesex).*

And it Started with a Hen Raid !

W HILE we were behind the line in March 1918 some chickens were stolen from the next village and traced to our billet by the feathers.

As the culprits could not be found our O.C. punished the whole company by stopping our leave for six months.

A few days later we " moved up " just as Jerry broke through further south. The orderly sergeant one night read out orders, which finished up with Sir Douglas Haig's famous dispatch ending with the words : " All leave is now stopped throughout the Army till further orders." Thereupon a tousled head emerged from a blanket on the floor with this remark : " Blimey, they mean to find out who pinched those blinking chickens."—*J. Slack, 157 Engadine Street, Southfields, S.W.18.*

" I'm a Water-Lily "

T HIS incident took place on the Neuve Chapelle front early in 1916. Our platoon was known as the " Divisional Drainers," for it was our job to keep the trenches as free from water as possible.

One day, while we were working in a very exposed drain about three feet deep, Jerry was unusually active with his whizzbangs, and we were repeatedly shelled off the job. During one of our periodical " dives " for cover, one of the boys (a native of Canning Town) happened to be " left at the post," and instead of gaining a dry shelter was forced to fling himself in the bottom of the drain, which had over two feet of weedy water in it.

Just as he reappeared, with weeds and things clinging to his head and shoulders, an officer came to see if we were all safe.

On seeing our weed-covered chum he stopped and said, " What's the matter, Johnson ? Got the wind up ? "

Johnson, quick as lightning, replied, " No, sir ; camouflage. I'm a water-lily."—*F. Falcuss (late 19th Batt. N.F.), 51, Croydon Grove, West Croydon.*

Not Knowin' the Language

A TEAM of mules in November 1916 was taking a double limber up to the line in pitch darkness on the Béthune–La Bassée road. A heavy strafe was on, and the road was heavily shelled at intervals from Beavry onwards.

On the limber was a newly-joined padre huddled up, on his way to join advanced battalion headquarters. A shell burst 60 yards ahead, and the mules reared ; some lay down, kicked over the traces, and the wheel pair managed to get their legs over the centre pole of the limber.

"Would you mind trekkin' off up the road ? "

There was chaos for a few minutes. Then the padre asked the wheel driver in a very small voice, " My man, can I do anything to assist you ? "

" Assist us," was the reply. " Yes, you can. Would you mind, sir, trekkin' off up the road, so as we can use language these blighters understand ? "—*L. C. Hoffenden (late 483rd Field Co. R.E.), " Waltonhurst," 16 Elmgate Gardens, Edgware.*

Churning in the Skies

A FTER returning from a night's " egg-laying " on Jerry's transport lines and dumps, my brother " intrepid airman " and I decided on tea and toast. To melt a tin of ration butter which was of the consistency of glue we placed it close to the still hot engine of the plane. Unknown to us, owing to the slant of the machine, the tin slipped backwards and spilled a goodly proportion of its melted contents over the propeller at the back. (Our planes were of the " pusher " type.)

Next day as we strolled into the hangar to look the bus over we found our Cockney mechanic, hands on hips, staring at the butter-splattered propeller.

" Sufferin' smoke, sir," he said to me, with a twinkle, " wherever was you flyin' lars' night — *through the milky way?*"— *Ralph Plummer (late 102 Squadron R.A.F. Night-Bombers), Granville House, Arundel Street, Strand.*

Larnin' the Mule

ON the Somme I saw a Cockney driver having trouble with an obstinate mule. At last he got down from his limber and, with a rather vicious tug at the near-side rein said, " That's your left," and, tugging the off rein, " that's your right—now p'raps you'll know ! "—*E. B. (late Gunner, R.G.A.), Holloway Road, N.7.*

" Now p'raps you'll know ! "

" Dr. Livingstone, I Presoom "

EARLY in 1915 one of our Q.M. Sergeants was sent to Cairo to collect a gang of native labourers for work in the brigade lines. Whilst at breakfast one morning we saw him return from the train at Ismailia, leading a long column of fellaheen (with their wives and children) all loaded with huge bundles, boxes, cooking pots, etc., on their heads.

The Q.M.S., who was wearing a big white " solar topi " of the mushroom type instead of his regulation military helmet, was greeted outside our hut by the R.S.M., and as they solemnly shook hands a Cockney voice behind me murmured : " Doctor Livingstone, I presoom ? " The picture was complete !—*Yeo Blake (1st County of London Yeomanry), Brighton.*

The Veteran Scored

ONE morning, while a famous general was travelling around the Divisional Headquarters, his eagle eye spotted an old war hero, a Londoner, whose fighting days were over, and who now belonged to the Labour Corps, busy on road repairs. The fact was also noticed that although within the gas danger-zone the old veteran had broken standing orders by not working with his gas mask in position.

Accordingly the Corps Commander stopped his car and, getting out, started off in his own familiar way as follows :

C. C. : Good morning, my man ; do you know who is speaking to you ?

O. V. : No, sir !

C. C. : I am your Corps Commander, Sir ——, etc.

O. V. : Yes, sir.

C. C. : I'm pleased to have this opportunity of talking to one of my men.

O. V. : Yes, sir.

C. C. : I see you are putting your back into your work.

O. V. : Yes, sir.

C. C. : I also notice that you have evidently left your gas mask behind.

O. V. : Yes, sir.

C. C. : Now supposing, my man, a heavy gas cloud was now coming down this road towards you. What would you do ?

O. V. (after a few moments' pause) : Nothing, sir.

C. C. : What ! Why not, my good man ?

O. V. : Because the wind is the wrong way, sir.

Exit C. C.—*T. J. Gough, Oxford House, 13 Dorset Square, N.W.1.*

Old Moore Was Right

ONE of my drivers, a Cockney, called one of his horses Old Moore——" 'cos 'e knows every blinkin' fing like *Old Moore's Almanac.*"

One evening, as we were going into the line, we were halted by a staff officer and warned of gas. Orders were given at once to wear gas helmets. (A nose-bag gas-mask had just been issued for horses.)

After a while I made my way to the rear of the column to see how things were. I was puffing and gasping for breath, when a cheery voice called out, " Stick it, sargint."

Wondering how any man could be so cheery in such circumstances, I lifted my gas helmet, and lo ! there sat my Cockney driver, with his horses' masks slung over his arm and his own on top of his head like a cap-comforter.

" Why aren't you wearing your gas helmet ? " I asked.

He leaned over the saddle and replied, in a confidential whisper, " Old Moore chucked his orf, so there ain't no blinkin' gas abaht—'*e* knows."

We finished the rest of that journey in comfort. Old Moore had prophesied correctly.—*S. Harvey (late R.F.A.), 28 Belmont Park Road, Leyton, E.10.*

He Wouldn't Insult the Mule

ONE day, while our Field Ambulance was on the Dorian front, Salonika, our new colonel and the regimental sergeant-major were visiting the transport lines. They came across a Cockney assiduously grooming a pair of mules—rogues, both of them.

"... because I didn't want to hurt his feelings."

Said the R.S.M.: " Well, Brown, what are the names of your mules ? "

Brown: " Well, that one is Ananias, because his looks are all lies. This one is Satan, but I nearly called him something else. It was a toss-up."

With a smile at the C.O., the sergeant-major remarked: " I would like to know what the other name was. Tell the colonel, what was it ? "

Brown: " Well, I was going to call him ' Sergeant-Major,' but I didn't want to hurt his feelings."—" *Commo* " (*ex-Sergeant, R.A.M.C.*), *London, N.1.*

" Don't Touch 'em, Sonny ! "

WE had just come back from Passchendaele, that land of two options
—you could walk on the duck boards and get blown off or you
could step off them yourself and get drowned in the shell-holes.

A draft from home had made us up to strength, and when Fritz treated
us to an air raid about eight miles behind the line I am afraid he was
almost ignored. Anyway, our Cockney sergeant was voicing the opinion
that it wasn't a bad war when up rushed one recruit holding the chin
strap of his tin hat and panting, " Aero—aero—aeroplanes." The
sergeant looked at him for a second and said, " All right, sonny, don't
touch 'em."

A flush came to the youngster's face, and he walked away—a soldier.—
*R. C. Ida, D.C.M. (late 2nd Royal Berks), 39 Hoylake Road, East Acton,
W.3.*

" Ze English—Zey are all Mad ! "

EARLY in 1915 an Anti-Aircraft Brigade landed at Dunkirk. Their
guns were mounted in armoured cars, the drivers for which were
largely recruited from London busmen.

By arrangement with the French staff it was decided that the pass-
word to enable the drivers to pass the French lines should be the French
word *aviation.*

The men were paraded and made to repeat this word, parrot fashion,
with orders to be careful to use it, as it was said that French sentries
had a nasty habit of shooting first and making any inquiries afterwards.

About a month later I asked my lorry driver how he got on with the
word. " Quite easy, sir," said he. " I leans aht over the dash and
yells aht ' 'ave a ration,' and the Frenchies all larfs and lets me by."

A bit worried about this I interviewed the French Staff Officer and
asked him if the men were giving the word satisfactorily.

" Oh," he said, " zose men of yours, zey are comique. Your man, he
says somezing about his dinner, and ze ozzers zey say ' Ullo, Charlie
Chaplin,' and ' Wotcher, froggy '—all sorts of pass-words."

I apologised profusely. " I will get fresh orders issued," I said, " to
ensure that the men say the correct word."

" No," replied the French officer, " it ees no use. We know your
men now. Ze English will never alter—*zey are all mad*."—*G. H. Littleton
(Lieut.-Col.), 10 Russell Square Mansions, Southampton Row, W.C.1.*

Mixed History

THE Scene : Qurnah, Mesopotamia.
Cockney Tommy—obviously an old Sunday school boy—fed up
with Arabs, Turks, boils, scorpions, flies, thirst, and dust : " Well, if
this is the Garden of Eden, no wonder the Twelve Apostles 'opped it ! "
—*G. T. C., Hendon, N.W.4.*

Got His Goat!

WE, a Field Company of the R.E.'s in France, were on the move to a new sector, and amongst our " properties " was a mobile " dairy " —a goat.

"Nanny" travelled on top of a trestle-wagon containing bridging gear, with a short rope attached to her collar to confine her activities. But a "pot-hole" in the narrow road supplied a lurch that dislodged her, with the result that she slid overboard, and the shortness of the rope prevented her from reaching the ground.

"Nanny, you'll hang next time!"

The driver of the wagon behind saw her predicament, and, dismounting, ran to her assistance, shouting for the column to halt. Then he took Nanny in his arms to relieve the weight on her neck, whilst others clambered aboard and released the rope.

Nanny was then put on her legs while her rescuer stood immediately in front, watching her recover.

This she speedily did, and, raising her head for a moment, apparently discerned the cause of her discomfiture peering at her. At any rate, lowering her head, she sprang and caught Bermondsey Bill amidships, sending him backwards into a slimy ditch at the side of the road.

As he lay there amidst the undergrowth he yelled, "Strike me pink, Nanny! You'll hang next time."—*E. Martin, 78 Chelverton Road, Putney, S.W.*15.

A Difficult Top Note

SOMEWHERE in Palestine the band of a famous London division had been called together for very much overdue practice. The overture "Poet and Peasant" called for a French horn solo ending on a difficult top note.

After the soloist had made many attempts to get this note the bandmaster lost his temper and gave the player a piece of his mind.

Looking at the battered instrument, which had been in France, the Balkans, and was now in the Wilderness, and was patched with sticking-plaster and soap, the soloist, who hailed from Mile End, replied : "Here, if you can do it better you have a go. I don't mind trying it on an *instrument*, but I'm darned if I can play it on a cullender."—*D. Beland, 17 Ridgdale Street, London, E.3.*

"... but I'm darned if I can play it on a cullender."

Home by Underground

A COLD, wet night in France. My company was making its way up a communication trench on the right of the Arras-Cambrin road. It was in some places waist deep in mud. I was in front next to my officer when the word was passed down that one of the men had fallen into the mud and could not be found. The officer sent me back to find out what had happened.

On reaching the spot I found that the man had fallen into the mouth of a very deep dug-out which had not been used for some time.

Peering into the blackness, I called out, "Where are you ? "

Back came the reply : "You get on wiv the blinkin' war. I've fahnd the Channel Tunnel and am going 'ome."

I may say it took us six hours to get him out—*H. F. B. (late 7th Batt. Middlesex Regt.), London, N.W.2.*

A Job for Samson

DURING Allenby's big push in Palestine the men were on a forced night march, and were tired out and fed up. An officer was trying to buck some of them up by talking of the British successes in France and also of the places of interest they would see farther up in Palestine.

He was telling them that they were now crossing the Plains of Hebron where Samson carried the gates of Gaza, when a deep Cockney voice rang out from the ranks, " What a pity that bloke ain't 'ere to carry this pack of mine ! "—*C. W. Bowers, 25 Little Roke Avenue, Kenley, Surrey.*

Jerry Wins a Bet

IN the Salient, 1916 : Alf, who owned a Crown and Anchor board of great antiquity, had it spread out on two petrol cans at the bottom of a shell-hole.

Around it four of us squatted and began to deposit thereon our dirty half and one franc notes, with occasional coins of lesser value. The constant whistle of passing fragments was punctuated by the voice of Alf calling upon the company to " 'ave a bit on the 'eart " or alternately " to 'ave a dig in the grave " when a spent bullet crashed on his tin hat and fell with a thud into the crown square. " 'Struth," gasped Alf, " old squarehead wants to back the sergeant-major." He gave a final shake to the cup and exposed the dice—one heart and two crowns. " Blimey," exclaimed Alf, " would yer blinkin' well believe it ? Jerry's backed a winner. 'Arf a mo," and picking up the spent bullet he threw it with all his might towards the German lines, exclaiming, " 'Ere's yer blinking bet back, Jerry, and 'ere's yer winnings." He cautiously fired two rounds.—*G. S. Raby (ex-2nd K.R.R.C.), Shoeburyness, Essex.*

Lucky he was Born British

MANY ex-soldiers must remember the famous Major Campbell, who (supported by the late Jimmy Driscoll), toured behind the lines in France giving realistic demonstrations of bayonet fighting.

I was a spectator on one occasion when the Major was demonstrating " defence with the naked hands." " Now," he shouted as Jimmy Driscoll (who acted the German) rushed upon him with rifle and bayonet pointed for a thrust, " I side-step " (grasping his rifle at butt and upper band simultaneously) ; " I twist it to the horizontal and fetch my knee up into the pit of his stomach, so ! And then, as his head comes down, I release my right hand, point my fore and third fingers, so ! and stab at his eyes."

" Lor ! " gasped a little Cockney platoon chum squatting beside me, " did yer see that lot ? Wot a nice kind of bloke he is ! Wot a blinkin' stroke of luck he was born on our side ! " —*S. J. Wilson (late 1/20th County London Regt.), 27 Cressingham Road, Lewisham.*

You Never Can Tell

SCENE : Turk trench, Somme, on a cold, soaking night in November, 1916. A working party, complete with rifles, picks, and spades, which continually became entangled in the cats' cradle of miscellaneous R.E. wire, is making terribly slow progress over irregular trench-boards hidden under mud and water. Brisk strafing ahead promising trouble.

Impatient officer (up on the parapet) : " For heaven's sake, you lads, get a move on ! You're not going to a funeral ! "

Cockney voice (from bottom of trench) " 'Ow the dooce does '*e* know ! "
—*W. Ridsdale, 41 Manor Road, Beckenham, Kent.*

The Window Gazer

IN the early part of 1915, when the box periscope was in great use in the trenches, we received a draft of young recruits. One lad, of a rather inquisitive nature, was always looking in the glass trying to find Jerry's whereabouts.

An old Cockney, passing up and down, had seen this lad peeping in the glass. At last he stopped and addressed the lad as follows :

" You've been a-looking in that bloomin' winder all the die, an' nah yer ain't bought nuffink."—*E. R. Gibson (late Middlesex Regt.), 42 Maldon Road, Edmonton, N.9.*

" I Don't Fink "

AFTER we landed in France our officer gave us a lecture and told us that our best pal in this world was our rifle. He warned us that on no account must we part with it. A couple of nights later Gunner Brown, a Cockney, was on guard. When the visiting officer approached him and said, " Your rifle is dirty, gunner," he replied, " I don't fink so sir, 'cos I cleaned it." " Give it to me," said the officer sternly, which Brown did. Then the officer said, " You fool, if I were an enemy in English uniform I could shoot you." To which Brown replied, " I don't fink you could, sir, 'cos I've got the blinkin' bolt in my pocket."—*E. W. Houser (late 41st Division, R.F.A.) 22 Hamlet Road, Southend.*

Why the Attack *Must* Fail

NOVEMBER 1918. The next day we were to move up in readiness for the great advance of the 3rd Army.

Some of us were trying to sleep in a cellar when the silence was broken by a small voice : " I'm sure this attack will go wrong, you chaps ! I feel it in my bones ! "

It can be imagined how this cheerful remark was received, but when the abuse had died down, the same voice was heard again : " Yes, I knows it. Some blighter will step orf wi' the wrong foot and we'll all 'ave to come back and start again ! "—" *D* " *Coy., M.G.C. (24th Batt.), Westcliff.*

The " Shovers "

DURING the retreat of 1918 I was standing with my company on the side of the road by Outersteene Farm, outside Bailleul, when three very small and youthful German Tommies with helmets four sizes too

" Luv us, 'Arry ; look what's shovin' our Army abaht ! "

large passed on their way down the line as prisoners for interrogation. As they reached us I heard one of my men say to another : " Luv us, 'Arry, look what's shovin' our Army abaht ! "—*L. H. B., Beckenham.*

Rehearsal—Without the Villain

A SMALL party with a subaltern were withdrawn from the line to rehearse a raid on the German line. A replica of the German trenches had been made from aircraft photographs, and these, with our own trench and intervening wire, were faithfully reproduced, even to shell-holes.

The rehearsal went off wonderfully. The wire was cut, the German trenches were entered, and dummy bombs thrown down the dugouts.

Back we came to our own trenches. "Everything was done excellently, men," said the subaltern, "but I should like to be sure that every difficulty has been allowed for.   Can any man think of any point which we have overlooked ? "

" Yus," came the terse reply—" Jerry."—*Edward Nolan* (*15th London Regt.*), 41 *Dalmeny Avenue, S.W.*16.

Poetry Before the Push

DURING February and March 1918 the 1/13th Battalion London Regiment (the Kensingtons), who were at Vimy Ridge, had been standing-to in the mornings for much longer than the regulation hour because of the coming big German attack.   One company commander— a very cheery officer—was tired of the general "wind up" and determined to pull the legs of the officers at Battalion H.Q.   It was his duty to send in situation reports several times a day.   To vary things he wrote a situation report in verse, sent it over the wire to B.H.Q., where, of course, it was taken down in prose and read with complete consternation by the C.O. and adjutant !

It showed the gay spirit which meant so much in the front line at a time when everyone's nerves were on edge.   It was written less than two days before the German offensive of March 21.   Here are the verses :

(C Company Situation Report 19/3/18)

There is nothing I can tell you
  That you really do not know—
Except that we are on the Ridge
  And Fritz is down below.

I'm tired of " situations "
  And of " wind " entirely " vane."
The gas-guard yawns and tells me
  " It's blowing up for rain."

He's a human little fellow
  With a thoughtful point of view,
And his report (uncensored)
  I pass, please, on to you.

" When's old Fritzie coming over ?
  Does the General really know ?
The Colonel seems to think so,
  The Captain tells us ' No.'

" When's someone going to tell us
  We can ' Stand-to ' as before ?
An hour at dawn and one at dusk,
  Lor' blimey, who wants more ? "

The word " vane " in the second verse refers, of course, to the weather-vane used in the trenches to indicate whether the wind was favourable or not for a gas attack.—*Frederick Heath* (*Major*), 1/13th *Batt. London Regt.* (*Kensingtons*).

'Erb's Consolation Prize

A NARROW communication trench leading up to the front line ; rain, mud, shells, and everything else to make life hideous.

Enter the ration party, each man carrying something bulky besides his rifle and kit.

One of the party, a Londoner known as 'Erb, is struggling with a huge mail-bag, bumping and slipping and sliding, moaning and swearing,

" Never mind, 'Erb, perhaps there's a postcard in it for you ! "

when a voice from under a sack of bread pipes : " Never mind, 'Erb ; perhaps there's a postcard in it for you ! "—*L. G. Austin* (24*th London Regiment*), 8 *Almeida Street, Upper Street, Islington, N.1.*

Rum for Sore Feet

W HILST doing duty as acting Q.M.S. I was awakened one night by a loud banging on the door of the shack which was used as the stores. Without getting up I asked the reason for the noise, and was told that a pair of boots I had issued that day were odd—one was smaller than the other. The wearer was on stable piquet, and could hardly walk.

I told him he would have to put up with it till the morning—I wasn't up all night changing boots, and no doubt I should have a few words to say when I did see him !

"Orl right, Quarter," came the reply, "I'm sorry I woke yer—but could yer give us a tot of rum to stop the pain ? "—*P. K. (late 183rd Batt. 41st Div. R.F.A.), Kilburn, N.W.6.*

Two Guineas' Worth

IN France during November 1914 I received an abrupt reminder that soldiering with the Honourable Artillery Company entails an annual subscription.

The battalion had marched out during the night to a small village named Croix Barbée to carry out some operation, and returned at day-break to its "lodging" near La Couture, another village some four or five miles away.

Being a signaller, I had the doubtful privilege of owning a bicycle, which had to be pushed or carried every inch of the way. On the march back the mud was so bad that it was impossible for me to keep up with the battalion, owing to the necessity every quarter of a mile or so of cleaning out the mudguards.

I was plodding along all by myself in the early hours of daylight, very tired of the bike and everything else, and I approached an old soldier of the Middlesex Regiment sitting by the roadside recovering slowly from the strain of the fatiguing night march.

He looked at me and, with a twinkle in his eye, said, "Well, mate, 'ad yer two guineas wurf yet ? "—*J. H. May, Ravenswood, Ashford, Middlesex.*

The Four-footed Spy

WHILST we were at Arras a horse was found entangled in some barbed wire, having presumably strayed from the German lines. He was captured by a rifleman and brought back to the horse lines to be used by the transport driver.

A Cockney groom was detailed to look after him. The two never seemed to agree, for the groom was always being bitten or kicked by "Jerry."

One morning the picket discovered that "Jerry" was missing, and concluded that he must have broken away during the night. The matter was reported to the sergeant, who went and routed out the groom. "What about it ? Ain't you goin' to look for 'im ? " said the sergeant.

"Not me, sarge! I always said the blighter was a blinkin' spy ! " replied the groom.—*J. Musgrave (late 175th Infantry Brigade), 52 Cedar Grove, South Ealing, W.5.*

Not Every Dog has his Night

OUR battalion arrived in a French village late on the night of September 25, 1915, after marching all day in pouring rain. To add to our troubles no billets were available (the place was teeming with reserve troops for the attack at Loos).

We were told to find some sort of shelter from the rain and get a good night's rest, as we were to move up to the attack on the morrow.

" . . . A very fed-up dog."

My chum, a Londoner, and I scouted round. I found room for one in an already overcrowded stable ; my chum continued the search. He returned in a few minutes to tell me he had found a spot. I wished him good night and went to sleep.

In the morning, when I came out of the stable, I saw the long legs of a Guardsman (who proved to be my chum) protruding from a dog kennel. Beside them sat a very fed-up dog !—*F. Martin (late 1st Batt. Scots Guards), 91 Mostyn Road, Brixton, S.W.*

The Brigadier's Glass Eye

A BRIGADIER of the 54th Infantry Brigade (18th Division), who had a glass-eye, and his Cockney runner, were on their way up the line when they observed a dead German officer who had a very prominent gold tooth.

The next day, passing by the same spot, the Brigadier noticed that the gold tooth was missing.

" I see that his gold tooth has gone, Johnson," he said.

" Yessir."

" I suppose someone will take my glass eye, if I am knocked out."

" Yessir. I've put meself dahn fer that, fer a souvenir ! "—W. T. Pearce, " Southernhay," Bethune Avenue, Friern Barnet, N.11.

The Chaplain-General's Story

I N June 1917 I shared a G.H.Q. car with the Chaplain-General to the Forces, Bishop Gwynne, who was on his way from St. Omer to Amiens, whilst I was on my way to the Third Army School at Auxi-le-Château.

During the journey our conversation turned to chaplains, and the bishop asked me whether I thought the chaplains then coming to France were of the right type, especially from the point of view of the regimental officers and men. My reply was that the chaplains as a whole differed very little from any other body of men in France : they were either men of the world and very human, and so got on splendidly with the troops, or else they were neither the one nor the other, cut very little ice, and found their task a very difficult one.

The Bishop then told me the following story, which he described as perfectly true :

" A chaplain attached to a London regiment made a practice of always living in the front line whenever the battalion went in to the trenches rather than remaining with Battalion Headquarters some way back, and he had his own dug-out over which appeared the words ' The Vicarage.'

" One day a young Cockney in the line for the first time was walking along the trench with an older soldier, and turning a corner suddenly came on ' The Vicarage.'

" ' Gorblimey, Bill ! ' he said, ' who'd 'ave fought of seein' the b—— vicarage in the front line ? '

" Immediately the cheery face of the padre popped out from behind the blanket covering the entrance and a voice in reply said : ' Yes ! And who'd have thought of seeing the b—— vicar too ? ' "

" That's the kind of chaplain," said the Bishop, " I'm trying to get them to send out to France."—(Brig.-Gen.) R. J. Kentish, C.M.G., D.S.O., Shalford Park, Guildford.

A Thirst Worth Saving

DURING the summer of 1917 our battalion—the 1/5th Buffs—formed part of General Thompson's flying column operating between the Tigris and the Shatt Al-'Adhaim.

One morning we discovered that the native camel drivers had deserted to the enemy's lines, taking with them the camels that were carrying our water.

No man had more than a small cup of water in his bottle yet we waited orders until dawn the next day, when a 'plane dropped a message for us to return to the Tigris.

I shall not dwell on that 20-mile march back to the river over the burning sand—I cannot remember the last few miles of it myself. None of us could speak. Our lips and tongues were bursting.

When we reached the Tigris we drank and drank again—then lay exhausted.

The first man I heard speak was " Busty " Johnson, who, with great effort hoarsely muttered : " Lumme, if I can only keep this blinkin' first till I goes on furlough ! "—*J. W. Harvey (late 1/5th Buffs, M.E.F.)*, 25 *Queen's Avenue, Greenford Park, Middlesex.*

Points of View

ON a wet and cold winter's night in the hills south of Nablus (Palestine) a sentry heard sounds as of slipping feet and strange guttural noises from the direction of the front line. He waited with his rifle at the port and then challenged : " Halt ! who goes there ? "

A thin, dismal voice came from the darkness. " A pore miserable blighter with five ruddy camels."

" Pass, miserable blighter, all's well," replied the sentry.

Into the sentry's view came a rain-soaked disconsolate-looking Tommy " towing " five huge ration camels.

" All's well, is it ? Coo ! Not 'arf ! " said he.—*W. E. Bickmore (late* " *C* " 303 *Brigade, R.F.A., 60th Div.),* 121 *Gouville Road, Thornton Heath, Surrey.*

Not the British Museum

THE Labyrinth Sector.

Three of us—signallers—having just come off duty in the front line, were preparing to put in a few hours' sleep, when a voice came floating down the dug-out steps : " Is Corporal Stone down there ? "

Chorus : " No ! "

Ten minutes later came the same voice : " Is Sergeant Fossell down there ? "

" Go away," replied our Cockney ; " this ain't the blinkin' British Museum ! "—*G. J. Morrison (late 14th London Regt.),* " *Alness,*" *Colborne Way, Worcester Park, Surrey.*

Jerry Would Not Smile

I MET him coming from the front line, one of "London's Own." He was taking back the most miserable and sullen-looking prisoner I have ever seen.

"Got a light, Jock?" he asked me. I obliged. "'Ave a Ruby Queen, matey?" I accepted.

"... and if that don't make a bloke laugh, well, it's 'opeless."

"Cheerful-looking customer you've got there, Fusie," I ventured, pointing to his prisoner.

He looked up in disgust. "Cheerful? Lummie, he gives me the creeps. I've orfered 'im a fag, and played 'Katie' and 'When this luvly war is over' on me old mouf orgin for him, but not a bloomin' smile. An' I've shown him me souvenirs and a photograph of me old woman, and, blimey, if that don't make a bloke laugh, well, it's 'opeless!"

And then, with a cheery " Mercy bokoo, matey," and a " Come on, 'Appy," to his charge, he pushed on.—*Charles Sumner (late London Scottish), Butler's Cottage, Sutton Lane, Heston, Middlesex.*

" Birdie " Had to Smile

WHILE I was serving with the Australians at Gallipoli in 1915 I was detailed to take charge of a fatigue party to carry water from the beach to the front line, a distance of about a mile.

Our way lay over rather dangerous and extremely hilly country. The weather was very hot. Each man in the party had to carry four petrol tins of water.

While trudging along a narrow communication trench we were confronted by General Birdwood and his A.D.C. As was the general's cheery way, he stopped, and to the man in front (one " Stumpy " Stewart, a Cockney who had been in Australia for some time) he remarked, " Well, my man, how do you like this place ? "

" Stumpy " shot a quick glance at the general and then blurted out, " Well, sir, 't'aint the sort of plice you'd bring your Jane to, is it ? "

I can see " Birdie's " smile now.—*C. Barrett (Lieut., Aust. Flying Corps, then 6th Aust. Light Horse), Charing Cross, W.C.*

Their Very Own Secret

WE were on a forced march to a sector on Vimy Ridge. It was a wicked night—rain and thick fog—and during a halt several of our men got lost. I was ordered to round them up, but I also got hopelessly lost.

I had been wandering about for some time when I came across one of our men—a young fellow from the Borough. We had both lost direction and could do nothing but wait.

At last dawn broke and the fog lifted. We had not the slightest idea where we were, so I told my friend to reconnoitre a hill on the right and report to me if he saw anyone moving, while I did the same on the left.

After a while I heard a cautious shout, and my companion came running towards me, breathless with excitement, and in great delight gasped, " Sergeant, sergeant ! Germans ! Germans ! Fousands of 'em —and there's nobody but you and me knows anyfing abaht it ! "— *G. Lidsell (late Devon Regt.), Brixton, S.W.9.*

Window Cleaners Coming !

WE were passing through Ypres, in 1915, in a Wolseley Signals tender when we came upon a battalion of the Middlesex on their way out to rest, very tired and very dirty.

Our cable cart ladders, strapped to the sides of the lorry, caught the eyes of one wag. " Blimey, boys," he cried, " we're orl right nah ; 'ere comes the blinkin' winder-cleaners."—*" Sigs.," Haslemere, Surrey.*

5

First Blow

IT was outside Albert, during the Somme attack, that I met a lone Army Service Corps wagon, laden with supplies. One of the horses was jibbing, and the driver, a diminutive Cockney, was at its head,

" An' besides, he kicked me first."

urging it forward. As I approached I saw him deliberately kick the horse in the flank.

I went up to the man and, taking out notebook and pencil, asked him for his name, number, and unit, at the same time remonstrating with him severely.

" I wasn't doin' 'im no 'arm," pleaded the man ; " I've only got my gum-boots on, and, besides, 'e kicked me first."

I tore up my entry, mounted my motor-cycle, and left an injured-looking driver rubbing a sore shin.—*R. D. Blackman* (*Capt., R.A.F.*), 118 *Abbey Road, St. John's Wood, N.W.6.*

M.M. (Mounted Marine)

AFTER riding for several hours one wet, windy, and miserable night, with everyone soaked to the skin and fed up generally, we were halted in a field which, owing to the heavy rain, was more like a lake.

On receiving the order to dismount and loosen girths, one of our number remained mounted and was busy flashing a small torch on the water when the sergeant, not too gently, inquired, " Why the dickens are

you still mounted, and what the deuce are you looking for anyway ? "
To which a Cockney voice replied, " Blimey, sergeant, where's the
landing stage ? "—" *Jimmy* " (*late Essex Yeomanry*).

His German 'Arp

HAVING been relieved, after our advance at Loos in 1915, we were
making our way back at night.

We had to pass through the German barbed wire, which had tins tied
to it so that it rattled if anyone tried to pass it.

Our sergeant got entangled in it and caused a lot of noise, whereupon

" **When it comes to the German 'arp you're a washaht.** "

a Cockney said : " You're orl right on the old banjo, sergeant, but when
it comes to the German 'arp you're a blinkin' washaht."—*W. Barnes*,
M.M. (*late 1st Bn. K.R.R.C.*), 63 *Streatfeild Avenue, East Ham.*

Jack went a-Riding

EARLY in 1916 we were on outpost duty at a place called **Ayun Musa**, about four miles east of Suez.

One day a British monitor arrived in the Gulf of Suez, and we were invited to spend an hour on board as the sailors' guests. The next day the sailors came ashore and were our guests.

" Don't ask me—ask the blinkin' 'oss "

After seeing the canteen most of them were anxious for a ride on a horse. So we saddled a few horses and helped our guests to mount. Every horse chose a different direction in the desert.

One of the sailors was a Cockney. He picked a fairly fresh mount, which soon " got away " with him. He lost his reins and hung round the animal's neck for dear life as it went at full gallop right through the Camp Commandant's quarters.

Hearing the commotion, the Commandant put his head out of his bivouac and shouted, " What the dickens do you mean galloping through here ? "

Back came the retort, " Don't ask me—ask the blinkin' 'oss."—*H. F. Montgomery (late H.A.C.), 33 Cavenham Gardens, Ilford.*

Bitter Memories

DURING an attack near Beer-Sheba, Palestine, our regiment had been without water for over twenty-four hours. We were suffering very badly, as the heat was intense. Most of us had swollen tongues and lips and were hardly able to speak, but the company humorist, a Cockney, was able to mutter, " Don't it make you mad to fink of the times you left the barf tap running ? "—*H. Owen (late Queen's Royal West Surrey Regt.), 18 Edgwarebury Gardens, Edgware, Middlesex.*

Tommy " Surrounded " Them

IT was in July 1916. The Somme Battle had just begun. The troops in front of us had gone over the top and were pushing forward. We were in support and had just taken over the old front line.

Just on our right was a road leading up and through the German lines. Looking up this road we saw a small squad strolling towards us. It was composed of four Germans under the care of a London Tommy who was strolling along, with his rifle under his arm, like a gamekeeper. It made quite a nice picture.

When they reached us one of our young officers shouted out : " Are you looking for the hounds ? "

Then the Cockney started : " Blimey, I don't know abaht looking for 'ounds. I got four of 'em 'ere—and now I got 'em I don't know where to dump 'em."

The officer said : " Where did you find them ? "

" I surrounded 'em, sir," was the reply.

Our officer said : " You had better leave them here for the time being."

" Right-o, sir," replied the Cockney. " You hang on to 'em until I come back. I'm going up the road to get some more. There's fahsends of 'em up there."—*R. G. Williams, 30 Dean Cottages, Hanworth Road, Hampton, Middlesex.*

Shell-holes and Southend

MY pal (a Battersea boy) and I were two of a draft in 1916 transferred from the K.R.R.s to the R.I.R.s. On the first night in the trenches we were detailed for listening post. My pal said : " That's good. I'll be able to tell father what No Man's Land is like, as he asked me."

After we had spent what was to me a nerve-wracking experience in the mud of a shell-hole, I asked him what he was going to tell his father. He said : " It's like Southend at low tide on the fifth of November."—*F. Twohey (late 14th Batt. R.I.R.), 31 Winchester Road, Edmonton.*

" Make Me a Good 'Orse "

HAVING come out of action, we lay behind the line waiting for reinforcements of men and horses. The horses arrived, and I went out to see what they were like.

I was surprised to see a Cockney, who was a good groom, having trouble in grooming one of the new horses. Every time he put the brush between its forelegs the animal went down on its knees.

" Gawd bless farver an' make me a good 'orse."

At last in desperation the Cockney stepped back, and gazing at the horse still on its knees, said : " Go on, yer long-faced blighter. ' Gawd bless muvver, Gawd bless farver, an' make me a good 'orse.' "—*Charles Gibbons (late 3rd Cavalry Brigade), 131 Grove Street, Deptford, S.E.8.*

The Lost Gumboot

AN N.C.O. in the Engineers, I was guiding a party of about seventy Royal Fusiliers (City of London Regt.) through a trench system between Cambrin, near Loos, and the front line. About half-way the trenches were in many places knee-deep in mud. It was about 2 a.m.

and shelling made things far from pleasant. Then word came up that we had lost touch with the tail-end of the party, and a halt was called, most of us standing in mud two feet deep.

The officer in charge sent a message back asking why the tail-end had failed to keep up. The reply came back in due course : " Man lost his gumboot in the mud." The officer, becoming annoyed at the delay, sent back the message : " Who's the fool who lost his gumboot ? "

I heard the message receding into the distance with the words " fool " " gumboot " preceded by increasingly lurid adjectives. In about three or four minutes I heard the answer being passed up, getting louder and louder : " Charlie Chaplin," " CHARLIE CHAPLIN," " CHARLIE CHAP-LIN." Even our sorely-tried officer had to laugh.—*P. Higson, Lancashire.*

" Compree ' Sloshy ' ? "

DURING one of the Passchendaele advances in 1917 my battery was situated astride a board roadway leading over the ridge. After this particular show was over I happened to be in the telephone dug-out when prisoners started coming back.

One weary little lance-jack in a London regiment arrived in charge of an enormous, spectacled, solemn-looking Fritz. As he reached the battery position he paused to rest and look at the guns.

Leaning against the side of the dug-out he produced a cigarette end and, lighting it, proceeded to make conversation with his charge which, being out of sight, I was privileged to overhear.

" Ain't 'arf blinkin' sloshy 'ere, ain't it, Fritz ? Compree sloshy ? " No reply.

He tried again. " Got a cushy job these 'ere artillery blokes, ain't they ? Compree cushy ? " Still no answer.

He made a third attempt. " S'pose you're abart fed up with this blinkin' guerre. Compree guerre ? " Again the stony, uncomprehending silence ; and then :

" Garn, yer don't know nuffink, yer don't, yer ignorant blighter. Say another blinkin' word and I'll knock yer blinkin' block orf."—*A. E. Joyce (late R.F.A.), Swallowcroft, Broxbourne Road, Orpington, Kent.*

Looking-Glass Luck

DURING the second battle of Ypres, in May 1915, I was attached to the 1st Cavalry Brigade, and after a terrific strafing from Fritz there was a brief lull, which gave us a chance for a " wash and brush up."

While we were indulging in the luxury of a shave, a Cockney trooper dropped his bit of looking-glass.

Seeing that it was broken I casually remarked, " Bad luck for seven years." And the reply I got was, " If I live seven years to 'ave bad luck it'll be blinking good luck."—*J. Tucker, 46 Langton Road, Brixton, S.W.*

Mine that was His

JUST before our big push in August 1918 we were resting in " Tank Wood." The place was dotted with shell holes, one of which was filled with rather clean water, evidently from a nearby spring. A board at the edge of this hole bore the word " MINE," so we gave it a wide berth.

Imagine our surprise when later we saw " Tich," a lad from the Old Kent Road, bathing in the water. One of our men yelled, " Hi, Tich, carn't yer read ? "

" Yus," replied " Tich," " don't yer fink a bloke can read 'is own writing ? "—*Walter F. Brooks (late R.W. Kent Regt.)*, 141 *Cavendish Road, Highams Park, E.4.*

" Geography " Hour

JUST before going over the top a private, wishing to appear as cheerful as possible, turned to his platoon sergeant and said : " I suppose we will be making history in a few minutes, sergeant ? "

" No," replied the sergeant : " our first objective is about 250 yards straight to the front. What you have to do is to get from here to there as quickly as your legs will carry you. We are making geography this morning, my lad ! "—" *Arras," London, S.W.1.*

To the General, About the Colonel

THE colonel of the regiment, gifted with the resonant voice of a daredevil leader, was highly esteemed for his rigid sense of duty, especially in the presence of the enemy.

The Germans had been troubling us a lot with gas, and this kept everyone on the *qui vive*.

Accompanied by the colonel, the divisional commander was making his usual inspection of the front line intent on the alertness of sentries.

In one fire-bay the colonel stopped to give instructions regarding a ventilating machine which had been used to keep the trench clear of gas after each attack.

Meanwhile the general moved on towards the other end of the firebay, where the sentry, fresh out from the reserve battalion recruited in Bermondsey, stood with his eyes glued to the periscope.

A natural impulse of the general as he noticed the weather-vane on the parapet was to test the sentry's intelligence on " gas attack by the enemy," so as he approached the soldier he addressed him in a genial and confiding manner : " Well, my lad, and how's the wind blowing this morning ? "

Welcoming a little respite, as he thought, from periscope strain, by way of a short " chin-wag " with one or other of his pals, the unsuspecting sentry rubbed his hands gleefully together as he turned round with the reply: " 'Taint 'arf so dusty arter all." Then, suddenly through the corner of his eye he caught sight of his colonel at the other end of the fire-bay. His face instantly changed its cheerful aspect as he breathlessly whispered to his inquirer, " Lumme, the ole man ! 'Ere, mate, buzz orf quick—a-a-an' don't let 'im cop yer a-talkin' to the sentry on dooty, or Jerry's barrage will be a wash-aht when the Big Noise starts 'is fireworks ! "—*William St. John Spencer (late East Surrey Regiment),* " *Roydsmoor," Arneson Road, East Molesey, Surrey.*

Bow Bells—1917 Style

WE were going up the line at Bullecourt in April 1917. I have rather bad eyesight and my glasses had been smashed. Being the last of the file I lost touch with the others and had no idea where I was. However, I stumbled on, and eventually reached the front line.

" Take those bells orf."

Upon the ground were some empty petrol cans tied up ready to be taken down to be filled with water. I tripped up amongst these and created an awful din, whereupon an angry voice came from out the gloom. —" I don't know 'oo or wot the dickens you are, but for 'eaven's sake take those bells orf ! "—*W. G. Root (late 12th London Regt.), 24 Harrington Square, N.W.1.*

5*

" The Awfentic Gramerphone ! "

THIS happened on that wicked March 21, 1918.
During a lull in the scrapping, a lone German wandered too near, and we collared him. He was handed over to Alf, our Cockney cookie.

Things got blacker for us. We could see Germans strung out in front of us and on both flanks—Germans and machine guns everywhere.

" Well, boys," said our major, " looks as if it's all up with us, doesn't it ? "

" There's this abaht it, sir," said Alf, pointing to his prisoner ; " when it comes to chuckin' our 'ands in, we've got the awfentic gramerphone to yell ' Kamerad ! '—ain't we ? "—*C. Vanon*, 33 *Frederick Street, W.C.1.*

The Muffin Man

TWO companies of a London regiment were relieving each other on a quiet part of the line, late in the evening of a dismal sort of day. The members of the ingoing company were carrying sheets of corrugated iron on their heads for the purpose of strengthening their position.

A member of the outgoing company, observing a pal of his with one of these sheets on his head, bawled out : " 'Ullo, 'Arry, what'cher doing of ? " to which came the laconic reply : " Selling muffins, but I've lost me blinkin' bell."—*H. O. Harries*, 85 *Seymour Road, Harringay, N.8.*

The Holiday Resort

EARLY in October 1915 a half company of the 3rd Middlesex Regiment occupied a front-line sector at Givenchy, known as the " Duck's Bill," which ran into the German line.

In spite of our proximity to the enemy our chief annoyance was occasional sniping, machine gunning, rifle grenades, and liquid fire, for the area had been given over mainly to mining and counter-mining.

It was expected that the " Duck's Bill " would " go up " at any moment, so it was decided to leave only one officer in charge, with instructions to keep every available man engaged either in furiously tunnelling towards the enemy to counter their efforts, or in repairing our breastworks, which had been seriously damaged in a German attack.

My men worked like Trojans on a most tiring, muddy, and gruesome task.

At last we were relieved by the Leicestershire Regiment, and one of my men, on being asked by his Leicester relief what the place was like, replied : " Well, 'ow d'yer spend yer 'olidies, in the country or at the seaside ? 'Cos yer gits both 'ere as yer pleases : rabbit 'unting (pointing to the tunnelling process) and sand castle building (indicating the breast-work repairs), wiv fireworks in the evening."

The Leicesters, alas ! " went up " that evening.—*S. H. Flood (late Middlesex Regiment and M.G.C.), " Prestonville," Maidstone Road, Chatham, Kent.*

The " Tich " Touch

WE had survived the landing operations at Murmansk, in North Russia, and each company had received a number of sets of skis, which are very awkward things to manage until you get used to them.

On one occasion when we were practising, a " son of London," after repeated tumbles, remarked to his pals, who were also getting some

" Trying to cut aht Little Tich in the long-boot dance."

" ups and downs " : " Fancy seein' me dahn Poplar way wiv these fings on ; my little old bunch of trouble would say, ' What's 'e trying ter do nah ? Cut aht Little Tich in the long-boot dance ? ' "—*C. H. Mitchell (late Staff-Sergt. A.S.C.), 7 Kingsholm Gardens, Eltham, S.E.9.*

Smart Men All

ONE of the usual orders had come through to my battalion of the Middlesex Regiment for a number of men to be detailed for extra regimental duties which would be likely to take them away from the battalion for a considerable time. The company I commanded had to provide twenty men.

It was a golden opportunity to make a selection of those men whose physical infirmities were more evident than the stoutness of their hearts. Together with my company sergeant-major I compiled a list of those who could best be spared from the trenches, and the following day they were paraded for inspection before moving off.

As I approached, one of the men who had been summing up his comrades and evidently realised the reason for their selection, remarked in a very audible Cockney whisper, " What I says is, if you was to search the 'ole of Norvern France you wouldn't find a smarter body o' men ! "— " Nobby " (late Captain, Middlesex Regiment), Potters Bar, Middlesex.

" You'd Pay a Tanner at the Zoo ! "

DURING the floods in Palestine in 1917 I had to be sent down the line with an attack of malaria. Owing to the roads being deep in water, I was strapped in an iron chair pannier on the back of a camel. My sick companion, who balanced me on the other side of the camel, was a member of the London Regiment affectionately known as the Hackney Gurkhas.

The Johnnie patiently trudged through the water leading the camel, and kept up the cry of " Ish ! Ish ! " as it almost slipped down at every step.

I was feeling pretty bad with the swaying, and said to my companion, " Isn't this the limit ? "

" Shurrup, mate ! " he replied. " Yer don't know when yer well orf. You'd 'ave to pay a tanner for this at the Zoo ! "—Frederick T. Fitch (late 1/5th Batt. Norfolk Regt.), The Gordon Boys' Home, West End, Woking, Surrey.

Smoking Without Cigarettes

MOST ex-soldiers will remember the dreary monotony of " going through the motions " of every movement in rifle exercises.

We had just evacuated our position on the night of December 4–5, 1917, at Cambrai, after the German counter-attack, and, after withstanding several days' severe battering both by the enemy and the elements, were staggering along, tired and frozen and hungry, and generally fed up.

When we were deemed to be sufficiently far from the danger zone the order was given to allow the men to smoke. As practically everyone in the battalion had been without cigarettes or tobacco for some days the permission seemed to be wasted. But I passed the word down, " ' C ' Company, the men may smoke," to be immediately taken up by a North Londoner : " Yus, and if you ain't got no fags you can go through the motions."—H. H. Morris, M.C. (late Lieut., 16th Middlesex Regt.), 10 Herbert Street, Malden Road, N.W.5.

An Expensive Light

WINTER 1915, at Wieltje, on the St. Jean Road. We were on listening post in a shell-hole in No Man's Land, and the night was black.

Without any warning, my Cockney pal Nobby threw a bomb towards the German trench, and immediately Fritz sent up dozens of Verey lights. I turned anxiously to Nobby and asked, " What is it ? Did you spot anything ? " and was astonished when he replied, " I wanted ter know the time, and I couldn't see me blinkin' watch in the dark."—*E. W. Fellows, M.M. (late 6th Battn. D.C.L.I.), 33 Dunlace Road, Clapton, E.5.*

Modern Conveniences

A TOMMY plugging it along the Arras-Doullens road in the pouring rain. " Ole Bill," the omnibus, laden with Cockneys going towards the line, overtakes him.

TOMMY : " Sitting room inside, mate ? "

COCKNEY ON BUS : " No, but there's a barf-room upstairs ! "— *George T. Coles (ex-Lieut., R.A.F.), 17 Glebe Crescent, Hendon, N.W.4.*

" There's a barf-room upstairs ! "

The Trench Fleet

A CERTAIN section of the line, just in front of Levantie, being a comparatively peaceful and quiet spot, was held by a series of posts at intervals of anything up to three hundred yards, which made the task of bringing up rations an unhappy one, especially as the trenches in this sector always contained about four feet of water.

One November night a miserable ration party was wading through the thin slimy mud. The sentry at the top of the communication trench, hearing the grousing, splashing, and clanking of tins, and knowing full well who was approaching, issued the usual challenge, as per Army Orders : " 'Alt ! 'Oo goes there ? "

Out of the darkness came the reply, in a weary voice : " Admiral Jellicoe an' 'is blinkin' fleet."—*W. L. de Groot (late Lieut., 5th West Yorks Regt.), 17 Wentworth Road, Golders Green, N.W.11.*

The Necessary Stimulant

ON the St. Quentin front in 1917 we were relieved by the French Artillery. We watched with rather critical eyes their guns going in, and, best of all, their observation balloon going up.

The ascent of this balloon was, to say the least, spasmodic. First it went up about a hundred feet, then came down, then a little higher and down again.

This was repeated several times, until at last the car was brought to the ground and the observer got out. He was handed a packet, then hastily returned, and up the balloon went for good. Then I heard a Cockney voice beside me in explanatory tones : " There ! I noo wot it was all the time. 'E'd forgotten his vin blong ! "—*Ernest E. Homewood (late 1st London Heavy Battery), 13 Park Avenue, Willesden Green, N.W.2.*

A Traffic Problem

A DARK cloudy night in front of Lens, two patrols of the 19th London Regt., one led by Lieut. R——, the other by Corporal B——, were crawling along the barbed wire entanglements in No Man's Land, towards each other.

Two tin hats met with a clang, which at once drew the attention of Fritz.

Lieut. R—— sat back in the mud, while snipers' and machine-gun bullets whistled past, and in a cool voice said, " Why don't you ring your perishing bell ? "—*L. C. Pryke (late 19th London Regt.), " Broughdale," Rochford Avenue, Rochford, Essex.*

Scots, Read This !

ON the afternoon of Christmas Day, 1915, three pipers, of whom I was one, went into the trenches at Loos, and after playing at our Battalion H.Q., proceeded to the front line, where we played some selections for the benefit of the Germans, whose trenches were very close at this point. Probably thinking that an attack was imminent, they sent up innumerable Verey lights, but, deciding later that we had no such intention, they responded by singing and playing on mouth-organs.

Having finished our performance, my friends and I proceeded on our way back, and presently, passing some men of another regiment, were asked by one of them : " Was that you playin' them bloomin' toobs ? " We admitted it.

" 'Ear that, Joe ? " he remarked to his pal. " These blokes 'ave bin givin' the 'Uns a toon."

" Serve 'em right," said Joe, " they started the blinkin' war."—*Robert Donald Marshall (late Piper, 1st Bn. London Scottish), 83 Cranley Drive, Ilford.*

Met His Match

A LONDON Tommy was standing near the leave boat at Calais, which had just brought him back to France on his way to the firing line. It was raining, and he was trying to get a damp cigarette to draw. Just then a French soldier approached him with an unlighted cigarette

Poilu : " Allumette ? "
Tommy : " 'Allo, mate." (Shakes.)

in his hand, and, pointing to Tommy's cigarette, held out his hand and exclaimed " Allumette ? "

The Tommy sadly shook hands and replied "Allo, Mate."—*A. J. Fairer, Mirigama, Red Down Road, Coulsdon, Surrey.*

Why Jerry was " Clinked "

ON August 8, 1918, as our battery began the long trail which landed us in Cologne before Christmas we met a military policeman who had in his charge three very dejected-looking German prisoners. " Brummy," our battery humorist, shouted to the red-cap : " 'Ullo, Bobby, what are yer clinkin' those poor old blokes for ? "

" Creatin' a disturbance on the Western Front," replied the red-cap.— *Wm. G. Sheppard (late Sergeant, 24th Siege Bty., R.A.), 50 Benares Road, Plumstead, S.E.18.*

Stick-in-the-Mud

WE were in reserve at Roclincourt in February 1917, and about twenty men were detailed to carry rations to the front line. The trenches were knee-deep in mud.

After traversing about two hundred yards of communication trench we struck a particularly thick, clayey patch, and every few yards the order " Halt in front ! " was passed from the rear.

The corporal leading the men got very annoyed at the all-too-frequent halts. He passed the word back, " What's the matter ? " The reply was, " Shorty's in the mud, and we can't get 'im out."

Waiting a few minutes, the corporal again passed a message back : " Haven't you got him out yet ? How long are you going to be ? " Reply came from the rear in a Cockney voice : " 'Eaven knows ! There's only 'is ears showin'."—*G. Kay, 162 Devonshire Avenue, Southsea, Hants.*

" If That can stick it, I can ! "

OWING to the forced marching during the retreat from Mons, men would fall out by the roadside and, after a rest, carry on again.

One old soldier, " Buster " Smith, was lying down puffing and gasping when up rode an officer mounted upon an old horse that he had found straying.

Going up to " Buster " the officer asked him if he thought he could " stick it."

" Buster " looked up at the officer and then, eyeing the horse, said : " If *that* can stick it, *I* can," and, getting up, he resumed marching.— *E. Barwick, 19 St. Peter's Street, Hackney Road, E.2.*

Wheeling a Mule

IN November '15 we were relieved in the early hours of the morning. It had been raining, raining most of the time we were in the trenches, and so we were more or less wet through and covered in mud when we came out for a few days' rest.

About two or three kilometres from Bethune we were all weary and fed-up with marching. Scarcely a word was spoken until we came across an Engineer leading a mule with a roll of telephone wire coiled round a wheel on its back. The mule looked as fed-up as we were, and a Cockney in our platoon shouted out, " Blimey, mate, if you're goin' much furver wiv the old 'oss yer'll 'ave to turn it on its back and wheel it."—*W. S. (late Coldstream Guards), Chelsea, S.W.3.*

Three Brace of Braces

WHILE I was serving with the 58th Siege Battery at Carnoy, on the Somme, in 1916, a young Cockney of the 29th Division was discovered walking in front of three German prisoners. Over his shoulders he had three pairs of braces.

" . . . while I got their ' harness ' they can't get up to any mischief."

A wag asked him if he wanted to sell them, and his reply was : " No, these Fritzies gets 'em back when they gets to the cage. But while I got their ' harness' they can't get up to any mischief."—*E. Brinkman,* 16 *Hornsey Street, Holloway Road, N.7.*

" Bow Bells " Warning

AT the beginning of March 1918, near Flesquieres, we captured a number of prisoners, some of whom were put in the charge of " Nipper," a native of Limehouse.

I heard him address them as follows : " Nah, then, if yer wants a fag yer can have one, but, blimey, if yer starts any capers, I'll knock ' Bow Bells ' aht of yer Stepney Church."—*J. Barlow (20th London Regt.),* 18 *Roding Lane, Buckhurst Hill, Essex.*

" 'Ave a Sniff "

MY father tells of a raw individual from London Town who had aroused great wrath by having within a space of an hour given two false alarms for gas. After the second error everyone was just drowsing off again when a figure cautiously put his head inside the dug-out, and hoarsely said : " 'Ere, sergeant, yer might come and 'ave a sniff."—*R. Purser, St. Oama, Vista Road, Wickford, Essex.*

The Dirt Track

WHILE my regiment was in support at Ecurie, near Arras, I was detailed to take an urgent message to B.H.Q.

I mounted a motor-cycle and started on my way, but I hadn't gone far when a shell burst right in my path and made a huge crater, into which I slipped. After going round the inside rim twice at about twenty-five miles an hour, I landed in the mud at the bottom. Pulling myself clear of the cycle, I saw two fellows looking down and laughing at me.

" Funny, isn't it ? " I said.

" Yus, matey, thought it was Sanger's Circus. Where's the girl in the tights wot rides the 'orses ? "

Words failed me.—*London Yeomanry, Brixton, S.W.*

Babylon and Bully

AFTER a dismal trek across the mud of Mespot, my batman and I arrived at the ruins of Babylon. As I sat by the river under the trees, and gazed upon the stupendous ruins of the one-time mightiest city in the world, I thought of the words of the old Psalm—" By the waters of Babylon we sat down and wept——"

And this was the actual spot !

Moved by my thoughts, I turned to my batman and said, " By Jove, just think. This is really *Babylon* ! "

" Yes, sir," he replied, " but I'm a-wonderin' 'ow I'm goin' to do your bully beef up to-night to make a change like."—*W. L. Lamb (late R.E., M.E.F.), " Sunnings," Sidley, Bexhill-on-Sea.*

Twice Nightly

AN attack was expected, and some men were kept in reserve in an underground excavation more closely resembling a tunnel than a trench.

After about twenty hours' waiting in knee-deep mud and freezing cold, they were relieved by another group.

As they were filing out one of the relief party said to one of those coming out, " Who are you ? "

" 'Oo are we ? " came the reply. " Cahn't yer see we're the fust 'ouse comin' aht o' the pit ? "—*K. Haddon, 379 Rotherhithe New Road, North Camberwell, S.E.16.*

In Shining Armour

A HORRIBLE wet night on the Locre-Dranoutre Road in 1914. A narrow strip of pavé road and, on either side, mud of a real Flanders consistency.

I was on my lawful occasions in a car, which was following a long supply column of five-ton lorries.

I need scarcely say that the car did not try to forsake the comparative security of the pavé, but when a check of about a quarter of an hour

" 'Ere, ally off the perishin' pavé, you knight in shinin' armour."

occurred, I got down from the car and stumbled through the pouring rain, well above the boot-tops in mud, to the head of the column.

Impasse barely describes the condition of things, for immediately facing the leading lorry was a squadron of French Cuirassiers, complete with " tin bellies " and helmets with horse-hair trimmings.

This squadron was in command of a very haughty French captain, who seemed, in the light of the lorry's head-lamps, to have a bigger cuirass and helmet than his men.

He was faced by a diminutive sergeant of the A.S.C., wet through, fed up, but complete with cigarette.

Neither understood the other's language, but it was quite obvious that neither would leave the pavé for the mud. Did the sergeant wring his hands or say to the officer, " Mon Capitaine, je vous en prie, etc." ? He did not. He merely stood there, and, removing his cigarette from his mouth, uttered these immortal words :

" 'Ere, ally off the perishing pavé, you son of a knight in shinin' armour ! "

And, believe me or believe me not, that is what the haughty one and his men did.—" *The Ancient Mariner," Sutton, Surrey.*

" A Blinkin' Paper-Chase ? "

ONE pitch black rainy night I was bringing up the rear of a party engaged in carrying up the line a number of trench mortar bombs known as " toffee-apples."

We had become badly tailed-off during our progress through a maze of communication trenches knee-deep in mud, and as I staggered at last into the support trench with my load I spied a solitary individual standing on the fire-step gazing over the parapet.

" Seen any Queen's pass this way ? " I inquired.

" Blimey," he replied, apparently fed-up with the constant repetition of the same question, " wot 'ave you blokes got on to-night—a blinkin' piper-chise ? "—*W. H. Blakeman (late Sergt., Queen's R.W.S. Regt.), 22 Shorts Road, Carshalton.*

Biscuits—Another Point of View

IN April 1915 my battalion was on the way up to take over a line of " grouse-butts "—there were no continuous trenches—in front of a pleasure resort by the name of Festubert.

Arrived at Gore, a couple of miles or so from the line, we ran into some transport that had got thoroughly tied up, and had a wait of about half-an-hour while the joy-riders sorted themselves out. It was pitch dark and raining hard, and the occasional spot of confetti that came over added very little to the general enjoyment.

As I moved up and down my platoon, the usual profane but humorous grousing was in full spate. At that time the ration arrangements were not so well organised as they afterwards became, and for some weeks the bulk of our banquets had consisted of bully and remarkably hard and unpalatable biscuits. The latter were a particularly sore point with the troops.

As I listened, one rifleman held forth on the subject. " No blinkin' bread for five blinkin' weeks," he wound up—" nothin' but blinkin' biscuits that taste like sawdust an' break every tooth in yer perishin' 'ed. 'Ow the 'ell do they expect yer to fight on stuff like that ? " " Whatcher grousin' about ? " drawled another weary voice. " Dawgs *lives* on biscuits, and they can fight like 'ell ! "—*S. B. Skevington (late Major, 1st London Irish Rifles), 10 Berkeley Street, W.1.*

His Bird Bath

A BATTALION of the Royal Fusiliers (City of London Regiment) was in support, and a private was endeavouring to wash himself as thoroughly as possible with about a pint of water in a mess-tin.

A kindly disposed staff officer happened to come along, and seeing the man thus engaged, said, " Having a wash, my man ? "

" Wish I was a blinkin' canary : I could have a bath then."

Back came the reply, " Yus, and I wish I was a blinkin' canary. I could have a bath then."—*R. G. Scarborough, 89 Tennyson Avenue, New Malden, Surrey.*

Ducking 'em—then Nursing 'em

AFTER the Cambrai affair of November 1917 our company came out of the line, but we had to salvage some very large and heavy shells.

We had been carrying the shells in our arms for about an hour when I heard a fed-up Cockney turn to the sergeant and say : " 'Ere 'ave I been duckin' me nut for years from these blinkin' fings—blimey, and nah I'm nursin' 'em ! "—*Rfn. Elliott (late 17th K.R.R.C.), 9 Leghorn Road, Harlesden, N.W.*

Salonika Rhapsody

THREE of us were sitting by the support line on the Salonika front, conditions were fairly bad, rations were short and a mail was long overdue. We were fed-up. But the view across the Vardar Valley was some compensation.

The wadis and plains, studded with bright flowers, the glistening river and the sun just setting behind the distant ridges and tinting the low clouds, combined to make a perfect picture. One of my pals, with a poetic temperament, rhapsodised on the scene for several minutes, and then asked our other mate what he thought. "Sooner see the blinkin' Old Kent Road!" was the answer of the peace-time costermonger.— *W. W. Wright*, 24 *Borthwick Road, E.*15.

A Ticklin' Tiddler

IN January 1915, near Richebourg, I was one of a ration-party being led back to the front line by a lance-corporal. The front line was a system of breast-works surrounded by old disused trenches filled with seven feet or so of icy-cold water.

It was a very dark moonless night, and near the line our leader called out to those in the breast-works to ask them where the bridge was. He was told to step off by the broken tree. He did so and slid into the murky depths—the wrong tree!

We got him out and he stood on dry (?) land, shining with moisture, full of strange oaths and vowing vengeance on the lad who had mis-directed him.

At stand-down in the dawn (hours afterwards) he was sipping his tot of rum. He had had no chance of drying his clothes. I asked how he felt.

"Fresh as a pansy, mate," was his reply. "Won'erful 'ow a cold plunge bucks yer up! Blimey, I feel as if I could push a leave train from 'ere to the base. 'Ere, put yer 'and dahn my tunic and see if that's a tiddler ticklin' me back."—*F. J. Reidy (late* 1st *K.R.R.s)*, 119 *Mayfair Avenue, Ilford.*

Biscuits and Geometry

DURING a spell near St. Quentin our company existed chiefly on biscuits—much to the annoyance of one of our officers, who said he detested dogs' food.

One evening he met the Cockney corporal who had just come up in charge of the ration party.

OFFICER : " Any change to-night, corporal ? "

CORPORAL : " Yessir ! "

OFFICER : " Good ! What have we got ? "

CORPORAL : " Rahnd 'uns instead of square 'uns, sir."—*R. Pitt (late M.G.C.)*, 54 *Holland Park Avenue, W.*11.

All that was Wrong with the War

TAKING up ammunition to the guns at Passchendaele Ridge, I met a few infantrymen carrying duck-boards.

My mule was rather in the way and so one of the infantrymen, who belonged to a London regiment, gave him a push with his duck-board.

Naturally, the mule simply let out and kicked him into a shell-hole full of water.

We got the unlucky fellow out, and his first action was to shake his fist

" . . . and that's mules."

at the mule and say : " There's only one thing I don't like in this blinking war and that's those perishin' mules ! "—*H. E. Richards (R.F.A.), 67 Topsham Road, Upper Tooting, S.W.17.*

Not a Single Cockney

IN 1917, when we were acting as mobile artillery, we had halted by the roadside to water and feed our horses, and were just ready to move off when we were passed by a column of the Chinese Labour Corps, about 2,000 of them.

After they had all passed, a gunner from Clerkenwell said : " Would yer believe it ? All that lot gorn by and I never reckernised a Townie ! " —*C. Davis (late Sergeant, R.A., 3rd Cavalry Division), 7 Yew Tree Villas, Welling, Kent.*

Sanger's Circus on the Marne !

ON the way from the Marne to the Aisne in September 1914 the 5th Cavalry Brigade passed a column of Algerian native troops, who had been drawn up in a field to allow us to continue along the nearby road.

The column had all the gaudy appearance of shop windows at Christmas. There were hooded vehicles with stars and crescents blazoned on them, drawn by bullocks, mules, and donkeys. The natives themselves were dressed, some in white robes and turbans, others in red " plus four " trousers and blue " Eton cut " jackets ; and their red fezzes were adorned with stars and crescents. Altogether a picturesque sight, and one we did not expect to meet on the Western Front.

On coming into view of this column, one of our lead drivers (from Bow) of a four-horse team drawing a pontoon wagon turned round to his wheel driver, and, pointing to the column with his whip, shouted, " Alf ! Sanger's Circus ! "—*H. W. Taylor (late R.E.), The Lodge, Radnor Works, Strawberry Vale, Twickenham.*

" Contemptible " Stuff

WHEN the rumour reached us about a medal for the troops who went out at the beginning, a few of us were sitting in a dug-out outside Ypres discussing the news.

" Mac " said : " I wonder if they'll give us anything else beside the medal ? "

Our Cockney, Alf, remarked : " You got a lot to say about this 'ere bloomin' ' gong ' (medal) ; anybody 'd fink you was goin' ter git one."

" I came out in September '14, any way," said Mac.

Alf (very indignant) : " Blimey, 'ark at 'im ! You don't arf expect somefink, you don't. Why, the blinkin' war was 'arf over by then."—*J. F. Grey (late D.L.I. and R.A.O.C.), 247 Ducane Road, Shepherd's Bush, W.12.*

A Cockney on Horseback—Just

WE were going out to rest after about four months behind the guns at Ypres, and the drivers brought up spare horses for us to ride. One Cockney gunner was heard to say, " I can't ride ; I've never rode an 'orse in me life." We helped him to get mounted, but we had not gone far when Jerry started sending 'em over. So we started trotting. To see our Cockney friend hanging on with his arms round the horse's neck was quite a treat !

However, we eventually got back to the horse lines where our hero, having fallen off, remarked : " Well, after that, I fink if ever I do get back to Blighty I'll always raise me 'at to an 'orse."—*A. Lepley (late R.F.A.), 133 Blackwell Buildings, Whitechapel, E.1.*

A Too Sociable Horse

WE were asleep in our dug-out at Bray, on the Somme, in November 1915. The dug-out was cut in the bank of a field where our horse lines were.

One of the horses broke loose and, taking a fancy to our roof, which was made of brushwood and rushes, started eating it.

Suddenly the roof gave way and the horse fell through, narrowly missing myself and my pal, who was also a Cockney.

" They want to come to bed wiv us."

After we had got over the shock my pal said, " Well, if that ain't the blinkin' latest. These long-eared blighters ain't satisfied with us looking after them—they want to come to bed with us."—*F. E. Snell (late 27th Brigade, R.F.A.), 22 Woodchester Street, Harrow Road, W.2.*

General Salute !

WHILE " resting " at Bully-Grenay in the winter of 1916 I witnessed the following incident :

Major-General ———— and his A.D.C. were walking through the

village when an elderly Cockney member of a Labour battalion (a typical London navvy) stumbled out of an estaminet. He almost collided with the general.

Quickly pulling himself together and exclaiming " Blimey, the boss ! " he gave a very non-military salute ; but the general, tactfully ignoring his merry condition, had passed on.

In spite of his pal's attempts to restrain him, he overtook the general, shouting " I did serlute yer, didn't I, guv'nor ? "

To which the general hastily replied : " Yes, yes, my man ! "

" Well," said the Cockney, " here's anuvver ! "—*A. J. K. Davis (late 20th London Regt., att. 73rd M.G.C.), Minnis Croft, Reculver Avenue, Birchington.*

Wipers-on-Sea

SCENE, " Wipers " ; Time, winter of 1917.
    A very miserable-looking R.F.A. driver, wet to the skin, is riding a very weary mule through the rain.

Voice from passing infantryman, in the unmistakable accent of Bow Bells : " Where y' goin', mate ? Pier an' back ? "—*A. Gelli (late H.A.C.), 27 Langdon Park Road, Highgate, N.6.*

He Rescued His Shirt

DURING the latter stages of the war, with the enemy in full retreat, supply columns and stores were in most cases left far behind. Those in the advance columns, when marching through occupied villages, often " won " articles of underclothing to make up for deficiencies.

Camberwell Alf had a couple of striped " civvy " shirts, and had lent a less fortunate battery chum one of these on the understanding that it would be returned in due course. The same evening the battery was crossing a pontoon bridge when a mule became frightened at the oscillation of the wooden structure, reared wildly, and pitched its rider over the canvas screen into the river.

Camberwell Alf immediately plunged into the water and rescued his unfortunate chum after a great struggle.

Later the rescued one addressed his rescuer : " Thank yer, Alf, mate."

" Don't yer ' mate ' me, yer blinkin' perisher ! " Alf replied. " Wot the 'ell d'yer mean by muckin' abaht in the pahny (water) wiv my shirt on ? "—*J. H. Hartnoll (late 30th Div. Artillery), 1 Durning Roud, Upper Norwood, S.E.19.*

A Smile from the Prince

ONE morning towards the end of May 1915, just before the battle of Festubert, my pal Bill and I were returning from the village bakery on the Festubert road to our billets at Gorre with a loaf each, which we had just bought.

Turning the corner into the village we saw approaching us a company of the Grenadier Guards in battle order, with a slim young officer at the head carrying a stick almost as tall as himself. Directly behind the officer was a hefty Guardsman playing " Tipperary " on a concertina.

We saluted the officer, who, after spotting the loaves of bread under our arms, looked straight at us, gave us a knowing smile and acknowledged our salute. It was not till then that we recognised who the officer was. It was the Prince of Wales.

" Lumme ! " said Bill. " There goes the Prince o' Wales hisself a-taking the guard to the Bank o' England ! "—*J. F. Davis*, 29 *Faunce Street, S.E.17.*

" Just to Make Us Laugh "

WE were one of those unlucky fatigue parties detailed to carry ammunition to the forward machine gun positions in the Ypres sector. We started off in the dusk and trudged up to the line. The transport dumped the " ammo " at a convenient spot and left us to it. Then it started raining.

The communication trenches were up to our boot tops in mud, so we left them and walked across the top. The ground was all chalky slime and we slipped and slid all over the place. Within a very short time we were wet through and, to make matters worse, we occasionally slipped into shell-holes half full of water (just to relieve the monotony !).

We kept this up all night until the " ammo " had all been delivered ; then the order came to march back to billets at Dranoutre. It was still pouring with rain, and when we came to Shrapnel Corner we saw the famous notice board : " Avoid raising Dust Clouds as it draws Enemy's Shell Fire."

We were new to this part of the line and, just then, the idea of raising dust clouds was extremely ludicrous.

I asked my pal Jarvis, who came from Greenwich, what he thought they put boards like that up for. His reply was typically Cockney : " I 'spect they did that just to make us laugh, as we cawnt go to the picshures."—*Mack (late M.G.C.), Cathcart, The Heath, Dartford.*

No Use Arguing with a Mule

WHILST " resting " after the Jerusalem battle, my battalion was detailed for road-making. Large stones were used for the foundation of the road and small and broken stones for the surface. Our job was to find the stones, *assisted by* mules.

A mule was new to Joe Smith—a great-hearted boy from Limehouse way—but he must have heard about them for he gingerly approached the one allotted to him, and as gingerly led him away into the hills.

Presently Joe was seen returning, but, to our amazement, he was struggling along with the loaded baskets slung across his own shoulders, and the mule was trailing behind. When I asked why *he* was carrying the load, he replied : " Well, I was loading 'im up wiv the stones, but he cut up rusty, so to save a lot of argument, I reckoned as 'ow I'd better carry the darned stones meself."—*A. C. Wood*, 56 *Glasslyn Road, N.*8.

Kissing Time

IT was towards the end of '18, and we had got old Jerry well on the run. We had reached a village near Lille, which had been in German occupation, and the inhabitants were surging round us.

" Take the rough with the smooth."

A corporal was having the time of his life, being kissed on both cheeks by the girls, but when it came to a bewhiskered French papa's turn the corporal hesitated. " Nah, then, corporal," shouted one of our boys, " be sporty ! Take the rough with the smooth ! "—*G. H. Harris (late C.S.M.*, 8*th London Regt.*), 65 *Nelson Road, South Chingford, E.*4.

" Playin' Soldiers "

WE were in the Cambrai Salient, in support in the old Hindenburg Line. Close to us was a road where there were a ration dump and every other sort of dump. Everybody in the sector went through us to get rations, ammunition, stores, etc.

There was just room in the trench for two men to pass. Snow had been on the ground for weeks, and the bottom of the trench was like glass. One night at stand-to the Drake Battalion crowded past us to get rations. On their return journey the leading man, with two sandbags of rations round his neck and a petrol can of water in each hand, fell over at every other step. Things were further complicated by a party of R.E.'s coming down the line with much barbed wire, in which this unfortunate " Drake " entangled himself.

As he picked himself up for the umpteenth time, and without the least intention of being funny, I heard him say : " Well, if I ever catch that nipper of mine playin' soldiers, I won't 'arf knock 'is blinkin' block orf."
—*A. M. B. (late Artists Rifles), Savage Club, W.C.2.*

Per Carrier

DURING the occupation of the " foreshores of Gallipoli " in 1915 the troops were suffering from shortage of water.

I and six more, including Tich, were detailed to carry petrol cans full of water up to the front line. We had rather a rough passage over very hilly ground, and more than one of us tripped over stones that were strewn across the path, causing us to say a few strong words.

By the time we reached our destination we were just about all in, and on being challenged " Halt ; who goes there ? " Tich answered : " Carter Paterson and Co. with ' Adam's ale,' all nice and frothy ! "—*D. W. Jordan (late 1/5th Essex, 54th Division), 109a Gilmore Road, Lewisham, S.E.13.*

" Enemy " in the Wire

I WAS in charge of an advanced post on the Dorian front, Salonica, 1917, which had been often raided by the Bulgars, and we were advised to be extra wary. In the event of an attack we were to fire a red flare, which was a signal for the artillery to put over a barrage.

About 2 a.m. we heard a commotion in our wire, but, receiving no answer to our challenge, I decided to await further developments. The noise was soon repeated in a way that left no doubt in my mind that we were being attacked, so I ordered the section to open fire and sent up the signal for the guns.

Imagine our surprise when, after all was quiet again, we heard the same noise in the wire. One of the sentries was a Cockney, and without a word he crawled over the parapet and disappeared in the direction of the noise.

A few minutes later came the sound of smothered laughter, and the sentry returned with a hedgehog firmly fixed in an empty bully tin. It was the cause of our alarm !

After releasing the animal from its predicament, the sentry said : " We'd better send the blighter to the Zoo, Corp, wiv a card to say ' this little pig put the wind up the troops, caused a fousand men to open fire, was bombed, machine-gunned, and shelled.' Blimey ! I'd like to see the Gunner officer's face if he knew this."—*D. R. Payne, M.M.* (*ex-Worcester Regt.*), 40 *High Street, Overton, Hants.*

Straight from the Heart

UNDER canvas at Rousseauville with 27th Squadron, R.F.C., early 1918—wet season—raining hard—everything wet through and muddy—a " fed-up " gloomy feeling everywhere.

We were trying to start a 3-ton lorry that was stuck in the mud on the aerodrome. After we had all had a shot at swinging the starting handle, the very Cockney driver of the lorry completely exhausted himself in yet another unsuccessful attempt to start up. Then, leaning against the radiator and pushing his cap back, he puffed out :

" I dunno ! These perishin' lorries are enough to take all the flamin' romance out of any blinkin' camp ! "—*R. S. W.* (*Flying-Officer, R.A.F. Reserve*), 52 *Cavendish Road, N.W.*6.

Smile ! Smile ! SMILE ! !

CONVERSATION between two Cockney members of a North Country regiment whilst proceeding along the Menin road in March 1918 as members of a wiring party :

1st : I'm fed up with this stunt.

2nd : Same 'ere. 'Tain't 'arf a life, ain't it ? No rest, no beer, blinkin' leave stopped—er, got any fags ?

1st : No, mate.

2nd : No fags, no nuffink. It's only us keepin' so ruddy cheerful as pulls us through.—*V. Marston*, 232 *Worple Road, Wimbledon, S.W.*20.

War's Lost Charm

TIME, winter of 1917 : scene, a track towards Langemarck from Pilkem. Weather and general conditions—Flanders at its worst. My companion that night was an N.C.O. " out since 'fourteen," and we had plodded on in silence for some time. Suddenly behind me there was a slither, a splash, and a smothered remark as the sergeant skidded from the duckboard into an especially dirty shell hole.

I helped him out and asked if he was all right. The reply came, " I'm all right, sir ; but this blinkin' war seems to have lost its charm ! "—*J. E. A. Whitman* (*Captain, late R.F.A.*), *The Hampden Club, N.W.*1.

Taking It Lying Down

THE 1st Battalion of the 25th Londons was preparing to march into Waziristan.

Old Bert, the cook, diligently loading up a kneeling camel with dixies, pots and pans, and general cooking utensils, paused for a bit, wiped the sweat from his brow, and stood back with arms akimbo gazing with satisfaction upon his work.

Then he went up to the camel, gave him a gentle prod, and grunted " Ooush, yer blighter, ooush " (i.e. rise). The camel turned gently over

" Don't yer understand yer own langwidge, yer kitten ? "

on his back, unshipping the whole cargo that Bert had worked so hard upon, and kicked his legs in the air.

Poor old Bert looked at the wreckage and exclaimed, more in sorrow than in anger : " Blimey, don't yer understand yer own langwidge, yer kitten ? "—*T. F. Chanter*, 16 *Atalanta Street, Fulham.*

The First Twenty Years

IT was round about Christmas 1917, and we were resting (?) at " Dirty Bucket Corner." The Christmas present we all had in view was a return to the line in front of Ypres.

On the day before we were due to return the Christmas post arrived,

and after the excitement had abated the usual " blueness " settled in—
the craving for home comforts and " Blighty."

My partners in the stretcher-bearing squad included a meek and
mild man (I believe he was a schoolmaster before the war) and a Cockney
from Seven Dials. We used to call him " Townie."

Although the ex-schoolmaster would have had cause in more normal
times to rejoice—for the post contained a letter telling him that he
had become the father of a bonny boy—the news made him morbid.

Of course, we all congratulated him. Meanwhile " Townie " was
busy with a pencil and writing pad, and after a few minutes handed to
the new parent a sheet of paper folded in half. The recipient unfolded
it and looked at it for several seconds before the rest of us became
interested and looked over his shoulder.

The paper was covered with lines, circles, and writing that appeared
to us like " double-Dutch."

" What's this ? " the father asked.

" That's a map I drawed fer yer kid. It'll show him where the old
pot and pan is when he's called up," and he concluded with this afterthought : " Tell 'im ter be careful of that ruddy shell-hole just acrost
there. I've fallen in the perishin' thing twice this week."—" *Medico* "
(58*th* (*London*) *Division*), *Clapham Common, S.W.11.*

Shell as a Hammer

AT one time the area just behind Vimy Ridge was plentifully sprinkled
with enemy shells which had failed to explode. As these were considered a great source of danger they were indicated by " danger boards "
nailed to pointed stakes driven into the ground.

On one occasion, seeing a man engaged in so marking the resting-
place of a " dud "—he was a cheerful Cockney, who whistled as he went
about his job—I was much amused (though somewhat scared) to see
him stop at a nearby shell, select a " danger board," pick up the shell,
and proceed to use it as a hammer to drive the stake into the ground !—
H. S. A. (*late Lieut., Suffolk Regt.*), *Glebe Road, Cheam.*

Sore Feet

AFTER the first battle of Ypres an old driver, whom we called
" Krongie," had very bad feet, and one day reported sick at the
estaminet where the M.O. held office.

After the examination he ambled up the road, and when he was about
50 yards away the M.O.'s orderly ran out and called : " Krongie, when you
get to the column tell the farrier the M.O.'s horse has cast a shoe."

" Krongie " : " Ho, yus. You tell 'im ter give the blinkin' *cheval* a
couple of number nines like he gave me for *my* feet."—*P. Jones* (*R.H.A.*),
6 *Ennis Road, N.4.*

My Sword Dance—by the C.O.

A BITTERLY cold morning in winter, 1916, in the Ypres Salient. I was on duty at a gas alarm post in the front line when along came the colonel.

He was the finest soldier and gentleman I ever had the pleasure to serve under (being an old soldier in two regiments before, I had experienced a few C.O.s). It was said he knew every man's name in the regiment. No officer dare start his own meal until every man of his company had been served. No fatigue or working party ever went up the line, no matter at what hour, without the colonel first inspected it.

He had a mania for collecting spare ammunition, and more than once was seen taking up to the front line a roll of barbed wire over his shoulder hooked through his stick. To him every man was a son, and to the men's regret and officers' delight he soon became a general.

This particular morning he approached me with " Good morning, Walker. You look cold. Had your rum ? " To which I replied that I had, but it was a cold job remaining stationary for hours watching the wind.

" Well," said the C.O., " do this with me." With that he started marking time at a quick pace on the duck-boards and I did likewise. We kept it up for about two minutes, while others near had a good laugh.

" Now you feel better, I know. Do this every ten minutes or so," he said, and away he went to continue his tour of inspection.

My Cockney pal in the next bay, who, I noticed, had enjoyed the scene immensely, said, " Blimey, Jock, was he giving you a few lessons in the sword dance or the Highland Fling ? "—" *Jock* " *Walker* (*late Royal Fusiliers*), 29 *Brockbank Road, Lewisham, S.E.*13.

A Big Bone in the Soup

IN Baghdad, 1917, " Buzzer " Lee and I were told off to do " flying sentry " round the officers' lines from 3 to 5 a.m. Well, we commenced our duty, and Buzzer suggested we visit the mess kitchen to see all was well, and in case there was anything worth " knocking off " (as he called it) in the way of char or scran (tea or bread and butter).

The mess kitchen was in darkness, and Buzzer began scrounging around. After a while he said : " I've clicked, mate ! Soup in a dixie ! " By the light of a match he found a cup, removed the dixie lid, and took a cup of the " soup."

" We're in the market this time, mate," said Buzzer, and took out a cupful for me.

" It don't taste like Wood's down the New Cut," I said, doubtfully.

He dipped the cup again and exclaimed : " ' 'Ere, I've fahnd a big bone ! "

It was a new broom-head, however ; it had been left in the dixie to soak for the night !—*G. H. Griggs* (*late Somerset L.I.*), 3 *Ribstone Street, Hackney, E.*9.

6

"I Shall have to Change Yer!"

IN the Ypres Salient in July 1915 Headquarters were anxious to know which German regiment was facing us. An immense Cockney corporal, who was particularly good on patrol, was instructed to secure a prisoner.

"I shall have to take yer aht to-night and change yer."

After a night spent in No Man's Land he returned at dawn with a capture, an insignificant little German, trembling with fear, who stood about five foot nothing.

Lifting him on to the fire-step and eyeing him critically, the corporal thus addressed him : " You won't do for our ole man ; I shall have to take yer aht to-night and change yer ! "—*S. Back, Merriams Farm, Leeds, near Maidstone.*

Scots Reveille

OURS was the only kilted battalion in the division, and our bagpipes were often the subject of many humorous remarks from the other regiments.

On one occasion, while we were out resting just behind the line at

" There goes them perishin' ' toobs ' agin."

Château de la Haye, we were billeted opposite a London regiment. Very early in the morning the bagpipes would sound the Scottish reveille—a rather long affair compared with the usual bugle call—and it did not please our London friends to be awakened in this manner.

One morning while I was on early duty, and just as the pipers were passing, a very dismal face looked out of a billet and announced to his pals inside, " There goes them perishin' ' toobs ' again."—*Arthur R. Blampied, D.C.M. (late London Scottish), 47 Lyndhurst Avenue, Streatham Hill, S.W.2.*

In the Negative

A BATTALION of the London Regiment had been having a particularly gruelling time in the trenches, but some of the men were cheered with thoughts of impending leave. In fact, permission for them to proceed home was expected at any moment.

At this time the Germans started a " big push " in another sector, and all leave was suddenly cancelled.

An N.C.O. broke the news to the poor unfortunates in the following manner : " All you blokes wot's going on leaf, ain't going on leaf, 'cause you're unlucky."

In spite of the great disappointment, this way of putting it amused even the men concerned. The real Cockney spirit !—*S. C., Brighton.*

" An' That's All that 'Appened "

B EFORE going up the line we were stationed at Etaples, and were rather proud of our cook-house, but one day the colonel told the sergeant-major that he had heard some of the most unparliamentary language he had ever heard in his life emanating from the cook-house.

The sergeant-major immediately called at the cook-house to find out the cause of the trouble, but our Cockney cook was very indignant. " What, *me* Lord Mayor ? [slang for ' swear ']. No one's ever 'eard me Lord Mayor."

" Don't lie to me," roared the sergeant-major. " What's happened here ? "

" Nuffin'," said the cook, " except that I slopped a dixie full of 'ot tea dahn Bill's neck. I said ' Sorry, Bill,' and Bill said ' Granted, 'Arry,' an' that's all what's 'appened."—*Ryder Davies (late 1st Kent Cyclists, Royal West Kents), 20 Villa Road, S.W.9.*

Watching them " Fly Past "

O UR first big engagement was a counter-attack to recapture the trenches lost by the K.R.R.'s and R.B.'s on July 30, 1915, when " Jerry " used liquid fire for the first time and literally burned our chaps out.

To get into action we had to go across open country in full view of the enemy. We began to get it " in the neck " as soon as we got to " Hell Fire Corner," on our way to Zillebeke Lake. Our casualties were heavy, caused by shell fire, also by a German aeroplane which was flying very low overhead and using its machine gun on us.

My pal, Wally Robins (later awarded M.M., promoted corporal, and killed at Lens), our company humorist, was looking up at the 'plane when a shell landed, killing several men in front of him.

As he fell I thought he too had caught it. I rushed to him anxiously and said, " Are you hurt ? "

This was his reply : " I should think I am. I wish they would keep their bloomin' aeroplanes out of the way. If I hadn't been looking up at that I shouldn't have fallen over that blinkin' barbed wire stake."— *E. W. Fellows, M.M. (late Corporal, 6th Battn., D.C.L.I.), 33 Dunlace Road, Clapton, E.5.*

High Necks and Low

AFTER the first Battle of Ypres in 1914 the Scots Guards were being relieved by a well-known London regiment.

A diminutive Cockney looked up at a six-foot Guardsman and asked him what it was like in the front line.

" 'Oo's neck ? "

" Up to your neck in mud," said the Guardsman.

" Blimey, oo's neck ? " asked the little chap.—*H. Rogers (late 116th Battery, 1st Div. R.F.A.), 10 Ashley Road, Richmond, Surrey.*

Too Light—by One Rissole

DURING the night before my Division (21st) attacked, on October 4, 1917, my unit was in the tunnel under the road at " Clapham Junction," near Hooge.

Rations having failed to arrive, each man was given a rissole and a packet of chewing-gum. We went over about 6 a.m., and, despite rather severe losses, managed to push our line forward about 1,300 yards.

When we were back in " rest " dug-outs at Zillebeke, our officer happening to comment on our " feed " prior to the attack, my mate said : " Yus. Blinkin' good job for old Jerry we never had two rissoles a man— we might have shoved him back to Berlin ! "—*C. Hartridge, 92 Lancaster Street, S.E.1.*

Psyche—" at the Barf ! "

I WAS billeting at Witternesse, near Aire, for a battery coming out of the line for rest and training prior to the August 1918 push.

I was very anxious to find a place where the troops could have a much-needed bath. The only spot was a barn, in which were two rusty old iron baths.

Further inspection showed that one was in use. On being asked who he was, the occupant stood up and replied in a Cockney voice : " Sikey at the Barf ! "—*H. Thomas, " Ivydene," Herne Grove, East Dulwich, S.E.22.*

A Juggler's Struggles

WE were disembarking at Ostend in 1914. Each man was expected to carry as much stores as he could. Our Cockney Marine was struggling down the gangway—full marching order, rifle slung round his neck, kitbag under his arm, and a box in each hand.

As he balanced the boxes we heard him mutter, " S'pose, if I juggle this lot orlright they'll poke annuver in my mouf."—*Thomas Bilson (late Colour-Sergeant, Royal Marines), 56 The Strand, Walmer, Kent.*

Almost a Wireless Story

SIR SIDNEY LAWFORD was to inspect our wagon lines in Italy, and we had received notice of his coming. Consequently we had been up since about 5 a.m. making things ship-shape.

One of the fatigues had been picking up all the spare wire lying about —wire from hay and straw bales, telephone wire, barbed wire, wire from broken hop poles, miscellaneous wire of all sorts.

Sir Sidney Lawford arrived about 11 a.m. with a number of his staff, dismounted . . . and promptly tripped over a piece of wire. Imagine our chagrin. However, the feeling passed away when a Cockney driver (evidently one of the wire-collecting fatigue) said in a voice audible to everyone as he peeped from under the horse he was supposed to be grooming: "Blimey, if he ain't fallen over the only piece of blinking wire in Italy!"—*F. Praid (late Lieut., R.F.A., 41st Div.), 88a High Street, Staines.*

When the S.M. Got Loose

WE were behind the lines at Merville in 1914. It was raining hard and it was night. "Smudger" Smith, from Lambeth, was on night guard. The horses were pulling their pegs out of the mud and

"Wot, yer loose again, yer blighter?"

getting loose, and "Smudger" was having a busy time running around and catching them and knocking the pegs in again with a mallet.

The sergeant-major, with a waterproof sheet over his head, visited the lines. "Smudger," seeing something moving about in the dark, crept up, and muttered, "Wot, yer loose again, yer blighter?"—and down went the sergeant-major.—*W. S. (late Queen's Bays), 2 Winsover Road, Spalding.*

Mons, 1914—Not Moscow, 1812 !

IN 1914 we of the 2nd Cavalry Brigade were going up to support the infantry somewhere near Mons, and when nearing our destination we saw several wounded being carried from the line.

Following them, seemingly quite unconcerned, was an infantry transport driver, who cut a queer figure. He was wearing a stocking hat,

" Napoleon's retreat from Moscow ain't in it wiv this ! "

and was mounted on an old mule. Thrown over the mule, with the tail-end round the mule's neck, was a German's blood-bespattered overcoat.

One of our troop addressed the rider thus : " Many up there, mate ? "

He answered : " Millions ! You 'ave a go. We can't shift 'em. They've took root, I fink."

He then dug both heels into the mule and, looking round with a bored expression, exclaimed : " Talk about Napoleon's blinkin' retreat from Moscow, it ain't ruddy well in it wiv this ! "

And he rode on.—*W. Baker (late 3rd Hussars)*, 35 *Tunstall Road, Brixton, S.W.9.*

The S.M. knew " Mulese "

DURING the Somme offensive in 1916 I was one of a party carrying rations up to the front line. We came upon a mule which was having a few pranks and pulling the chap who was leading it all over the road.

This man turned out to be an old Cockney pal of mine in the East Surreys. I said, " Hello, Jim, what's the matter ? "

" Blimey," he replied, " 'e won't do nuffink for me, so I'm taking 'im back to our sergeant-major, as 'e talks the mule langwidge."—*C. A. Fairhead (late R.W. Kent Regt.),* 16 *Council Cottages, Ford Corner, Yapton, Sussex.*

Lost : One Star

WE were on our way to the front line trenches one wet and dreary night when our subaltern realised that we were lost. He asked our sergeant if he could see the North Star. My Cockney pal, fed up, as we all were, turned to me and said : " Pass the word back and ask if anyone 'as got a Nawth Star in his pocket."—*H. J. Perry,* 42 *Wells House Road, Willesden Junction, N.W.10.*

Simpler than Sounding It

AFTER leaving Gallipoli in December 1915 our battalion (4th Essex) were in camp near the pyramids in Egypt.

" Pro Tem." we reverted to peace-time routine, and brought the buglers into commission again. One bugler was making a rather rotten show at sounding the " fall-in "—his " lip " being out of practice, I suppose—when a bored Cockney roared out, " Go rahnd and tell 'em."—*H. Barlow,* 5 *Brooklands, Abbs Cross Lane, Hornchurch.*

Under the Cart

THE place was a rest billet, which we had just reached after a gruelling on the Somme. Time, 12.30 a.m., dark as pitch and pouring with rain.

A despatch-rider arrived with an " urgent " message from H.Q., " Must have the number of your water-cart."

Out of bed, or its substitute, were brought the regimental sergeant-major, the orderly-room clerk, and the quartermaster-sergeant (a director of a London shipping firm bearing his name). All the light we had was the end of a candle, and as the Q.M.S. was crawling in the mud under the water-cart trying to find the number the candle flickered, whereupon the

Cockney sergeant-major exclaimed : " For Heaven's sake, stop that candle from flickerin', or our blinkin' staff will think we're signalling to Jerry ! "

The look on the Q.M.S.'s face as he sat in the mud made even the soaked despatch-rider laugh.

" What's the number of your water-cart ? " became a byword with the boys.—*W. J. Smallbone (late R.M.S., 56th Field Ambulance, 18th Division), 22 Stoneycroft Road, Woodford Bridge, Woodford Green, Essex.*

The Lion Laughed up his Sleeve

I HAD been driving a lorry all day in the East African bush with a Cockney escort. When we " parked " for the night I invited the escort to sleep under cover in the lorry, as I was going to do. But he refused, saying proudly that he had slept in the open since he had landed in Africa. So, undressing, he proceeded to make the rim of the rear wheel his pillow, covering himself with a blanket and greatcoat.

About 1 a.m. I was awakened by hearing someone climbing over the tail-board. Responding to my challenge the Cockney said : " It's all right. The blighter's been and pinched my blanket and greatcoat. It's a good job I had my shirt on." We found next morning that a lion had run off with them : about 100 yards away they lay, and one sleeve was torn out of the coat.—*H. J. Lake, 40a Chagford Street, N.W.1.*

The Carman's Sarcasm

WHILE our allies, the Portuguese, were holding part of the line to the left of Festubert, a Portuguese officer rode up on the most emaciated and broken-down old " crock " I had set eyes on.

He dismounted and was looking round for somewhere to tether the horse, when one of our drivers, a Cockney carman in " civvy " life, cast a critical eye over the mount and bawled out, " Don't worry abaht tying it up, mate. *Lean it up agin this 'ere fence."—A. G. Lodge (Sergeant, 25th Division Artillery), 12 Derinton Road, S.W.17.*

Burying a Lorry

DURING the Battle of the Somme, near Ginchy, a R.A.S.C. motor-lorry ran off the main track in the darkness and got stuck in the mud. The driver came to our battery near by and asked for help, so six gunners and I volunteered and set out with shovels.

On arriving at the scene, there was the motor-lorry almost buried to the top of the wheels. We all stood around surveying the scene in silence, wondering how best to make a start, when the Cockney member of the volunteer party burst out with : " Lummy, the quickest way out of this is to shovel some more blinkin' dirt on top, an' bury it."— *H. Wright (ex-Sig./Bdr., C/74 Bde., R.F.A.), 45 Colehill Lane, Fulham, S.W.6.*

Striking a Bargain

DURING the battle of the Narrows at the Dardanelles (March 18, 1915) I was in charge of No. 3 stokehold in H.M.S. *Vengeance*. The front line of ships engaged consisted of *Irresistible, Ocean, Vengeance,* and an old French battleship, the *Bouvet*. The stokers off watch were the ambulance party and fire brigade.

When the battle was at its height one of the fire brigade, a Cockney,

" Give us yer week's ' navy ' and I'll let yer aht."

kept us informed of what was going on, and this is the news we received down the ash hoist :

" *Ocean* and *Irresistible* 'as gorn darn, the Froggy's gone up in smoke : our blinkin' turn next.

" Pat, give us yer week's ' navy ' (rum ration) and I'll lift this bloomin' 'atch (armoured grating) and let yer aht ! "—" *Ajax*," 23 *King's Drive, Gravesend, Kent.*

Bugling in 'Indoostanee

AFTER the evacuation of Gallipoli a transport was conveying British troops to Egypt.

The O.C. wanted a trumpeter or bugler to follow him around during the daily lifeboat parade and to sound the " Dismiss " at the end. The only one available was an Indian trumpeter, who had not blown a trumpet or bugle since 1914. He was ordered for the duty.

On the first day, immediately after the inspection was over, the O.C. gave orders for the trumpeter to sound the " Dismiss." After the trumpeter had finished, the O.C., with a look of astonishment on his face, gasped, " What's that ? I never heard it sounded like that before."

Came a Cockney voice from the rear rank, " 'E sounded it in Indoostanee, sir."—*M. C., Surrey.*

" For 'eaven's sake, stop sniffin' ! "

OUR sector of the line at Loos was anticipating a raid by the Germans and the whole battalion was ordered to " stand to " all night.

Double sentries were posted at intervals of a few feet with orders to report any suspicious shadows in No Man's Land.

All eyes and ears were strained in an effort to locate any movement in the darkness beyond the parapet.

Strict silence was to be maintained, and the guns had been ordered to hang fire so that we might give the Germans a surprise welcome if they came over.

The ominous stillness was broken at last by a young Cockney saying to his pal standing with him on the fire-step : " For 'Eaven's sake, stop sniffin', Porky. How d'yer fink we'll 'ear Jerry if he comes acrorst ? "
—*C. J. Blake, 29a Collingbourne Road, Shepherd's Bush, W.12.*

Babes in the Salonika Wood

I WAS with the Salonika Force on the Dorian front. One night while an important raid was on my platoon was told off to seize a big wood between the lines and make sure it was clear of Bulgars, who could otherwise have enfiladed the main raiding party.

The orders were " absolute silence, and no firing unless the other side fires first." I halted my men behind a fold in the ground near the wood and called up two men and told them to creep forward and see if the wood was occupied.

It was nasty work as the first news of any Bulgars would almost certainly have been a bayonet in the back from somebody perfectly concealed behind a tree.

I asked them if the instructions were quite clear and one of them, Charlie, from Limehouse, whispered back :

" Yessir ! We're going to be the Babes in the Wood, and if the Wicked Uncles is out to-night we don't fire unless they fires first. Come on, George (to his companion), there's going to be some dirty work for the Little Robin Redbreasts to-morrer ! "—*A. Forsyth (late Army Cyclist Corps), 65 St. Martin's Lane, W.C.2.*

Bringing it Home to Him

FOR several months in 1917 matches were rationed in a Y.M.C.A. rest-camp canteen, somewhere in France. There entered during this time a war-worn Cockney, a drawn, tired look still in his eyes, and the mud of the trenches on his uniform and boots. He asked for cigarettes and matches, and was told there were no matches.

" Wot, no matches ? 'Ow am I goin' ter light me fags, miss ? "

" You see matches are rationed now," I said, " and the few we are allowed run out at once.

With a weary sigh, as if a great truth had dawned upon him, he said pathetically :

" Lumme, that do bring the war 'ome to a bloke, don't it, miss ? "— *Miss H. Campbell, Pennerly Lodge, Beaulieu, Hants.*

After the Feast

THE company dinner on Christmas Day 1917 was eaten in a large barn at Ribemont, on the Somme, and before this extra special feast began an affable " old sweat," one Billy Williams, of London Town, volunteered for the clearing-up party.

It was a long sitting and some considerable time before the men began to wander back to their billets, and it fell to the most capable of the orderlies to clear up the debris.

This had just been accomplished to the satisfaction of the orderly officer when out of the barn strode old Billy carrying a dixie full of beer. " Where are you going with that, Williams ? " asked the officer.

Springing smartly to attention, and with a pained look upon his face, old Billy replied : " This 'ere, sir ? Sick man in the 'ut, sir ! "—*R. E. Shirley (late The London Regiment),* 5 *Staunton Road, Kingston, Surrey.*

Wait for the " Two Pennies, Please "

NEAR the River Struma, on the Salonika front, in March 1917 our brigade H.Q. was on the extreme right of the divisional artillery and near a French artillery brigade.

For the purpose of maintaining communication a French telephonist was quartered in our dug-out. Whenever he wished to get into communication with his headquarters he unmercifully thumped the field telephone and in an excitable voice called out : " *'Ullo, mon capitaine,*" five or six times in half as many seconds.

Greatly impressed by one of these sudden outbursts, the adjutant's batman—a typical Cockney—exclaimed in a hurt voice : " Nah then, matey, jest cool yerself a bit till the young lidy tells yer to put in yer two coppers ! "—*F. G. Pickwick (301 Brigade R.F.A.),* 100 *Hubert Grove, Stockwell, S.W.9.*

The General Goes Skating

ONE horribly wet day during the winter of 1915 I met the Brigadier paying his morning visit to the front line and accompanied him along my section of the trench. Entering one fire-bay, the gallant General slipped and sat down uncommonly hard in the mud.

" 'Ere, chum, get up ; this ain't a skatin' rink."

Discipline stifled any desire on my part for mirth, but to my horror, the sentry in that bay, without turning away from his periscope, called over his shoulder in unmistakable Cockney accents: " 'Ere, chum, get up ; this ain't a blinkin' skatin' rink ! "

Fortunately the General's sense of humour was equal to the occasion, and he replied to the now horror-stricken sentry with an affable " Quite." —" *Company Commander," Orpington, Kent.*

" To Top Things Up "

DURING the early part of 1916 a few picked men from the North Sea Fleet were sent on a short tour of the Western Front to get an accurate idea of the work of the sister Service. One or two of these men were attached to my company for a few days in January when we were at Givenchy—a fairly lively spot at that time. The morning after their arrival there was some pretty heavy firing and bombing, which soon died down to normal.

Later in the day, as I was passing down the line, I asked one of our guests (an out-and-out Londoner) what he thought of things. He shook his head mournfully. " I thought the blighters was coming over after all that gunfire this morning, sir," he said. " I been in a naval action ; I been submarined ; I been bombed by aeroplanes ; and, blimey, I did 'ope I'd be in a bay'nit charge, just to top things up."—*L. V. Upward (late Capt. R.N.), 14 Lyndhurst Road, Hampstead, N.W.3.*

Luck in the Family

A COCKNEY R.A.S.C. driver had been knocked down and badly injured by a staff-officer's car.

On recovering consciousness in hospital, he highly amused the doctor by exclaiming, " Well, me gran'farver was kicked by a Derby winner, me farver knew Dr. Crippen, an' 'ere's me gets a blighty orf a brass-'at's Rolls-bloomin'-Royce. It's funny 'ow luck runs in famblys ! "—*J. F. C., Langdon Park Road, N. 6.*

" I'm Drownded "

WE were going into the line in front of Cambrai, in November 1917, and were walking in single file. The night was pitch black. Word came down at intervals from the leading file, " 'Ware wire," " 'Ware shell-hole."

My pal, a Cockney, was in front of me. Suddenly I heard a muffled curse—he had deviated and paid the penalty by falling into a particularly deep shell-hole filled with mud and water.

I stumbled to the edge of the hole and peered down and saw his face. I asked him if he was all right, and back came the reply, " Blimey, I'm drownded, so let the missus know I died like a sailor."

Three days later he did die . . . like a soldier.—*Ex-Rfn. John S. Brown, 94 Masterman Road, East Ham, E.6.*

Not a New World's Wonder

THE regiment had reached Hebuterne after marching from St. Amand, and a party of us was detailed to carry stuff up to the front line.

One of our number, a hefty Cockney, besides being in full marching order, had a bag of bombs and a couple of screw pickets. A sergeant then handed him some petrol tins. With a look of profound disgust, the

" There's only seven wonders."

Cockney dropped the tins and remarked, " Chuck it, mate ; there's only seven wonders in this blinkin' world."—*W. G. H. Cox (late 16th London Regt.*), 9 *Longstaff Crescent, Southfields, S.W.*18.

Lads of the Village

WHILE en route from the Western to the Italian front we were held up at an Italian wayside station and, hearing that we had some time to wait, our cook says, " Nah's our chance to make some tea."

So we dragged our boiler on to the end of the platform, scrounged some wood, and soon had the fire going and the water on the boil. " Nah we will get the tea and sugar," says the cook. When we returned we found that the chimney of the boiler had disappeared, smoke and flames were roaring up, and the water was ruined by soot.

An Italian soldier was standing by, looking on. " Somebody's pinched our chimbley," gasped the cook, " and I've got an idea that this Italian fellow knows somefing abaht it."

Back came the reply from the Italian, in pure Cockney : " I ain't pinched yer chimbley, mate ! "

" What ! yer speak our lingo ? " says the cook. " What part of the Village do yer come from ? "

" Clerkenwell," was the reply.

" Give us yer mitt," says the cook. " I'm from the same parish. And nah I knows that yer couldn't 'ave pinched our chimbley. It must have been one of them scrounging Cockneys."—*H. Howard, 26 Hanover Street, Islington, N.1.*

Before 1914, When Men Worked

NIGHT after night, for three weeks, with never a night off, we took ammunition up for the guns at Ypres in 1917. Sometimes we couldn't get back until 5 a.m. or 6 a.m.—and the day was spent feeding and gr ,ming the horses, cleaning harness, and a hundred odd jobs besides.

We had built a bit of a shack, and in this I was writing a letter home, and one of my drivers noticed my handwriting on the envelope.

" Coo, Corp ! You can't 'arf write ! 'Ow did yer learn it ? " he said.

I told him I had been in an insurance office before I joined up.

" Lumme ! " he exclaimed, " did yer *work* once, Corp ? "—*David Phillips (late R.F.A.), The Ship Inn, Soham, near Ely, Cambridgeshire.*

Their Fatigue

IN August 1915, our Division was moved to the Loos area in preparation for the battle which began on September 25, and I well remember the long march which brought us to our destination—the mining village of Nœux-les-Mines, about a mile from Mazingarbe.

We ended the hard and tiring journey at a spot where a huge slag-heap towered above our heads to a height of seventy or eighty feet. On our arrival here there were the usual fatigue parties to parade, and with everyone tired and weary this was an unthankful duty.

The youngest Cockney in my section, who was always cheerful, hearing me detailing men for fatigue, shouted out, " Come on, mites ; paride with spoons and mess-tins. The blinking fattygue party will shift this perishin' slag-heap from 'ere to Mazingarbe."—*Herbert W. Bassett (Cpl. attached 47th London Division), 41 Argyle Road, Sevenoaks, Kent.*

Teaching Bulgars the Three-card Trick

AT Butkova, on the right of Lake Doiran, in 1917, we had surprised the Bulgar and had pushed forward as far as the foot of the Belashitsa Mountains, the reserve position of the enemy.

After a sharp encounter we retired, according to plan, and on the return to our lines we heard murmurings in a nullah to our right.

"Find der lidy—dere you are—over yer go—under yer go—nah find 'er!"

Motioning to me and the section corporal, our platoon commander advanced cautiously towards the nullah and you can imagine our surprise when we discovered " Dido " Plumpton calmly showing the " three-card trick " to the two Bulgar prisoners he had been detailed to escort. He was telling his mystified audience : " Find der lidy— dere you are—over yer go—under yer go—*nah* find 'er ! "—*Alfred Tall (late 2nd East Kents), 204 Hoxton Street, N.1.*

3. HOSPITAL

" Tich " Meets the King

IN a large ward in a military hospital in London there was a little Cockney drummer boy of eighteen years who had lost both legs from shell fire. In spite of his calamity and the suffering he endured from numerous operations for the removal of bone, he was one of the cheeriest boys in the ward.

At that time many men in the ward had limbs amputated because of frost-bite, and it was quite a usual thing for a visitor to remark, " Have you had frost-bite ? "

Nothing made Tich so furious as the suggestion that *he* should have lost his limbs by any, to his mind, second-rate way. If he were asked, " Have you had frost-bite ? " he would look up with disgust and reply, " Naow—a flea bit me ! " If, however, he was asked, " Were you wounded ? " he would smile and say, " Not 'arf ! "

A visit was expected from the King, and the Tommies kept asking Tich what he would say if the King said, " Have you had frost-bite ? " " You wite ! " said Tich.

I was standing with the Sister near to Tich in his wheel-chair when the King approached. His Majesty at once noticed Tich was legless, and said in his kind way, " Well, my man, how are you getting on ? "

" Splendid, sir ! " said Tich.

" How did it happen ? " asked the King.

" Wounded, sir—shell," replied Tich, all smiles.

Tich's opinion of the King soared higher than ever.—*M. A. Kennedy (late V.A.D., Royal Military Hospital, Woolwich), 70 Windmill Hill, Enfield, Middlesex.*

Putting the Lid on It

IT was " clearing day " at the 56th General Hospital, Wimereux. Nurses and orderlies were having a busy morning getting ready the patients who were going to Blighty. Nearly all of them had been taken out to the waiting ambulances except my Cockney friend in the bed next to mine, who had just had an arm amputated and was very ill.

Two orderlies came down the ward bearing a stretcher with an oblong box fixed on to it (to prevent jolting while travelling). They placed it beside my friend's bed, and, having dressed him, put him in the box on the stretcher. Then a nurse wrapped him up in blankets, and after she had finished she said : " There you are. Feeling nice and comfortable ? "

" Fine," said he, " but don't put the lid on before I have kissed the orderly good-bye."—*E. C., Hackney, E.8.*

Riddled in the Sands

ONE of the finest exhibitions of Cockney spirit I saw during the war occurred in Mesopotamia after the Battle of Shaiba (April 1915), in which we had completely routed the Turkish army.

We were busy evacuating the wounded in boats across the six-mile stretch of water which separated us from Basra. A sergeant who had been hit by no fewer than six machine-gun bullets was brought down in a

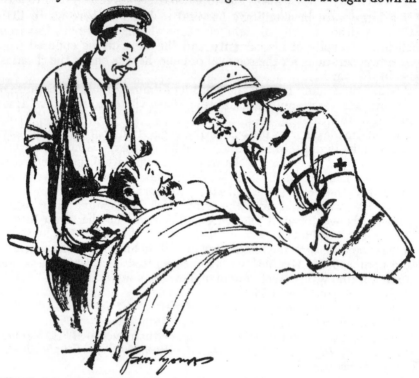

"Don't drop me in the water, sir. I'm so full of holes I'd be sure to sink."

stretcher to be put in one of the boats. As I superintended this manœuvre he said to me : " Don't drop me in the water, sir. I'm so full of holes I'd be sure to sink ! "—*F. C. Fraser (Lieut.-Col., Ind. Med. Service),* 309 *Brownhill Road, Catford, S.E.*6.

Season !

A COCKNEY soldier, badly hit for the third time, was about to be carried once more on board the ambulance train at Folkestone. When the bearers came to his stretcher, one said to the other, " What's it say on his ticket? "

" Season ! " said a voice from the stretcher.—*Rev. A. T. Greenwood, Wallington, Surrey.*

Where's the Milk and Honey ?

A MEDICAL Officer of a London division in Palestine was explaining to a dying Cockney in his field ambulance at Bethlehem how sorry he was that he had no special comforts to ease his last moments, when the man, with a cheery grin, remarked : " Oh, that's all right, sir. Yer reads as 'ow this 'ere 'Oly Land is flowing with milk and 'oney ; but I ain't seen any 'oney myself, and in our battery there's 15 men to a tin o' milk."—*E. T. Middleton, 32 Denmark Road, West Ealing, W.13.*

" Lunnon "

HE was my sergeant-major. Having on one occasion missed death literally by inches, he said coolly : " Them blighters can't 'it 'arf as smart as my missus when she's roused." I last saw him at Charing Cross Station. We were both casualties. All the way from Dover he had moaned one word—" Lunnon." At Charing Cross they laid his stretcher beside mine. He was half conscious. Suddenly he revived and called out, his voice boyish and jolly : " Good 'ole Charin' Crawss," and fell back dead.—*G. W. R., Norwich, Norfolk.*

Sparing the M.O.

IT was during some open warfare in France. The scene a small room full of badly wounded men ; all the remainder have been hurriedly removed, or rather, not brought in here. There are no beds ; the men lie on the floor close together.

I rise to stretch my back after dressing one. My foot strikes another foot. A yell of agony—the foot was attached to a badly shattered thigh.

An insistent, earnest chorus : " You *didn't* 'urt him, sir. 'E often makes a noise like that."

I feel a hand take mine, and, looking down, I see it in the grasp of a man with three gaping wounds. " It *wasn't* your fault, sir," he says, in a fierce, hoarse whisper.

And then I realise that not a soul in that room but takes it for granted that my mental anguish for my stupidity is greater than his own physical pain, and is doing his best to deaden it for me—one, at any rate, at great cost to himself.

In whose ranks are the world's great gentlemen ?—*" The Clumsy Fool," Guy's Hospital, E.C.*

" Robbery with Violence "

A COCKNEY soldier had his leg shattered. When he came round in hospital the doctors told him they had been obliged to take his leg off.

" Taken my leg off ? Blimey ! Where is it ? Hi, wot yer done wiv it ? Fer 'Eaven's sake, find my leg, somebody ; it's got seven and a tanner in the stocking."—*S. W. Baker, 23 Trinity Road, Bedford.*

Seven His Lucky Number

SCENE : the plank road outside St. Jean. Stretcher-bearers bringing down a man whose left leg had been blown away below the knee. A man coming up recognises the man on the stretcher, and the following conversation ensues :

" Hello, Bill ! " Then, catching sight of the left leg : " Blimey ! You ain't 'arf copped it."

The Reply : A faint smile, a right hand feebly pointing to the left sleeve already bearing *six* gold stripes, and a hoarse voice which said, " Anuvver one, and seven's me lucky number."—*S. G. Wallis Norton, Norton House, Peaks Hill, Purley.*

Blind Man's Buff

THE hospital ship *Dunluce Castle*, on which I was serving, was taking the wounded and sick from Gallipoli. Among the wounded brought on board one evening was a man who was badly hurt about his face. Our M.O. thought the poor chap's eyes were sightless.

Imagine our surprise when, in the morning, finding that his eyes were bandaged, he pulled himself to a sitting posture in bed, turned his head round and cried out, " S'y, boys, who's fer a gime of blind man's buff ? "

I am glad to say that the sight of one eye was saved.—*F. T. Barley, 24, Station Avenue, Prittlewell, Southend.*

Self-Supporting

AFTER being wounded at Ypres in July 1917, I was being sent home. When we were all aboard, an orderly came round with life-belts.

When he got to the next stretcher to me, on which lay a man who had his arm and leg in splints, he asked the usual question (" Can you look after yourself if anything happens going across ? "), and received the faint answer : " Lumme, mate, I've enough wood on me to make a raft."— *A. E. Fuller (36th Battery R.F.A.), 21 Pendragon Road, Downham Estate, Bromley.*

In the Butterfly Division

ON arriving at the hospital at Dames Camiers, we were put to bed. In the next bed to mine was a young Cockney who had lost three fingers of his right hand and his left arm below the elbow.

The hospital orderly came to take particulars of our wounds, etc. Having finished with me, he turned to the Cockney. Rank, name, and regimental number were given, and then the orderly asked, " Which division are you from ? "

" Why, the 19th," came the answer ; and then, as an afterthought, " that's the butterfly division, yer know, but I've 'ad me blinkin' wings clipped."—*H. Redford (late R.F.A.), 49 Anselm Road, Fulham, S.W.6.*

An Unfair Leg-Pull

I WAS working in a surgical ward at a base hospital, and among the patients was a Tommy with a fractured thigh-bone. He had his leg in a splint and, as was customary in these cases, there was an extension at the foot-piece with a heavy weight attached to prevent shortening of the leg.

This weight was causing him a good deal of pain, and as I could do nothing to alleviate it I asked the M.O. to explain to him the necessity for the extension. He did so and ended up by saying, " You know, we want your leg to be straight, old man."

The Tommy replied: "Wot's the good of making that leg strite w'en the uvver one's bowed?"—*Muriel A. Batey (V.A.D. Nurse), The North Cottage, Adderstone Crescent, Newcastle-upon-Tyne.*

He Saw It Through

IN the big general hospital at Colchester the next bed to mine was occupied by a typical Cockney who was very seriously wounded. It was little short of marvellous that he was alive at all.

Early one morning he became so ill that the hospital chaplain was sent to administer the Last Sacrament and the little Londoner's parents were telegraphed for.

About nine o'clock he rallied a little, and apparently realised that the authorities had given him up as hopeless, for with a great effort he half-sat up and, with his eyes ablaze, cried: " Wot? You fink I'm goin' ter die? Well, you're all wrong! I've bin in this war since it started, an' I intends to be in it at the finish. So I just *won't* die, to spite yer, see ? "

His unconquerable spirit pulled him through, and he is alive—and well —to-day !—*A. C. P. (late 58th (London) Division), Fulham, S.W.6.*

As Good as the Pictures

IN Salonika during 1916 I was taken to a field hospital, en route for the Base Hospital.

All merry and bright when lying down, but helpless when perpendicular, was a comrade in the next bed to me. We were to be moved next day.

I was interested in him, as he told me he belonged to " Berm-on-Sea," which happens to be my birth-place. Well, close to our marquee were the dump and transport lines, which we could plainly see through the entrance to the marquee.

Sister was taking our temperatures when we heard an explosion. Johnnie had " found " the dump. An officer ran through the marquee, ordering everyone to the dug-outs, and they promptly obeyed.

I looked at Bermondsey Bill. He said: " We are beat. Let's stop and watch the fireworks."

We were helpless on our feet. I tried to walk, but had to give it up. A new commotion then began, and Bill exclaimed : " Blimey, 'ere comes

Flying Fox rahnd Tattenham Corner." It was a badly-wounded and panic-stricken mule. It dashed through our marquee, sent Sister's table flying, found the exit and collapsed outside.

Sister returned (she was the right stuff) and said: " Hello, what's happened here? And you boys still in bed! Hadn't you better try and get to the dug-outs? "

Bermondsey Bill said: " We'll stick it aht nah, Sister, an' fancy we're at the pictures."—*J. W. Fairbrass, 131 Sutton Dwellings, Upper Street, Islington, N.1.*

Room for the Comforter

AT Etaples in 1916 I was in a hospital marquee with nothing worse than a sprained ankle. A Y.M.C.A. officer was visiting us, giving a cheery word here and there, together with a very welcome packet of cigarettes.

In the next cot to me was a young Cockney of the " Diehards," who had been well peppered with shrapnel. His head was almost entirely swathed in bandages, openings being left for his eyes, nose, and mouth.

" Well, old chap," said the good Samaritan to him, " they seem to have got you pretty badly."

" I'm all right, guv'nor—ser long as they leaves me an 'ole to put me fag in."—*A. E. Jeffreys (late 4th Q.O. Hussars), 24 Byne Road, Sydenham, S.E.26.*

" War Worn and Tonsillitis "

MY son, Gunner E. Smith (an " Old Contemptible "), came home on leave in September 1918, and after a day or two had something wrong with his throat. I advised him to see the M.O.

He went and came back saying, " Just look at this." The certificate said " War worn and tonsillitis."

He went to the hospital, and was kept in for three weeks. The first time I went to see him, he said, " What do you think of it? A 1914 man, and knocked over by a kid's complaint."—*F. Smith, 23 Saunders Road, Plumstead, S.E.18.*

" . . . Fort I was in 'Ell "

IT was at the American General Hospital in Rouen. There was the usual noise created by chaps under anæsthetic, swearing, shouting, singing, and moaning; but the fellow in the next bed to me had not stirred since they had brought him from the operating theatre many hours before.

Suddenly he sat up, looked around him in amazement, and said, " Strike, I've bin a-lying 'ere fer abaht two 'ours afraid ter open me peepers. I fort I was in 'ell."—*P. Webb (late E. Surreys), 68 Rossiter Road, Balham, S.W.12.*

Pity the Poor Fly !

AMONGST my massage patients at one of the general hospitals was a very cheery Cockney sergeant, who had been badly damaged by shrapnel. In addition to other injuries he had lost an eye.

One morning he was issued with a new eye, and was very proud of it. After admiring himself in a small mirror for a considerable time he turned to me and said, " Sister, won't it be a blinkin' sell for the fly who gets into my glass eye ? "—(*Mrs.*) *A. Powell*, 61 *Ritherdon Road, S.W.*17.

Temperature by the Inch

I WAS a patient in a general hospital in 1918, when a Cockney gunner was put into the bed next to mine. He was suffering from a severe form of influenza, and after ten days' treatment showed little sign of improvement.

One evening the Sister was going her rounds with the thermometers. She had taken our friend's temperature and registered it on the chart hanging over his head. As she passed to the next bed he raised himself and turned round to read the result. Then he looked over to a Canadian in a bed in the far corner of the ward, and this dialogue ensued :

Gunner : Canada !

Canadian : Hallo !

Gunner : Up agin.

Canadian : Go on ! How much ?

Gunner : 'Arf inch.

—*E. A. Taylor (late 4th London Field Ambulance), Drouvin, The Chase, Wallington, Surrey.*

" 'Arf Price at the Pickshers ! "

ON the way across Channel with a Blighty in 1917 I chummed up with a wounded Cockney member of the Sussex. His head was swathed in bandages.

" Done one o' me eyes in altergevver," he confided lugubriously. " Any blinkin' 'ow," he added in cheerier tones, " if that don't entitle a bloke to 'arf price at the pickshers fer the rest of 'is blinkin' natural I don't know wot will do ! "—*James Vance Marshall*, 15, *Manette Street, W.*1.

Twenty-four Stitches in Time

DURING the 1918 reverses suffered by the Turks on various fronts large numbers of mules were captured and sent to the veterinary bases to be reconditioned, sorted, and shod, for issue to various units in need of them. It was no mean feat to handle and shoe the worst-tempered brutes in the world. They had been made perfect demons through privation.

" Ninty," a shoeing-smith (late of Grange Road, Bermondsey), was laid out and savaged by a mule, and carried off to hospital. At night his bosom pal goes over to see how his " old china " is going on.

" 'Ow are ye, Ninty ? "

" Blimey, Ted, nineteen stitches in me figh an' five in me ribs. Ted—wot d'ye reckon they done it wiv ? A sewin' machine ? "—*A. C. Weekley (late Farrier Staff Sergeant, 20th Veterinary Hospital, Abbassair), 70 Denbigh Road, East Ham, E.6.*

His Second Thoughts

A BLUEJACKET who was brought into the Naval Hospital at Rosyth had had one of his legs blown off while he was asleep in his hammock. The late Mr. Thomas Horrocks Oppenshaw, the senior surgeon-in-charge, asked him what his first thought was when the explosion woke him up.

" My first thought was ' Torpedoed, by gum ! ' "

" And what did you think next ? "

" I think what I thought next was ' Ruddy good shot ! ' "—*H.R.A., M.D., Ilford Manor, near Lewes, Sussex.*

Hats Off to Private Tanner

THE following story, which emphasises the Cockney war spirit in the most adverse circumstances, and how it even impressed our late enemy, was related to me by a German acquaintance whose integrity is unimpeachable.

It was at a German prisoner-of-war clearing station in Douai during the summer of 1917, where wounded British prisoners were being cleared for prison-camp hospital.

A number of wounded of a London regiment has been brought in, and a German orderly was detailed to take their names and particulars of wounds, etc. Later looking over the orderly's list the German sergeant-major in charge came across a name written by the orderly which was quite unintelligible to the sergeant-major.

He therefore requested an intelligence officer, who spoke perfect English, to ask this particular man his name. The intelligence officer sought out the man, a Cockney, who had been severely wounded, and the following conversation took place.

I.O. : You are Number —— ?

Cockney : Yussir.

I.O. : What is your name ?

Cockney : Fourpence'a'penny.

I.O. : I understand this is a term of English money, not a name.

Cockney : Well, sir, I used to be called Tanner, but my right leg was took orf yesterday.

The final words of the intelligence officer, as related to me, were : " I could have fallen on the ' begrimed ruffian hero's ' neck and kissed him."—*J. W. Rourke, M.C. (ex-Lieut. Essex Regt.), 20 Mill Green Road, Welwyn Garden City.*

The Markis o' Granby

WOUNDED at Sheria, Palestine, in November 1917, I was sent to the nearest railhead in a motor-ambulance. A fellow-passenger —also from a London battalion—was wounded very badly in both thighs. The orderly who tucked him up on his stretcher before the start asked him if he would like a drink.

" No, thanks, chum—not nah," he replied ; " but you might arsk the driver to pull up at the ole Markis o' Granby, and we'll all 'ave one ! "

I heard later that he died in hospital.—*C. Dickens (late 2/20th London Regiment)*, 18 *Wheathill Road, Anerley, S.E.20.*

A One-Legged Turn

WOUNDED about half an hour after the final attack on Gaza, I awoke to consciousness in the M.O.'s dug-out.

" Poor old concert party," he said ; " you're the fifth ' Ragamuffin ' to come down."

Eventually I found myself sharing a mule-cart with another wounded man, but he lay so motionless and quiet that I feared I was about to journey from the line in a hearse.

The jolting of the cart apparently jerked a little life into him, for he asked me, " Got a fag, mate ? " With a struggle I lighted my one remaining cigarette.

After a while I asked him, " Where did you catch it, old fellow ? "

" Lumme," he replied, " if it ain't old George's voice." Then I recognised Sam, the comedian of our troupe.

" Got it pretty rotten in the leg," he added.

" Will it put paid to your comedy act, Sammy ? " I asked.

" Dunno," he replied with a sigh in his voice—" I'm tryin' to fink 'art a one-legged step dance."—*G. W. Turner (late 11th London Regt.)*, 10 *Sunny View, Kingsbury, N.W.9.*

4. HIGH SEAS

The Skipper's Cigar

BRADLEY (a Deptford flower-seller before joining up) was the "comic" of the stokers' mess deck.

He was always late in returning from shore leave. One Monday morning he returned half an hour "adrift," and was promptly taken before the skipper.

The skipper, a jovial old sort, asked him his reason for being adrift again, and Bradley replied:

"Well, sir, Townsend and me were waiting for the liberty boat, and I was telling him that if ever I sees the skipper round Deptford I'll let him 'ave a 'bob' bunch of flowers for a 'tanner,' and we looked round and the blinkin' boat was gorne."

The skipper smiled and dismissed him. On Christmas Day Bradley received a packet containing a cigar in it, with the following written on the box:

"For the best excuse of the year.—F. H. C., Capt."

I saw Bradley three years ago and he told me he still had that cigar in a glass case with his medals.—*F. H.* (*late Stoker, R.N.*), 18 *Little Ilford Lane, Manor Park, E.*12.

Breaking the Spell

WE were in a twelve-inch gun turret in a ship during the Dogger Bank action. The ship had been hit several times and big explosions had scorched the paint and done other damage. There came a lull in the firing, and with all of us more or less badly shaken there was a queer silence. Our captain decided to break it. Looking round at the walls of the turret he remarked in a Cockney, stuttering voice: "Well, lads, this blinking turret couldn't 'arf do with a coat of paint."— *J. Bone*, 84 *Victoria Road, Surbiton.*

A V.C.'s Story of Friendship

A TRANSPORT packed with troops and horses for the Dardanelles was suddenly hailed by a German cruiser and the captain was given a few minutes in which to abandon ship.

One young soldier was found with his arms round his horse's neck, sobbing bitterly, and when ordered to the boats he stubbornly refused to move. "Where my white-faced Willie goes *I* goes," he said proudly.

His loyalty to his dumb friend was rewarded, for the German cruiser fired twice at the transport, missed each time, and before a third effort British destroyers were on the scene to chase her away. It was then the young soldier had the laugh over his friends, for they in many cases arrived back on the ship half frozen and soaked to the skin!——*A Colonel, who wishes to remain anonymous: he holds the V.C., D.S.O., and M.C.*

The Stoker Sums it Up

I WAS on a large transport (normally a freighter), which had just arrived at a port on the East African coast, very rusty, and with a very un-naval-looking crew. We were taken in charge by a very small but immaculate gun-boat.

Orders were shouted to us by megaphone, and our men were leaning

" Do yer stop aht all night in 'er ? "

over the side watching the gun-boat rather enviously, when a Poplar stoker came up from below for a " breather," and summed up his mates' feelings in eight words.

Cupping his hands about his mouth, he shouted in a voice of thunder : " *Do yer stop aht all night in 'er ?* "—*R. N. Spence (late Lieutenant, R.N.V.R.), 214 Croydon Road, Beckenham.*

Channel Swimming his Next Job

DURING the war I had to fly a machine over to France. I had as passenger a Cockney Tommy who had recently transferred from the infantry to the R.F.C., and was joining his unit overseas.

Half-way over the Channel my engine failed and I glided down towards the nearest boat I could see. The landing was not very successful; the under-carriage struck the crest of a wave and the aeroplane hit the water almost vertically.

We were both thrown out, my passenger being somewhat badly knocked about in the process. We clung to the almost submerged

"I know me way across nah!"

wreckage and gazed hopefully towards the vessel I had sighted. She continued on her course, however.

The machine soon sank and we were left bobbing about in our life-belts. Things began to look far from bright, especially as my Cockney observer was in a pretty bad way by now. Suddenly the sun broke through the clouds, and the white cliffs of Grisnez, about eight miles away, stood out clearly.

"What's them hills, sir?" asked Tommy.

"Cape Grisnez, where Burgess landed after his Channel swim," I replied.

"Blimey," he said, "if we ever gets out of this perishing mess, and I can't get me old job back after the war, I'll be a blooming Channel swimmer. I know the ruddy way across nah."—"*Pilot R.F.C.*," *London, W.1.*

It Was a Collapsible Boat

I WAS one of the survivors of the transport ship *Leasowe Castle*. Just before she took her final plunge, I was standing on deck when an empty boat was seen drifting near by. Our section officer called for swimmers, and five or six men went overboard in a jiffy and brought the boat alongside.

There was a bit of a scuffle to get over the rail and into the boat, and one man jumped straight into her from a height of about thirty feet. To our dismay he went clean through—it was a collapsible boat !

No sooner had this happened than a typical Cockney voice said : " Blimey, he's got the anchor in his pocket, I'll bet yer ! "—*G. P. Gregory (late 272 M.G. Company), 107 Tunkar Street, Greenwich.*

Luck in Odd Numbers

WE were on board H.M.S. *Sharpshooter*, doing patrol off the Belgian coast. The signalman on watch, who happened to be a Cockney, suddenly yelled out : " Aeroplane on the starboard bow, sir."

The " old man," being fairly tired after a night of rain, said : " All right, it's only a friendly going back home."

About two minutes later the plane dropped three bombs, the last of which was much too close to be comfortable.

After our friend the signalman had wiped the splash off his face he turned round to the First Lieutenant and casually remarked : " Strike ! It's a thundering good job he wasn't hostile or he might have hit us."—*R. Walmsley, D.S.M., 47 Watcombe Road, South Norwood, S.E.25.*

" Your Barf, Sir ! "

WE were a mixed crowd on board the old *Archangel* returning " off leave " from Southampton to Havre on the night of January 6, 1917. The sea was calm, and a moon made conditions ideal for Jerry's " skimmers."

When we were well under way I chummed up with a typical son of the Mile End Road, one of the Middlesex men, and we talked for some time whilst watching the long, white zig-zag wake.

Then he suggested looking for a " kip." After nosing around several dark corners, a strip of carpet along the alley between the first-class cabins appealed to us, and quietly unslinging kit and putting our packs for a pillow, we made ourselves as comfortable as possible. During the process my pal jerked his thumb towards the closed doors and whispered " Orficers."

How long we had been asleep I don't know, but we were rudely awakened by a dull booming thud and a sound of splintering wood, and at the same time we were jolted heavily against the cabins. We hurriedly scrambled to our feet, looked at each other (no need to ask what had happened !), then grabbed our kit and made for the deck.

As my companion passed the last cabin he banged on the door with his fist and called out : " Oi, yer barf'll be ready in a minute, sir ! "—*A. E. Ulyett, 41 Smith Terrace, King's Road, Chelsea, S.W.3.*

" Mind My Coat "

MIDDLE watch, H.M.S. *Bulldog* on patrol off the Dardanelles : a dirty and a black night. A shout of " Man overboard ! " from the fore-gun crew. . . . We located an A.B. in the water, and with a long boat-hook caught his coat and pulled him towards the boat. As he drew nearer he cried : " Don't pull so bloomin' hard ; you'll tear my blinkin' coat ! "

Then we knew it was our " Ginger," from Poplar. Now " Ginger " has the life-saving medal. A few weeks after his ducking the ship struck a mine and the after-part went west : " Ginger " was discovered in the water, having gone in after a wounded sub-lieutenant who had been blown overboard.—*Henry J. Wood, D.S.M., 19 Gracechurch Street, E.C.3.*

" Wot's the Game—Musical Chairs ? "

IT was a bitterly cold day in December, somewhere in the North Sea. A section of mine-sweepers were engaged clearing an area well sown by Jerry's submarines. Suddenly the expected happened, and in a few minutes one of the sweepers was settling down fast by the stern.

Those who did not " go west " in the explosion were with difficulty picked up ; among them was a Cockney stoker rating. He arrived on board, wet, cold, and pretty well " pumped," and the bo'sun's peg of rum had almost disappeared between his chattering teeth when there was another explosion, and once again he was in a sinking ship.

His reply to the order " abandon ship," which he had heard for the second time within half an hour, was : " Wot blinkin' game's this— musical chairs ? "—*H. Waterworth, 32 Grasmere Road, Muswell Hill, N.10 (late Engineer-Lieutenant, R.N.R. (retired)).*

A Voice in the Dark

DAWN of a day in March 1917 found Submarine F3 on patrol near the Terschelling lightship. As we broke surface two German destroyers were seen only a few hundred yards away. We immediately dived again, and shortly afterwards the depth charges began to explode. Lower and lower we went until we touched the bottom.

Bangs to the right of us, bangs to the left of us, bangs above us— then one glorious big bang and out went the lights.

Deadly silence, and then out of the darkness came the voice of our Battersea bunting-tosser—" Anyone got six pennorth o' coppers ? "— *Frederick J. H. Alsford, 78 North Street, S.W.4.*

Why the Stoker Washed

H.M. Q ship 18 was sinking sixty miles off the French coast as the result of gunfire, after destroying a German submarine.

After getting away we had a hurried call-over and found that a Cockney fireman was missing. We hailed the ship which seemed about to take the plunge any minute, and at last the stoker appeared, spotlessly clean and dressed in " ducks."

He had to jump and swim for it. As we hauled him to our boat we asked him why he had waited to clean himself.

" Well," he explained, " if I am going to hell there's no need to let the blighter know I'm a stoker."—*Wm. C. Barnaby (late Chief Coxswain, R.N.), 7 Seville Street, Knightsbridge, S.W.1.*

Accounts Rendered

THE First-Lieutenant of a warship I was in, though a first-class sailor, had no great liking for clerical work, consequently the ship's store-books were perhaps not quite as they should have been.

" Well, *that* clears up those blessed accounts anyhow."

He therefore got an Able Seaman (who had been a London clerk in civil life) to give him a hand in his " off watches " in putting the books in order.

7

Shortly afterwards the ship stopped a torpedo and sank in eight minutes. Before the First-Lieutenant had very much time to look round he found himself in the " ditch."

As he was clambering out of the water on to the bottom of an upturned boat, he saw his " Chief Accountant " climbing up the other side, and the first thing he did was to reach out and shake hands with the A.B. across the keel of the boat, at the same time remarking, " Well, *that* clears up those blessed accounts anyhow."—*John Bowman* (*Able Seaman, R.N.V.R.*), 19 *Handel Mansions, W.C.1.*

An Ocean Greyhound

ON one occasion when the *Diligence* was " somewhere in the North Sea," shore leave was granted.

One of the sailors, a Cockney, returned to the ship with his jumper " rather swollen." The officer of the watch noticed something furry

" . . . To Nurse it Back to 'Ealth and Strength."

sticking out of the bottom of his jumper, and at once asked where he had got it from, fearing, probably, that he had been poaching.

The Cockney thought furiously for a moment and then said : " I chased it round the Church Army hut, sir, until it got giddy and fell over, and so I picked it up and brought it aboard to nurse it back to 'ealth and strength."—*J. S. Cowland,* 65 *Tylney Road, Forest Gate, E.7.*

Margate in Mespot.

OCTOBER 29, 1914—England declares war on Turkey and transports laden with troops sail from Bombay.

One evening, within a week, these transports anchor off the flat Mesopotamian coast at the top of the Persian Gulf. In one ship, a county

"Wot price this fer Margate ?"

regiment (95 per cent. countrymen, the remainder Cockney) is ordered to be the first to land. H.M.S. *Ocean* sends her cutters and lifeboats, and into these tumble the platoons at dusk, to be rowed across a shallow " bar."

Under cover of an inky darkness they arrive close to the beach by midnight. It is very cold, and all feel it the more because the kit worn is shorts and light khaki shirts.

In the stone-cold silence a whisper passes from boat to boat—" *Remove puttees ; tie boots round the neck ; at signal, boats to row in until grounded ; platoons to disembark and wade ashore.*"

So a shadowy line of strange-looking waders is dimly to be seen advancing through the shallow water and up the beach—in extended order, grim and frozen stiff. As dawn breaks they reach the sandy beach, and a few shots ring out from the distant Fort of Fas—but no one cares. Each and all are looking amazedly at the grotesque appearance of the line—silent, miserable figures, boots wagging round their necks, shorts rolled as high as possible, while their frozen fingers obediently cling to rifles and ammunition.

It is too much for one soul, and a Cockney voice calls out : " 'Ere, wot price this fer Margate ? "

The spell is broken. The Mesopotamian campaign begins with a great laugh !—*John Fiton, M.C., A.F.C., 9 High Grove, Welwyn Garden City, Herts.*

Urgent and Personal !

THE ss. *Oxfordshire*, then a hospital ship, was on her way down from Dar-es-salaam to Cape Town when she received an S.O.S. from H.M.T. *Tyndareus*, which had been mined off Cape Agulhas, very near the spot where the famous *Birkenhead* sank.

The *Tyndareus* had on board the 26th (Pioneer) Battalion, Middlesex Regiment, under the command of Colonel John Ward, then on their way to Hong Kong.

As the hospital boat drew near it was seen that the *Tyndareus* was very low in the water, and across the water we could hear the troops singing " Tipperary " as they stood lined up on the decks.

The lifeboats from both ships were quickly at work, every patient capable of lending a hand doing all he could to help. Soon we had hundreds of the Middlesex aboard, some pulled roughly up the side, others climbing rope-ladders hastily thrown down. They were in various stages of undress, some arriving clad only in pants.

On the deck came one who, pulled up by eager hands, landed on all fours with a bump. As he got up, hands and toes bleeding from contact with the side of the vessel, I was delighted to recognise an old London acquaintance. The following dialogue took place :

MYSELF : Hallo, Bill ! Fancy meeting you like this ! Hurt much ?

BILL : Not much. Seen Nobby Clark ? Has he got away all right ?

MYSELF (*not knowing Nobby Clark*) : I don't know. I expect so ; there are hundreds of your pals aboard.

BILL : So long. See you later. Must find Nobby ; he collared the " kitty " when that blinking boat got hit !—*J. P. Mansell (late) 25th Royal Fusiliers.*

Victoria ! (Very Cross)

WHILE I was an A.B. aboard H.M.S. *Aboukir* somewhere in the North Sea we received a signal that seven German destroyers were heading for us at full speed. We were ordered at the double to action stations.

My pal, a Cockney, weighing about 18 stone, found it hard to keep up

" Where's your station ? "
" Victoria—if I could only get there."

with the others, and the commander angrily asked him, " Where is your station ? "

To which the Cockney replied. " Victoria—if I could only get there."
—*J. Hearn, 24 Christchurch Street, S.W.*3.

He Saw the Force of It

IN February 1915 we beat out our weary patrol near the Scillies. Our ship met such heavy weather that only the bravest souls could keep a cheery countenance. Running into a growing storm, and unable to turn from the racing head seas, we beat out our unwilling way into the Atlantic.

Three days later we limped back to base with injured men, hatches stove in, winch pipes and boats torn away. Our forward gun was smashed and leaned over at a drunken angle.

Early in the morning the crew were taking a well-earned rest, and the decks were deserted but for the usual stoker, taking a breath of air after his stand-by watch. A dockyard official, seeing our damage, came on board, and, after viewing the wrecked gun at close quarters, turned to the stoker with the remark : " Do you mean to say that the sea smashed a heavy gun like that, my man ? "

The stoker, spitting with uncanny accuracy at a piece of floating wood overside, looked at the official : " Nah," he said, " it wasn't the blinking sea ; the ryne done it ! "—*A. Marsden* (*Engineer-Lieutenant-Commander, R.N.*), *Norbrook Cottage, Leith Park Road, Gravesend.*

New Skin—Brand New !

TWO mines—explosion—many killed—hundreds drowned. We were sinking fast. I scrambled quickly out of my hammock and up the hatchway. On deck, leaning against the bulkhead, was a shipmate, burned from head to foot. More amazing than fiction was his philosophy and coolness as he hailed me with, " 'Cher, Darby ! Got a fag ? I ain't had a 'bine since Pa died." I was practically " in the nude," and could not oblige him. Three years later I was taking part at a sports meeting at Dunkirk when I was approached by—to me—a total stranger. " What 'cher, Darby—ain't dead yet then. What ! Don't you remember H.M.S. *Russell* ? Of course I've altered a bit now—new skin—just like a two-year-old—brand new." Brand new externally, but the philosophy was unaltered.—" *Darby*," 405 *Valence Avenue, Chadwell Heath, Essex.*

A Zeebrugge Memory

DURING the raid on Zeebrugge, one of our number had his arms blown away. When things quietened a little my chum and I laid him on a mess table and proceeded to tend his wounds. My chum tried to light the mess-deck " bogey " (fire), the chimney of which had been removed for the action. After the match had been applied, we soon found ourselves in a fog. Then the wounded man remarked : " I say, chum ! If I'm going to die, let's die a white man, not a black 'un." The poor fellow died before reaching harbour.—*W. A. Brooks,* 14 *Ramsden Road, N* 11.

Another Perch in the Roost

ON the morning of September 22, 1914, when the cruisers *Aboukir*, *Hogue*, and *Cressy* were torpedoed, we were dotted about in the water, helping each other where possible and all trying to get some support. When one piece got overloaded it meant the best swimmers trying their luck elsewhere.

Such was my position, when I saw a piece of wreckage resembling a chicken coop, large enough to support four men. I reached it just ahead of another man who had been badly scalded.

We were both exhausted and unable to help another man coming towards us. He was nearly done, and my companion, seeing his condition, shouted between breaths: " Come along, ole cock. Shake yer bloomin' feavers. There's a perch 'ere for anover rooster."

Both were stokers on watch when torpedoed, and in a bad state from scalds. Exposure did the rest. I was alone, when picked up.—*W. Stevens (late R.M.L.I.), 23 Lower Range Road, Denton, near Gravesend.*

Uncomfortable Cargo

(A 12-in. shell weighs about 8 cwt. High explosives were painted yellow and "common" painted black.)

IN October 1914 H.M.S. *Venerable* was bombarding the Belgian coast and Thames tugs were pressed into service to carry ammunition to ships taking part in the bombardment.

The sea was pretty rough when a tug came alongside the *Venerable* loaded with 12-in. shells, both high explosive and common. Deck hands jumped down into the tug to sling the shells on the hoist. The tug skipper, seeing them jumping on the high explosives, shouted: " Hi! dahn there! Stop jumping on them yaller 'uns "; and, turning to the Commander, who was leaning over the ship's rail directing operations, he called out : " Get them yaller 'uns aht fust, guvnor, or them blokes dahn there 'll blow us sky high."—*A. Gill, 21 Down Road, Teddington, Middlesex.*

Good Old " Vernon "

SEVERAL areas in the North Sea were protected by mines, which came from the torpedo depot ship, H.M.S. *Vernon*. The mines floated several feet below the surface, being kept in position by means of wires attached to sinkers.

In my submarine we had encountered very bad weather and were uncertain of our exact position. The weather got so bad that we were forced to cruise forty feet below the surface.

Everything was very still in the control room. The only movements were an occasional turn of the hydroplanes, or a twist at the wheel, at which sat " Shorty " Harris, a real hard case from Shadwell.

Suddenly we were startled by a scraping sound along the port side. Before we could put our thoughts into words there came an ominous bump on the starboard side. *Bump! . . . bump! . . .* seven distinct thuds against the hull.   No one moved, and every nerve was taut.   Then " Shorty " broke the tension with, " Good old *Vernon*, another blinkin' dud."—*T. White*, 31 *Empress Avenue, Ilford.*

Any Time's Kissing Time !

A TORPEDO-BOAT destroyer engaged on transport duty in the Channel in 1916 had been cut in two by collision whilst steaming with lights out.   A handful of men on the after-part, which alone re-

" Ain't nobody a-goin' ter kiss me ? "

mained afloat, were rescued after several hours by another destroyer, just as the after-part sank.

A howling gale was raging and some of the survivors had to swim for it.

As the first swimmer reached the heaving side of the rescuing ship he was caught by willing hands and hauled on board.

When he got his breath he stood up and, shaking himself to clear the water somewhat from his dripping clothes, looked around with a smile at the " hands " near by and said : " *Well, ain't nobody a-goin' ter kiss me ?* "—*J. W., Bromley, Kent.*

The Fag End

THE captain of the troopship *Transylvania* had just called the famous " Every man for himself " order after the boat had received two torpedoes from a submarine.

The nurses had been got off safely in a boat, but our own prospects of safety seemed very remote. Along came a Cockney with his cigarettes and the remark, " Who'll 'ave a fag afore they get wet ? "—*A. W. Harvey, 97 Elderfield Road, Clapton, E.5 (late 10th London Regiment).*

" Spotty " the Jonah

ON board the s.s. *Lorrento* in 1917 with me was one " Spotty " Smith, A.B., of London. He had been torpedoed five times, and was reputed to be the sole survivor on the last two occasions. Such a Jonah-like reputation brought him more interest than affection from sailormen.

Approaching Bizerta—a danger spot in the South Mediterranean—one dark night, all lights out, " Spotty " so far forgot himself as to strike matches on deck. In lurid and forcible language the mate requested him " not to beat his infernal record on this ship."

" Spotty," intent on turning away wrath, replied, " S'elp me, sir, I've 'ad enough of me heroic past. This next time, sir, I made up me mind to go down with the rest of the crew ! "—*J. E. Drury, 77 Eridge Road, Thornton Heath.*

He Just Caught the Bus !

AFTER an arduous spell of patrol duty, our submarine had hove to to allow the crew a much-needed breather and smoke. For this purpose only the conning-tower hatch was opened so as to be ready to submerge, if necessity arose, with the minimum of delay.

Eager to take full advantage of this refreshing interlude, the crew had emerged, one by one, through the conning-tower and had disposed themselves in sprawling attitudes around the upper deck space, resting, reading, smoking.

Sure enough, soon the alarm was given, " Smoke seen on the horizon."

The order " Diving stations " was given and, hastily scuttling down the conning-tower, the crew rapidly had the boat submerging, to leave only the periscope visible.

The commander kept the boat slowly cruising with his periscope trained on the approaching smoke, ready for anything. Judge of his amazement when his view was obscured by the face of " Nobby " Clark (our Cockney A.B.) at the other end of the periscope. Realising at once that " Nobby " had been locked out (actually he had fallen asleep and had been rudely awakened by his cold plunge), we, of course, " broke surface " to collect frightened, half-drowned " Nobby," whose only ejaculation was : " Crikey ! I ain't half glad I caught the ole bus."—*J. Brodie, 177 Manor Road, Mitcham, Surrey.*

7*

Dinner before Mines !

"SOMEWHERE in the North Sea " in 1917, when I was a stoker on H.M.S. *Champion*, there were plenty of floating mines about.

One day, several of us were waiting outside the galley (cook house) for our dinners, and the cook, a man from Walworth, was shouting out the number of messes marked on the meat dishes which were ready for the men to take away.

He had one dish in his hand with no number marked on it, when a stoker rushed up and shouted : " We nearly struck a mine—missed it by inches, Cookey." But Cookey only shouted back : " Never mind about blinkin' mines nah ; is this *your* perishin' dish with no tally on it ? "—*W. Downs (late stoker, R.N.), 20 Tracey Street, Kennington Road, S.E.*

A Philosopher at Sea

WE were a helpless, sorry crowd, many of us with legs in splints, in the hold of a " hospital " ship crossing from Boulogne. The boat stopped dead.

" What are we stopping for, mate ? " one man asked the orderly.

" The destroyers wot's escortin' of us is chasin' a German submarine. I'm just a-goin' on deck agin to see wot's doin'." As he got to the ladder he turned to say : " Nah, you blokes : if we gits 'it by a torpedo don't go gettin' the ruddy wind up an' start rushin' abaht tryin' ter git on deck. It won't do yer wounds no bloomin' good ! "—*E. Bundy (late L/Corporal, 1/5th L.F.A., 47th Division), 4 Upton Gardens, Barkingside, Ilford, Essex.*

Extra Heavyweight

AMONGST the crew of our mine-sweeper during the war " Sparks," the wireless operator, was a hefty, fat chap, weighing about 18 stone. One day while clearing up a mine-field, laid overnight by a submarine, we had the misfortune to have four or five of the mines explode in the " sweep."

The explosion shattered every piece of glass in the ship, put the engines out of action, and nearly blew the ship out of the water.

" Bill," one of our stokers—a Cockney who, being off watch, was asleep in his bunk—sat up, yawned, and exclaimed in a sleepy voice : " 'Ullo, poor ole ' Sparks ' fallen out of 'is bunk again ! 'E'll 'urt 'isself one of these days ! "—*R.N.V.R., Old Windsor, Berks.*

Three Varieties

THE boat on which I was serving as a stoker had just received two new men as stokers.

On coming down the stokehold one of them seemed intent on finding out what different perils could happen to him.

After he had been inquiring for about an hour a little Cockney, rather bored, got up and said, " Now look here, mate. The job ain't so bad, looking at it in this light—you've three ways of snuffing it : one is *burnt* to death, the other is *scalded* to death ; or, if you're damn lucky, *drowned*. That's more chances than they have upstairs."—*B. Scott (late Stoker, H.M.S. " Marlborough "), 29 Stanley Road, Southend-on-Sea, Essex.*

He was a Bigger Fish

THE battleship in which I was serving was picking up survivors from a torpedoed merchantman in the North Atlantic. They had been drifting about for hours clinging to upturned boats and bits of gear that had floated clear of the wreckage.

Our boat had picked up three or four half-drowned men and was just

" Wot d'yer fink I am—a blinkin' tiddler ? "

about to return to the ship when we espied a fat sailor bobbing about with his arms around a plank. We pulled up close to him and the bow-man leaned out with a boat-hook and drew him alongside.

He seemed to have just strength enough left to grasp the gunwale, when we were surprised to hear him shout, in an unmistakable Cockney voice : " All right, cockey, un'itch that boat 'ook. Wot d'yer fink I am—a blinkin' tiddler ? "—*Leslie E. Austin, 6 Northumberland Avenue, Squirrels Heath, Romford, Essex.*

The " Arethusa " Touch

DURING the action off Heligoland in August 1914 the light cruiser *Arethusa* came under a hot fire. A shell penetrated the chief stoker's mess, knocked a drawer full of flour all over the deck, but luckily failed to explode.

A Cockney stoker standing in the mess had a narrow escape, but after surveying the wreckage and flour-covered deck all he said was : " Blowed if they ain't trying to make a blinkin' duff in our mess ! "—*C. H. Cook (Lieut., R.N.V.R.), 91 Great Russell Street, W.C.1.*

His Chance to Dive

DURING the early part of 1917, whilst I was serving with one of H.M. transports, we had occasion to call at Panama for coaling purposes before proceeding to England via New York.

One of our many Cockney sailors was a fine swimmer and diver. He took every opportunity to have what he termed " a couple of dives."

Owing to the water being rather shallow immediately along the quay, his diving exhibitions were limited to nothing higher than the forecastle, which was some 30 ft. His one desire, however, was to dive from the boat-deck, which was about 60 ft. Whilst steaming later in the front line of our convoy, which numbered about forty-two ships, we became the direct target of a deadly torpedo. Every soul dashed for the lifeboats.

After things had somewhat subsided I found our Cockney friend— disregarding the fact that our ship was badly damaged and was now listing at an almost impossible angle—posing rather gracefully for a dive. He shouted, " Hi ! hi ! Wot abaht this 'un ? I told yer I could do it easy ! " He then dived gracefully and swam to a lifeboat.—*Bobbie George Bull (late Mercantile Marine), 40 Warren Road, Leyton, E.10.*

Wot Abaht Wot ?

IN 1917 our job on an armed merchantman, H.M.A.S. *Marmora*, was to escort food ships through the danger zone. One trip we were going to Sierra Leone, but in the middle of the afternoon, when about two days out from Cardiff, we were torpedoed.

The old ship came to a standstill and we all proceeded to action stations. Just as we were training our guns in the direction of the submarine another torpedo struck us amidships and smashed practically all the boats on the port side.

" Abandon ship " was given, as we were slowly settling down by the bows. Our boat was soon crowded out, and there seemed not enough room for a cat. The last man down the life-line was " Tubby," our cook's mate, who came from Poplar.

When he was about half way down the boat was cut adrift and " Tubby " was left hanging in mid-air. " Hi ! " he shouted. " What abaht it ? "

Another Cockney (from Battersea) replied : " What abaht what ? "

" Abaht coming back for me."

" What do you take us for," said the lad from Battersea ; " do yer fink we all want the sack fer overcrowdin' ? "

" Tubby " was, of course, picked up after a slight immersion.—*C. Phelps (late R.M.L.I.), 36 Oxford Road, Putney, S.W.15.*

Water on the Watch

I WAS one of the crew of a patrol boat at the Nore in the winter of 1915. Most of the crew had gone to the dockyard to draw stores and provisions, and I was down in the forecastle when I heard a shout for

help. I nipped up on deck and discovered that our Cockney stoker had fallen overboard. He was trying to swim for dear life, though handicapped by a pair of sea boots and canvas overalls over his ordinary sailor's rig. A strong tide was running and was carrying him away from the boat.

I threw a coil of rope to him, and after a struggle I managed to haul him aboard. I took him down to the boiler room and stripped off his clothes.

Around his neck was tied a bootlace, on the end of which was hanging a metal watch, which he told me he had bought the day before for five shillings. The watch was full of sea water, and there was an air bubble inside the glass. As he held it in his hand he looked at it with disgust. When I said to him what a wonderful escape his

" A perishin' spirit level."

wife had had from being left a widow, he replied, " Yes, it was a near fing, ole' mate, but wot abaht me blinkin' bran' noo watch ? It's gone and turned itself into a perishin' spirit level, and I've dipped five bob."—*W. Carter, 55 Minet Avenue, Harlesden, N.W.10.*

A Gallant Tar

AN awe-inspiring sight met the eyes of the 29th Division as they came into view of Gallipoli on the morning of April 25, 1915. Shells from our ships were bursting all over that rugged coast, and those from the enemy bespattered the water around us.

While I gazed at the scene from the deck of the *Andania*, carried away by the grandeur of it all, my reverie was broken by a Cockney voice from the sailor in charge of the small boat that was to take us ashore.

" 'Op in, mate," said the sailor. " I've just lorst three boats. I reckon I'll soon have to take the blooming island meself."

His fourth trip was successfully accomplished, but the fifth, alas ! was fatal both to this gallant tar and to the occupants of his boat.—*G. Pull (late 1st R. Innis. Fus.), 20 Friars Place Lane, Acton, W.3.*

A Cap for Jerry

DAWN, September 1, 1917, H.M. destroyer *Rosalind* was engaged with enemy ships off Jutland. I was serving on one of the guns, and we were approaching the enemy at full speed. The ship was vibrating from end to end, and the gun fire, the bursting of shells, and the smell of the cordite had got our nerves at high tension.

When we were very near the enemy one of the German ships blew up completely in a smothering cloud of smoke.

At this time something went wrong with our ammunition supply, and we had used up all that we usually carried on the gun platform. One of the gun's crew, a Cockney, put his cap in the breech, and said " Quick ! Send 'em this to put the lid on that blinkin' chimney." We all had to laugh, and carried on.—*W. E. M. (late H.M.S. " Rosalind "), 19 Kimberley Road, Leytonstone, E.11.*

Give 'im 'is Trumpet Back

AFTER the *Britannia* was torpedoed in November 1918, and the order " Abandon Ship " had been given, the crew had to make their way as best they could to a destroyer which had pulled up alongside.

Hawsers were run from the *Britannia* to the destroyer, down which we swarmed. Some got across. Others were not so lucky. One of the unlucky ones who had a free bath was a Cockney stoker nicknamed " Shorty," who, after splashing and struggling about, managed to get near the destroyer.

To help him a burly marine dangled a rope and wooden bucket over the side, this being the only means of rescue available. The marine, who was puffing at a large meerschaum pipe, called out : " Here y'are, Shorty, grab 'old o' this bucket an' mind yer don't drown yerself in it."

" Shorty " makes sure of bucket, then wipes the water from his eyes, looks up to the marine, and says : " Garn, give the kid 'is trumpet back."—*G. Lowe (ex-R.M.L.I.), 18 Brocas Street, Eton, Bucks.*

Getting the Range

IT was on H.M. monitor *General Wolfe*, my first ship, and this was my first taste of actual warfare.

We were lying anchored off the Belgian coast, shelling an inland objective with our 18-in. gun, the ammunition for which, by the way, was stowed on the upper deck.

All ratings other than this gun's crew were standing by for " action stations." Just then the shore batteries opened fire on us. The first shot fell short, the next went over.

A Cockney member of my gun's crew explained it thus : " That's wot they calls a straddle," he said. " They finds our range that way—one short, one over, and the next 'arf way between. Got a 'bine on yer before it's too late ? "—*Regd. W. Ayres (late A.B., R.N.)*, 50 *Lewisham High Road, New Cross, S.E.14.*

Coco-nut Shies

EARLY in 1915 I was attached to one of our monitors in the Far East. We had painted the ship to represent the country we were fighting in. The ship's side was painted green with palm trees on it, and up the funnel we painted a large coco-nut tree in full bloom.

When we went into action, a shell penetrated our funnel, and a splinter caught my breech worker in the shoulder. After we had ceased fire we carried him below on a stretcher. Looking at the funnel, he said, " Blimey, Tom, 'appy 'Ampstead and three shies a penny. All you knock down you 'ave."

Later I went to see him in Zanzibar Hospital, and told him he had been awarded the D.S.M. He seemed more interested to know if the German had got his coco-nut than in his own award.—*T. Spring (late Chief Gunner's Mate, R.N.)*, 26 *Maidenstone Hill, Greenwich, S.E.10.*

" Any more for the ' Skylark ' ? "

PASSING through the Mediterranean in 1916, the P. & O. liner *Arabia*, returning from the East with a full complement of passengers, was torpedoed.

I was in charge of a number of naval ratings returning to England, who, of course, helped to get the boats away.

While some of my boys were getting out one of the port boats a woman passenger, who had on a Gieves waistcoat, rushed up, holding the air tube in front of her, and shouting hysterically, " Oh, blow it up some-body, will somebody please blow it up ? " A hefty seaman with a couple of blasts had the waistcoat inflated, and as he screwed up the cap said, " Look 'ere, miss, if yer 'oller like that Fritzy will 'ear yer and he *will* be angry. 'Ere you are, miss, boat all ready ; 'op in."

Then, turning round to the waiting passengers, he said, " Come on, any more for the ' Skylark ' ? "—*F. M. Simon (Commander, R.N., retd.)*, 99 *Lower Northdown Road, Margate.*

Still High and Dry

WHILST patrolling on an exceptionally dark night, the order being " No lights showing," we had the misfortune to come into collision with a torpedo boat. Owing to the darkness and suddenness of the collision we could not discover the extent of the damage, so the officer of the watch made a " round," accompanied by the duty petty officer.

Upon reaching a hatchway leading down to the stokers' mess deck, he called down : " Is there any water coming in down there ? " In answer a Cockney stoker, who was one of a number in their hammocks, was heard to reply : " I don't fink so ; it ain't reached my 'ammock yet."—*J. Norton (late Ldg. Stoker, R.N.), 24 Lochaline Street, Hammersmith, W.6.*

Trunkey Turk's Sarcasm

WE were serving in a destroyer (H.M.S. *Stour*) in 1915, steaming up and down the East Coast. As we passed the different coastguard stations the bunting-tosser had to signal each station for news.

One station, in particular, always had more to tell than the others. One day this station signalled that a merchant ship had been torpedoed and that German submarines were near the coast.

My Cockney chum—we called him Trunkey Turk because of his big nose—asked the bunting-tosser for his news as he was coming down from the bridge, and when he was told, said, " Why didn't you ask them if they saw a tin of salmon in their tot of rum to-day ? "—*J. Tucknott, 2 Wisbeach Road, West Croydon.*

Running Down the Market

ON board a destroyer in the North Sea in 1916. Look-out reports, " Sail ahead, sir."

The captain, adjusting his glasses, was able to make out what at first appeared to be a harmless fisherman.

As we drew nearer we could see by her bow wave that she had something more than sails to help her along : she had power.

" Action Stations " was sounded, the telegraphs to engine-room clanged " Full speed ahead." Our skipper was right. It was a German submarine, and as our foremost gun barked out we saw the white sails submerge.

Depth charges were dropped at every point where we altered course. Imagine our surprise to find the resulting flotsam and jetsam around us consisted of trestles, boards, paint-brushes, boxes, and a hat or two, which the crafty Germans had used to camouflage their upper structure.

The scene was summed up neatly by " Spikey " Merlin, A.B., a real product of Mile End Road : " Lor' luv old Aggie Weston, we've run dahn the blinkin' Calerdonian Markit."—*A. G. Reed (late R.N.), 15 William Street, Gravesend, Kent.*

Five to One against the " Tinfish "

H M.S. *Morea*, on convoy duty, was coming up the Channel when the silver streak of a " tinfish " was seen approaching the port side. The *Morea* was zig-zagging at the time, so more helm was given her to dodge the oncoming torpedo.

The guns' crews were at action stations and were grimly waiting for the explosion, when a Cockney seaman gunner sang out, " I'll lay five to one it doesn't hit us."

This broke the tension, and, as luck would have it, the torpedo passed three yards astern.—*J. Bowman* (R.N.), 19 *Handel Mansions, Handel Street, W.C.1.*

A Queer Porpoise

I N September 1914 I was in H.M.S. *Vanguard*, patrolling in the North Sea. One day four of us were standing on the top of the foremast turret, when all of a sudden my pal Nobby shouted to the bridge above us, " Periscope on the port bow, sir." At once the captain and signalman levelled their telescopes on the object. Then the captain looked over the bridge and shouted, " That's a porpoise, my man."

Nobby looked up at the bridge and said, " Blimey, that's the first time I've seen a porpoise wiv a glass eye."

He had no sooner said it than the ship slewed to port and a torpedo passed close to our stern, the signalman having spotted the wake of a torpedo.—*M. Froggat*, 136 *Laleham Road, Catford, S.E.*

" Hoctopus " with One Arm

A T the time when the German submarine blockade was taking heavy toll of all general shipping I was serving aboard a destroyer doing escort work in the Channel. One night three ships had been torpedoed in quick succession, and we understood they were carrying wounded.

We were kept pretty busy dodging from one place to another to pick up survivors, and during our " travels " a ship's boat was sighted close at hand. In the darkness we could just make out the figure of a soldier endeavouring to pull a full-sized oar.

After hailing the boat someone on our destroyer shouted, " Why didn't you get some more oars out ? " A voice replied : " Don't be so funny. D'yer fink I'm a hoctopus ? Our engines 'ave all conked aht." Which remark raised a laugh from the entire boatload.

On getting closer alongside the tragedy dawned on us. This Cockney was the only man (out of about thirty) who was sound enough to handle an oar, and he only had one arm and a half.—*H. G. Vollor (late Ldg.-seaman, R.N.)*, 73 *Playford-Road, Finsbury Park, N.4.*

Interrupted Duel

THE C.O. of my ship had his own way of punishing men who were brought before him for fighting.

He would send for the gunner's mate and tell him to have the two men up on the upper deck, in view of the ship's company, armed with single-sticks. The gunner's mate would get them facing each other, give them the first order of " Cutlass practice "—" Guard ! " then " Loose play." At that order they would go for each other hammer and tongs till one gave in.

Such a dispute had to be settled one day while we were patrolling the North Sea. The combatants were just getting warm to it when the alarm buzzers went—enemy in sight.

The gunner's mate, who was refereeing the combat, said : " Pipe dahn, you two bounders. Hop it to your action stations, and don't forget to come back 'ere when we've seen them off."

Fortunately they were both able to " come back."—*John M. Spring* (*late P.O., R.N.*), *Bank Chambers, Forest Hill, S.E.23.*

Enter Dr. Crippen

OUR ship, the s.s. *Wellington*, was torpedoed on August 14, 1917, and we were a despondent crew in the only two boats. The U-boat that had sunk our ship appeared and we were wondering what was going to happen to us.

As the U-boat bore down upon us my mate, Nigger Smith (from Shoreditch) spotted its commander, who wore large spectacles, on its conning tower bridge. " Blimey," said Nigger, " 'ere's old Crippen ! "—*J. Cane* (*late Gunner, R.M.*), *73 Rahere Street, E.C.1.*

The All-seeing Eye

MY pal Pincher and I volunteered out of the destroyer *Vulture* for the Q-boats, and got detailed for the same mystery ship. After a lot of drills—"Abandon ship," " Panic crews away," etc.—we thought we were hot stuff.

Knocking about the Channel one fine day the order came, " Panic crews to stations." Thinking it was drill, Pincher and I nipped into our boat, when the after fall carried away, letting Pincher, myself, and crew into the " drink."

Pincher must have caught sight of the periscope of a U-boat, for on coming up (although he couldn't swim much) he said when I grabbed him : " Lumme, I'm in for fourteen penn'orth ! " (14 days 10A, i.e. punishment involving extra work). " There's the skipper lookin' at me through 'is telescope, and they aven't piped 'ands to bathe yet."— *P. Willoughby* (*late R.N.*), *186 Evelyn Street, S.E.8.*

The Submarine's Gamps

WHILE patrolling in the Sea of Marmora a British submarine came across several umbrellas floating in the sea, presumably from a sunken ship. Some of them were acquired by the crew.

On the passage down the Dardanelles the submarine was damaged in the conning tower by gun-fire from the Turkish batteries, and water began to come in.

At this critical stage I overheard one sailor remark to another, " I say, Bill, don't you think it is about time we put those blinkin' umbrellas up ? "
—*Naval officer retired, Hampstead, N.W.*3.

Polishing up his German

ABOUT January 15, 1915, we were on patrol duty in the North Sea. Near daybreak we came across a number of German drifters, with carrier pigeons on board, that were suspected of being in touch with submarines.

We were steaming in line abreast, and the order was signalled for each ship to take one drifter in tow. Our Jerry objected to being towed to England, and cut our tow-rope, causing us a deal of trouble.

Our captain was in a rage and shouted down from the bridge to the officer of the watch, " Is there anyone on board who can speak German ? "

The officer of the watch called back, " Yes, sir ; Knight speaks German " —meaning an officer.

So the captain turned to the bos'n's mate and said, " Fetch him." The bos'n's mate sends up Able Seaman " Bogey " Knight, to whom the captain says, over his shoulder : " Tell those fellows that I'll sink 'em if they tamper with the tow again."

With a look of surprise Bogey salutes and runs aft. Putting his hands to his mouth, Bogey shouts :

" Hi ! there, drifterofsky, do yer savvy ? " and makes a cut with his

"I makes de shoot."

hand across his arm. " If yer makes de cut agin, I makes de shoot —(firing an imaginary rifle)—and that's from our skipper ! "

Bogey's mates laughed to hear him sprachen the German ; but Jerry didn't cut the tow again.—*E. C. Gibson,* 3 *Slatin Road, Stroud, Kent.*

5. HERE AND THERE

Answered

WE were a working party of British prisoners marching through the German barracks on our way to the parcel office. Coming towards us was a German officer on horseback. When he arrived abreast of us he shouted in very good English: " It's a long way to Tipperary, boys, isn't it ? " This was promptly answered by a Cockney in the crowd: " Yus ! And it's a ruddy long way to Paris, ain't it ? "—*C. A. Cooke, O.B.E. (late R.N.D.), 34 Brandram Road, Lee High Road, S.E.*

A Prisoner has the Last Laugh

SCENE : A small ward in Cologne Fortress, occupied by about twelve British prisoners of war.

Time : The German M.O.'s inspection. Action : The new sentry on guard in the corridor had orders that all must stand on the M.O.'s entry. Seeing the M.O. coming, he called out to us. We jumped to it as best we could, except one, a Cockney, who had just arrived minus one leg and suffering from other injuries.

Not knowing this, the sentry rushed over to him, yelling that he must stand. Seeing that no notice was being taken, he pointed his rifle directly at the Cockney. With an effort, since he was very weak and in great pain, the Cockney raised himself, caught hold of the rifle and, looking straight at it, said: " Dirty barrel—seven days ! "

The M.O., who had just arrived, heard the remark, and, understanding it, explained it to the sentry, who joined in our renewed laughter.—*A. V. White, 35 Mayville Road, Leytonstone, E.11.*

Not Yet Introduced

WE were prisoners of war, all taken before Christmas 1914, and had been drafted to Libau, on the Baltic coast.

Towards the end of 1916 a party of us were working on the docks when a German naval officer approached and began talking to us.

During the conversation he said he had met several English admirals and named some of them.

After a little while a Cockney voice from the rear of our party said, " 'Ave you ever met Jellicoe, mate ? "

The officer replied in the negative, whereupon the Cockney said, " Well, take yer bloomin' ships into the North Sea : he's looking for yer."—*F. A. F. (late K.O.Y.L.I.), 4 Shaftesbury Road, W.6.*

On the Art of Conversation

IN 1916 the British R.N.A.S. armoured cars, under Commander Oliver Locker-Lampson, went from Russia to Rumania to help to stem the enemy's advance.

One day, at the frontier town of Reni, I saw a Cockney petty officer engaged in earnest conversation with a Russian soldier. Finally, the two shook hands solemnly, saluted, and parted.

" Did he speak English ? " I asked when the Russian had gone away. " Not 'im," said the P.O.

" Perhaps you speak Russian ? " I asked, my curiosity aroused. " No bloomin' fear ! " he said, for all the world as if I had insulted him.

" Then how do you speak to each other ? "

" That's easy, sir," he said. " 'E comes up to me an' says ' Ooski, kooski, wooski, fooski.' ' Same to you,' says I, ' an' many of 'em, ol' cock.' ' Bzz-z-z, mzz-z-z, tzz-z-z,' says 'e. ' Thanks,' I says. ' Another time, ol' boy. I've just 'ad a couple.' ' Tooralski, looralski, pooralski,' 'e says. ' Ye don't say ! ' says I. ' An' very nice, too,' I says, ' funny face ! '

" 'Armony," he explained. " No quarrellin', no argifyin', only peace an' 'armony. . . . Of course, sir, every now an' again I says ' Go to 'ell, y' silly blighter ! ' "

" What for ? "

He looked at me coldly. " 'Ow do I know but what the blighter's usin' insultin' words to me ? " he asked.—*R. S. Liddell, Rosebery Avenue, E.C.1.*

Down Hornsey Way

HERE is a story of the Cockney war spirit at home. We called him " London " as he was the only Londoner in the troop. Very pale and slight, he gave the impression of being consumptive, yet he was quite an athlete, as his sprinting at the brigade sports showed.

We had been on a gunnery course up Hornsey way, and with skeleton kit were returning past a large field in which were three gas chambers used for gas drill. No one was allowed even to go in the field unless equipped with a gas-mask. Suddenly a voice called out, " Look, there's a man trying to get in yon chamber."

We shouted as loud as we could, but beyond waving his arms the figure —which looked to be that of a farm labourer—continued to push at the door. Then I saw " London " leap the gate of the field and sprint towards the chamber. When he was about 50 yards off the man gave a sudden lurch at the door and passed within. We called to " London " to come back, but a couple of seconds later he too was lost from view.

One minute—it seemed like an hour—two, three, five, ten, and out came " London." He dragged with him the bulky labourer. Five yards from the chamber he dropped. Disregarding orders, we ran to his assistance. Both his eyes were swollen, his lip was cut, and a large gash on the cheek-bone told not of gas, but of a fight.

He soon came to—and pointing to his many cuts said, " Serves me right for interfering. Thought the fellah might have been gassed, but there's none in there ; and hell—he *can* hit."—" *Selo-Sam,*" *late Yorks Dragoons.*

" . . . Wouldn't Come Off "

HE hailed from Walworth and was the unfortunate possessor of a permanent grin.

The trouble began at the training camp at Seaford when the captain was inspecting the company.

" Who are you grinning at ? " said he. " Beg parding," replied Smiler, " but I can't help it, sir. I was born like it."

On the " other side " it was the same. The captain would take Smiler's grin as a distinct attempt to " take a rise " out of him. The result was that all the worst jobs seemed to fall upon the luckless Londoner.

He was one of the " lucky lads " selected one night for a working party. While he was so engaged Jerry sent over a packet which was stopped by Smiler, and it was quickly apparent to him and to us that this was more than a Blighty one.

As I knelt by his side to comfort him he softly whispered, " Say, mate, has Jerry knocked the blinkin' smile off ? "

" No," I replied, " it's still there."

Then, with a strange light in his eyes, he said, " Won't the captain be darned wild when he hears about it ? "—*P. Walters (late Cpl., Royal Fusiliers*), 20 *Church Street, Woolwich, S.E.*18.

When in Greece . . . ?

ON a Greek island overlooking the Dardanelles, where we were stationed in 1916, my pal Sid and I were one day walking along a road when we saw approaching us a poor-looking knock-kneed donkey. On its back, almost burying it, was a huge pile of brushwood, and on top of this sat a Greek, whilst in front walked an elderly woman, probably his wife, also with a load of twigs on her back.

Sid's face was a study in astonishment and indignation. " Strewth ! " he muttered to himself. To the Greek he said, " Hi, 'oo the dickens d'you fink you are—the Lord Mayor ? Come down orf of there ! "

The Greek didn't understand, of course, but Sid had him down. He seemed to be trying to remonstrate with Sid, but Sid wasn't " 'avin' no excuses of that sort," and proceeded to reverse the order of things. He wanted " Ma " to " 'op up an' 'ave a ride," but the timid woman declined. Her burden, however, was transferred to the man's back, and after surveying him in an O.C. manner, Sid said : " Nah, pass on, an' don't let it 'appen again ! "—*H. T. Coad (late R.M.L.I.*), 30 *Moat Place, Stockwell, S.W.*9.

The Chef Drops a Brick

AT a prisoners of war camp, in Havre, it was my duty to make a daily inspection of the compound within the barbed wire, and also the officers' quarters.

In charge of the officers' mess was a little Cockney corporal, but practically all the cooking and other work was done by German prisoners.

We had just put on trial a new cook, a German, who had told us that he had been a chef before the war at one of the big London hotels.

I was making my usual inspection with my S. M., and when we came

" 'Ow long 'ave *you* bin a partner in the firm ? "

to the officers' mess he bawled out " 'Shun ! Officer's inspection, any complaints ? "

The new German cook apparently did not think that this applied to him, and, wanting to create a good impression, he strolled across to me in the best *maître d'hôtel* style, and exclaimed, " Goot mornung, sir. I tink ve are go'n to haf som rain."

Our little corporal appeared astounded at this lack of respect, and, going over to the German, he said in a loud voice : " Put thet knife dahn, an' stand to attention. Ve'r gorn to 'ave some rine, indeed ! " And then, in a louder voice, " *Ve* are. 'Ow long 'ave *you* bin a partner in the firm ? "—*Lieut. Edwin J. Barratt (Ex-" Queens " R.W. Surrey Regt.), 8 Elborough Street, Southfields, S.W.*18.

His " Read " Letter Day

AT Sorrel le Grand, which our division had just taken in 1917, we took up a good position for our machine gun in a small dug-out.

I was cleaning my revolver on one of the steps, and it accidentally went off.

To my surprise and horror the bullet struck one of my comrades (who was in a sitting position) in the centre of his steel helmet, creating a huge dent.

His remark was : " Lummy, it was a jolly good job I was reading one of my girl's letters," and then continued reading.—*Robt. Fisher (late Corpl., M.G.C.), 15 Mayesbrook Road, Goodmayes, Essex.*

Dan, the Dandy Detective

JERRY's front line trench and ours were not three hundred yards apart. Over that sinister strip of ground attack and counter-attack had surged and ebbed in a darkness often turned to day by Verey lights and star-shells. Brave men on each side had reached their objective, but " fell Sergeant Death " often took charge.

In our sector was a 1914 " Contemptible," who, despite mud and adverse conditions, made his New Army comrades smile at his barrack-room efforts to keep his uniform and equipment just so.

Of Coster ancestry, his name was Dan, and, of course, they called him Dandy. He felt distinctly annoyed when on several days an officer passed him in the trench with the third button of his tunic missing. " 'Is batman ought bloomin' well be for it," he soliloquised.

Another night visit to Jerry's trench, and again some poor fellows stay there for keeps. In broad noonday Dan is once more aggrieved by seeing an officer with a button missing who halts in the trench to ask him the whereabouts of B.H.Q. and other details. The tunic looked the same, third button absent, *but it was not the same officer.*

Now Dan's platoon sergeant, also a Londoner, was a man who had exchanged his truncheon for a more deadly weapon. Him Dan accosts : " I've a conundrum I'd like to arsk you, sergeant, as I don't see Sherlock 'Olmes nowhere. W'y do orficers lose their third button ? "

As became an ex-policeman, the sergeant's suspicions were aroused by the coincidence, so much so indeed that he made discreet enquiries and discovered that the original owner of a tunic minus a third button had been reported missing, believed dead, after a recent trench raid.

The adjutant very soon made it his business to intercept the new wearer and civilly invite him to meet the O.C. at B.H.Q. Result : a firing party at dawn.

When the news of the spy filtered through, Dan's comment was : " Once, when a rookie, I was crimed at the Tower for paradin' with a button missin', but I've got even now by havin' an orficer crimed for the same thing, even if he *was* only a blinkin' 'Un ! "—*H. G., Plaistow.*

The Apology

A HEAVILY-LADEN and slightly intoxicated Tommy, en route to France, entered the Tube at Oxford Circus. As the train started he lurched and trod heavily on the toes of a very distinguished "Brass Hat."

Grabbing hold of the strap, he leaned down apologetically and murmured: "*Sorry, Sergeant!*"—*Bert Thomas, Church Farm, Pinner, Middlesex.*

"Sorry, Sergeant!"

Too Scraggy

WE were prisoners in the infamous Fort Macdonald, near Lille, early in May 1917, rammed into the dungeons there for a sort of "levelling down process," i.e. starvation, brutal treatment, and general misery. After eleven days of it we were on our way, emaciated, silent, and miserable, to the working camps close behind the German lines, when a Cockney voice piped up :

" Nah then, boys, don't be down 'earted. They kin knock yer abaht and cut dahn yer rations, but, blimey, they won't *eat* us—not nah ! "— *G. F. Green, 14 Alma Square, St. John's Wood, N.W.8.*

So Why Worry ?

THE following, written by a London Colonel, was hung up in one of our dug-outs :

" When one is a soldier, it is one of two things. One is either in a dangerous place, or a cushy one. If in the latter, there is no need to worry. If one is in a dangerous place, it is one of two things. One is wounded, or one is not. If one is not, there is no need to worry. If the former, it is either dangerous or slight. If slight, there is no need to worry, but if dangerous, it is one of two alternatives. One dies or recovers. If the latter, why worry ? If you die you cannot. In these circumstances the real Tommy never worries."—*"Alwas," Windmill Road, Brentford, Middlesex.*

Commended by the Kaiser

AS prisoners of war we were unloading railway sleepers from trucks when a shell dump blew up. German guards and British prisoners scattered in all directions. Some of the Germans were badly wounded and, as shells continued to explode, no attempt was made by their comrades to succour them.

Seeing the plight of the wounded, a Cockney lad called to some fellow-prisoners crouching on the ground, " We can't leave 'em to die like this. Who's coming with me ? "

He and others raced across a number of rail tracks to the wounded men and carried them to cover.

For this act of bravery they were later commended by the then Kaiser. —*C. H. Porter (late East Surrey Regiment), 118 Fairlands Avenue, Thornton Heath, Surrey.*

Only Fog Signals

WE were resting in Poperinghe in December 1915. One morning about 4.30 a.m. we were called out and rushed to entrain for Vlamertinghe because Jerry was attacking.

The train was packed with troops, and we were oiling our rifle bolts and checking our ammunition to be ready for action. We had not proceeded far when Jerry started trying to hit the train with some heavy shells. Several burst very close to the track.

There was one young chap in our compartment huddled in a corner looking rather white. " They seem to be trying to hit the train," he said.

" Darkie " Webb, of Poplar, always cheerful and matter-of-fact, looked across at the speaker and said, " 'It the train ? No fear, mate, them's only signals ; there's fog on the line."—*B. Pigott (late Essex Regt.)*, 55 *Burdett Avenue, Westcliff-on-Sea.*

An American's Hustle

I WAS on the extreme right of the British line on March 22, 1918, and was severely wounded. I was picked up by the U.S. Red Cross.

There was accommodation for four in the ambulance, and this was apportioned between two Frenchmen, a Cockney gunner, and myself.

Anxious to keep our spirits up, the kindly Yankee driver said, " Cheer up ! I'll soon get you there and see you put right," and as if to prove his words he rushed the ambulance off at express speed, with the result that in a few moments he knocked down a pedestrian.

A short rest whilst he adjusted matters with the unfortunate individual, then off again at breakneck speed.

The Cockney had, up to now, been very quiet, but when our driver barely missed a group of Tommies and in avoiding them ran into a wagon, the Londoner raised himself on his elbow and in a hoarse voice said, " Naw then, Sam, what the 'ell are you playing at ? 'Aint yer got enough customers ? "—*John Thomas Sawyer (8th East Surreys)*, 88 *Wilcox Road, S.W.8.*

Truth about Parachutes

MOST English balloon observers were officers, but occasionally a non-commissioned man was taken up in order to give him experience.

On one such occasion the balloon burst in the air. The two occupants made a hasty parachute exit from the basket. The courtesy usually observed by the senior officer, of allowing the other parachute to get clear before he jumps, was not possible in this instance, with the result that the officer got entangled with the " passenger's " parachute, which consequently did not open.

Fortunately the officer's parachute functioned successfully and brought both men safely to earth. Upon landing they were rather badly dragged along the ground, being finally pulled up in a bush.

The " passenger," a Cockney sergeant, was damaged a good deal, but upon being picked up and asked how he had enjoyed his ride he answered, " Oh, it was all right, but a parachute is like a wife or a toof-brush—you reely want one to yourself."—*Basil Mitchell (late R.A.F.)*, 51 *Long Lane, Finchley, N.3.*

The Linguist

AN Indian mule driver had picked up a German hand grenade of the " potato masher " type, which he evidently regarded as a heaven-sent implement for driving in a peg. Two Tommies tried to dissuade him, but, though he desisted, he was obviously puzzled. So one of the

" Moi—vous—'im—avec Allah ! "

Cockneys tried to explain. " Vous compree Allah ? " he asked, and raised his hand above his head. Satisfied that the increasing look of bewilderment was really one of complete enlightenment, he proceeded to go through a pantomime of striking with the " potato masher " and, solemnly pointing in turn to himself, to the Indian, and to his companion, said : " Moi, vous, and 'im—avec Allah."—*J. F. Seignoir* (*Lt., R.A.*), 13 *Moray Place, Cheshunt, Herts.*

Billiards isn't all Cannons

MY regiment was in action on the Marne on September 20, 1914. We had been hammering, and had been hammered at, for some hours, until there were very few of us left, and those few, being almost all of them wounded or short of ammunition, were eventually captured and taken behind the German lines.

As we passed their trenches we saw a great number of German wounded lying about.

One of our lads, a reservist, who was a billiards marker in Stepney, although badly wounded, could not resist a gibe at a German officer.

" Strewth, Old Sausage and Mash," he cried, " your blokes may be good at the cannon game, but we can beat yer at pottin' the blinkin' red. Look at yer perishin' number board " (meaning the German killed and wounded). And with a sniff of contempt he struggled after his mates into captivity.—*T. C. Rainbird (late Pte., 1st West Yorks)*, 41 *Cavalry Crescent, Eastbourne, Sussex.*

Run ?—Not Likely

IT was the beginning of the spring offensive, 1918, and the 2nd Army Gun School, Wisques, was empty, as the men had gone into the line. A handful of Q.M.A.A.C. cooks were standing by.

I sent two little Cockney girls over to the instructors' château to keep the fires up in case the men returned suddenly. I went to the camp gate as an enemy bombing plane passed over. The girls had started back, and were half-way across the field. The plane flew so low that the men leaned over the side and jeered at us.

I held my breath as it passed the girls—would they shoot them in passing ? The girls did not hasten, but presently reached me with faces as white as paper.

" Why didn't you run ? " I said.

" Lor', mum," came the reply, " yer didn't think as 'ow we was a-goin' ter run with them there Germans up there, did ye ? Not much ! "— *C. N. (late U.A., Q.M.A.A.C.), Heathcroft, Hampstead Way, N.W.*

At " The Bow Bells " Concert

WHILST having a short spell away from the front line I attended a performance given in Arras by the divisional concert party, " The Bow Bells."

During one of the items a long-range shell struck the building, fortunately without causing any casualties among the audience.

Although front-line troops are not given to " windiness," the unexpectedness of this unwelcome arrival brought about a few moments' intense silence, which was broken by a Cockney who remarked, " Jerry *would* come in wivvaht payin'."—*L. S. Smith (late 1–7 Middlesex Regt., 56th Division, B.E.F.), 171 Langham Road, N.15.*

A Bomb and a Pillow

DURING part of the war my work included salving and destroying
" dud " shells and bombs in the back areas.   On one occasion in an
air-raid a " dud " bomb glanced through the side of a hut occupied by
some fitters belonging to an M.T. section of R.E.'s.

This particular bomb (weighing about 100 lb.), on its passage through
the hut had torn the corner of a pillow on which the owner's head was
lying and carried feathers for several feet into the ground.

We dug about ten feet down and then, as the hole filled with water
as fast as we could pump it out, we gave it up, the tail, which had become
detached a few feet down, being the only reward of our efforts.

While we were in the midst of our operations the owner of the pillow—
very " bucked " at being unhurt after such a narrow shave—came to
look on, and with a glance down the hole and a grin at me said, " Well,
sir, if I'd known it 'ud give yer so much trouble, I'd 'a caught it ! "
—*Arthur G. Grutchfield (late Major (D.A.D.O.S. Ammn.) R.A.O.C.),
Hill Rise, Sanderstead Road, Sanderstead, Surrey.*

Athletics in the Khyber Pass

DURING the Afghan operations I was resting my company on the
side of the road at the Afghan entrance to the Khyber Pass.   It was
mid-day and the heat was terrific, when along that heat-stricken road came
a British battalion.   They had marched 15 miles that morning from Ali
Musfd.   Their destination was Landi Kana, five miles below us on the
plain.

As they came round the bend a cheer went up, for they spotted specks
of white canvas in the distance.   Most of the battalion seemed to be on
the verge of collapse from the heat, but one Tommy, a Cockney, broke
from the ranks and had a look at the camp in the distance, and exclaimed :
" Coo !   If I 'ad me running pumps I could sprint it ! "—*Capt. A. G. A.
Barton, M.C., Indian Army, " The Beeches," The Beeches Road, Perry
Bar, Birmingham.*

Jack and his Jack Johnsons

IN September 1915 our battery near Ypres was crumped at intervals
of twenty minutes by 18-in. shells.   The craters they made could
easily contain a lorry or two.

One hit by the fifth shell destroyed our château completely.   Leaving
our dug-outs I found a gunner smoking fags under the fish-net camouflage
at Number One gun.

Asked sternly why he had not gone to ground, he replied, " Well,
yer see, sir, I'm really a sailor and when the earth rocks with Jack
Johnsons I feels at 'ome like.   Besides, the nets keeps off the flies."—
*G. C. D. (ex-Gunner Subaltern, 14th Div.), Sister Agnes Officers' Hospital,
Grosvenor Crescent, S.W.1.*

Even Davy Jones Protested

TOWARDS the final stages of the Palestine front operations, when Johnny Turk was retreating very rapidly, I was detailed with others to clear and destroy enemy ammunition that had been left behind.

When near the Sea of Galilee there was discovered a dump of aerial bombs, each approximately 25 lb. in weight. Thinking it quicker and attended by less risk than the usual detonation, I decided to drop them in the sea.

About ten bombs were placed aboard a small boat, and I with three others pushed out about two hundred yards. Two of the bombs were dropped overboard without ever a thought of danger when suddenly there was a heavy, dull explosion beneath us, and boat, cargo, and crew were thrown into the air.

Nobody was hurt. All clung to the remains of the boat, and we were brought back to our senses by one of our Cockney companions, who remarked : " Even Davy Jones won't have the ruddy fings." —*A. W. Owen (late Corporal, Desert Corps), 9 Keith Road, Walthamstow, E.17.*

" Parti ? Don't blame 'im ! "

ONE summer afternoon in 1915 I was asked to deliver an official letter to the Mayor of Poperinghe. The old town was not then so well known as Toc H activities have since made it. At the time it was being heavily strafed by long-range guns. Many of the inhabitants had fled.

I rode over with a pal. The door of the *mairie* was open, but the building appeared as deserted as the great square outside.

Just then a Belgian gendarme walked in and looked at us inquiringly. I showed him the buff envelope inscribed " *Monsieur le Maire,*" whereupon he smiled and said, " *Parti.*"

At that moment there was a deafening crash outside and the air was filled with flying debris and acrid smoke. In a feeling voice my chum quietly remarked, " And I don't blinkin' well blame 'im, either ! "— *F. Street, 13 Greenfield Road, Eastbourne.*